NEW OR
THE GUI

NEW ORDER IN THE GULF

The Rise of the UAE

Dina Esfandiary

I.B. TAURIS

LONDON • NEW YORK • OXFORD • NEW DELHI • SYDNEY

I.B. TAURIS
Bloomsbury Publishing Plc
50 Bedford Square, London, WC1B 3DP, UK
1385 Broadway, New York, NY 10018, USA
29 Earlsfort Terrace, Dublin 2, Ireland

BLOOMSBURY, I.B. TAURIS and the I.B. Tauris logo are trademarks of
Bloomsbury Publishing Plc

First published in Great Britain 2023

Cover design by Adriana Brioso
Cover image © UFUK SEZGEN/Alamy Stock Vector

A catalogue record for this book is available from the British Library.

A catalog record for this book is available from the Library of Congress.

ISBN: HB: 978-0-7556-4579-4
PB: 978-0-7556-4578-7
ePDF: 978-0-7556-4580-0
eBook: 978-0-7556-4581-7

Typeset by Newgen KnowledgeWorks Pvt. Ltd., Chennai, India
Printed and bound in Great Britain

To find out more about our authors and books visit www.bloomsbury.com
and sign up for our newsletters.

CONTENTS

Introduction 1

1 A critical moment: The 2011 Arab Spring 11

2 The US 'Pivot to Asia' 27

3 The 2015 Iran nuclear deal 43

4 The UAE's growing assertiveness 59

5 The perception of success 79

6 What this means for the Persian Gulf 99

Conclusion 115

Notes 125
Select Bibliography 185
Index 191

INTRODUCTION

For over a decade now, regional relations in the Persian Gulf focused largely on the competition for regional hegemony between Iran and Saudi Arabia, and the different layers of this rivalry. Today, while Saudi Arabia and Iran remain major regional powers, a growing assertiveness exists within the United Arab Emirates (UAE) and, increasingly, within some of its smaller Gulf Arab neighbours. This change has affected regional security and the way the Persian Gulf states interact among themselves and with the regional hegemons. Since 2011, three key regional events engrained this change: the 2011 Arab Spring, President Barack Obama's announced 'Pivot to Asia' and the 2015 nuclear deal with Iran. These events created opportunities and entrenched old fears that made the UAE more assertive. Abu Dhabi is the vanguard of change and a microcosm of what may prove to be a far greater process of change in the region.

Prior to 2011, the region was hostage to the rivalry between Iran and Saudi Arabia. The two countries are the largest regional actors with the most extensive reach, while the once-prominent Iraq, a third potential rival, never recovered from the US invasion in 2003. Several deep-seated structural factors limit 'significant security cooperation' between the two,[1] including size, distribution of resources, oil and location. The rivalry also encompassed 'national, cultural, ethnic and sectarian divisions', and was a 'function of domestic political developments in Iran and Saudi Arabia'.[2] After the 1979 Islamic Revolution in Iran, Ayatollah Ruhollah Khomeini's desire to export the revolution in the region and repeated challenges to the legitimacy of the Al Saud's reign in Saudi Arabia added an ideological dimension to the rivalry.[3] Both countries also developed opposing perspectives on how to ensure domestic and regional security. Riyadh and its allies focused on internationalizing regional security, while Iran for its part, believed in indigenizing regional security. As a result, after the removal of Iraq as the third major player in the Persian

Gulf region in 2003, the region was firmly split into two poles, Iran and Saudi Arabia. Yet Saudi Arabia's long-standing rivalry with Iran was not the only relationship shaping the Persian Gulf region, even if it was the dominant one. Riyadh's – at times turbulent – relation with its allies and smaller neighbours was also a major factor.

In general terms, from their birth in the early 1970s (except Oman, which gained its independence from Britain in 1951 and Kuwait in 1961), the other Arab Gulf states – Bahrain, Kuwait, Qatar, Oman and the UAE – fit into and indeed reinforced this regional duality, largely deferring to Riyadh on policy decisions affecting the region. This conformity was due to several factors. First, independence from the UK occurred in a rapid time frame – between 1971 and 1972 – and went against the wishes of the sheikhdoms, who wanted the UK to remain to protect them from overbearing neighbours like Iran.[4] Second, the smaller Gulf Arab countries feared Saudi hegemony and reprisals, especially in light of some of the small territorial disputes that existed among them. Third, their newly independent status meant that the political elites focused on managing their own internal dynamics and setting up state institutions. Internal threats to the leadership of the Gulf sheikhdoms were common during this early period. The sheikhdoms that would eventually come together to form the UAE, for example, could not agree on the form their country would take,[5] and after the federation's formation in 1971, internal political wrangling continued for the country's first two decades of existence.[6] In Oman, Qaboos bin Said al Said overthrew his father and became sultan in 1970, while an internal rebellion was underway in the Dhofar region.[7] In Qatar, six months after independence, Khalifa bin Hamad al Thani deposed his cousin, Ahmad bin Ali al Thani, the then emir of Qatar, in February 1972.[8] As a result, defaulting to Riyadh for major regional policy decisions and leadership was a convenient path to follow. The need for the smaller Gulf Arab states to guard against foreign threats from bigger and more capable neighbouring countries reinforced this trend of deference to Saudi Arabia. The arrival of Iranian troops on the disputed island of Tunbs on 30 November 1971, just as British troops left, only served to highlight the Iranian threat, which further worsened with the advent of the 1979 Islamic Revolution in Iran.

Despite this, relations between Saudi Arabia and its smaller neighbours were not without problems. The UAE and its neighbours feared that Saudi Arabia would impose its vision for the region, including its perception of regional threats and its policies, on them.[9] In fact, by 2009, the United States assessed that 'while publicly expressing close ties with Riyadh, the UAE privately regards the Kingdom as its second greatest security threat after Iran (Israel is not on the list).[10] As a result, despite the drive to pool resources under Saudi leadership with the formation of the Gulf Cooperation Council (GCC) in May 1981,[11] the smaller Gulf Arab states simultaneously tried to guard against an overbearing Saudi leader by ensuring they would retain decision-making and self-sufficiency in defence matters at least.[12] They avoided full military integration, and the 'UAE insist(ed) that when the (Peninsula Shield) force enters a member's territory the command structure reverts from Saudi Arabia to that of the host country.[13] On the whole, however, the role of Saudi Arabia as a natural leader for the smaller Gulf States was one that became established from their independence in the early 1970s onwards.

This distrust drove some of the smaller Gulf Arab countries to pursue their own foreign policy goals even as they remained under the leadership of Saudi Arabia. Bahrain, whose ruling Khalifa family is Saudi Arabia's closest ally, signed its own Free Trade Agreement with the United States, in an effort to set its own agenda and depart from relying solely on Riyadh.[14] Qatar too tried to develop a more independent foreign policy,[15] which at times resulted in a split from its GCC allies.[16] But until recently, the Gulf Arab states were able to keep their disagreements mainly behind closed doors, and they rarely pursued interests in open defiance of their close GCC allies.[17] The smaller Gulf Arab states were aware of their vulnerability to both internal and external security threats, which trumped concerns over Saudi hegemony. This drove them to tighten their ranks and continue to work together to address common external threats.

The UAE and its growing assertiveness

The UAE too began to chart a more independent foreign policy in the 1990s. It displayed a desire for self-sufficiency, evident in its deployment in Kosovo, for example.[18] But in the years following the Arab Spring, the nature and pace of its assertiveness changed. Abu Dhabi significantly increased its political and diplomatic activities in the region and beyond, and pursued the defence of its interests unilaterally – something it was not accustomed to doing – or with regional allies in a more active manner. The UAE exemplifies the broader shift that appears to be shaping the region. It is a case study in both its self-perception of growing strength and clout, and in the effect this change has had on its foreign policy in the region.

After the British announced their departure from the Persian Gulf, the emirates that would form the UAE had a particularly difficult time as their leaders were embroiled in lengthy and complicated negotiations over the formation of the country and its institutions,[19] including opposing interests, disputes over borders and islands, and the desire to prevent the central government from encroaching on the prerogatives of the ruling families. As a result, some of the ruling families did not buy into the idea of creating a federation.[20] It was only once external security threats became significant and coincided with the looming deadline of the British withdrawal that the 'vulnerability of the single emirates became clear even to their rulers and a somewhat uneasy union could be forced on seven of the nine protected states'.[21] The internal political wrangling continued in the first two decades of the UAE's existence,[22] affecting the way the country's leadership viewed its hold on power for years to come.

In the first few years of its existence, the UAE also found itself at odds with some of its Arab neighbours, including Saudi Arabia and Qatar, over claims to land.[23] Riyadh refused to recognize the UAE until 1974, after Abu Dhabi forfeited the disputed territories of Khor al Udaid, Khor Duwayham and Huwayat to Saudi Arabia.[24] This contributed to Abu Dhabi's wariness of Saudi hegemony, laying the foundations for its desire to become self-sufficient, and contributing to the lack of real integration among the GCC.[25] But Saudi Arabia was not the only problem. The UAE reconciled itself with the country's position as a small power sandwiched between Iran and Saudi Arabia. Abu Dhabi understood that it was 'still vulnerable to either an outright attack, or, more likely, collateral damage from a proximate conventional war'[26] and it harboured a 'concrete fear … that their bigger brethren would assume a hegemonic role'.[27] Abu Dhabi was fearful of the Iranian threat and wanted to contain Iran's hegemonic ambitions.[28] Iran did not help this perception. On 30 November 1971, as soon as the British left the region, the Shah of Iran sent Iranian troops to the lesser and greater Tunbs, and the Abu Musa islands. It was clear Iran was a real and long-standing threat to the country.[29] But still, the UAE as a whole could not agree on policy towards Iran, as the elite in each emirate viewed the threat differently.[30] Dubai, for example, maintained extensive ties with Iran and served as a transhipment hub for Iran-bound goods during the height of sanctions, while Abu Dhabi continued to call for a tougher line on Tehran. Despite all this, the two countries worked together when needed.[31] Nevertheless, throughout the 1980s and 1990s, Iran and the tensions with Saudi Arabia were the UAE's main foreign policy concerns.

While the UAE faced a number of foreign threats, it was also grappling with domestic issues related to state formation and the building of institutions.[32] The looseness of the federation was a problem for the UAE, which, along with the different rates of economic growth in each emirate, led to inequalities within the country.[33] The UAE is a rentier state based on the distribution of wealth, which means that as a wealthier country with smaller indigenous population, it has a stronger bargain.[34] Challenges to this ruling bargain have been numerous over the years, ranging from the problem posed by an increase in numbers of expats in the country, fostering a sense of being strangers in their own countries for Gulf nationals;[35] the increasing difficulty for nationals of reaching their ruling sheikhs – a cornerstone of the Bedouin political culture;[36] and the dramatic decline in the price of oil, giving the Gulf monarchies less disposable income.[37] As a result, a quest for economic diversification emerged.[38] This initially meant relying on energy-reliant, export-oriented industries like petrochemicals, metals, fertilizers and plastics.[39] But the emirates that were not resource rich – Dubai being a notable example – focused instead on infrastructure and attracting foreign investment.[40]

The UAE is 'presided over by a hybrid polity made up of seemingly modern governmental structures, which have been grafted onto traditional political structures that have undergone little or no evolution since the UAE's creation in 1971'.[41] As a result, the UAE emerged as a hybrid country: politically stagnant domestically but economically vibrant. The process of state formation was slow and painful, and many were unsure the country would endure. In 2009, Sheikh Zayed's long-time translator, Zaki Nusseibah, said,

> There was a lot of skepticism about whether this place would survive. All the journalists I took around then, the editors, the visiting dignitaries – they all looked at the Emirates and said it would not survive … They thought that the individual emirates would be absorbed by their bigger neighbors. You must remember, we had revolutions all around us – there was Communism and Marxism, and simply bigger neighbors like Iran and Saudi Arabia.[42]

The domestic difficulties meant that it was not surprising that at first, the UAE was conservative in its foreign policymaking. 'For much of its first few decades as a nation state, the UAE operated a conservative foreign and national security policy that was largely predicated on ensuring survival in the face of internal and external threats to the fragile unity and territorial integrity of the federation.'[43] During these years, and in the aftermath of the invasion of Kuwait in 1990, the UAE's leadership reconciled itself with its vulnerability as a small power.[44] It is in this context, and with the added challenge of not being an overly tightly knit federation, that Abu Dhabi devised a few guiding principles for its foreign policy. Under its first ruler, Sheikh Zayed (bin Sultan al Nahyan), the founder of the UAE and its first president, the country's foreign policy was largely 'idealistic' and 'Arab world-centered',[45] with limited objectives. Sheikh Zayed's son, Mohammed bin Zayed (MBZ), became increasingly prominent throughout the 1990s and had more ambitious goals for his country. He aimed to make the UAE as self-sufficient as possible while ensuring that foreign powers had a stake in its security; boost its international and regional influence in the defence of its political and economic interests; and develop lasting relations with friendly powers, especially Saudi Arabia,[46] while containing threats, predominantly Iran[47] and Islamism.[48] These goals continue today.

The UAE's desire to act more assertively is influenced by a range of factors, but the foreign policy context is the primary arena in which the changes were enabled, developed and enacted. For Abu Dhabi, the Arab Spring and President Obama's announced 'Pivot to Asia' highlighted the Iranian threat and the UAE's feeling of isolation, while providing an opportunity for it to fill an emerging void in the region. The 2015 nuclear deal with Iran worsened the feeling of abandonment, and gave Tehran the means to pursue what Gulf States viewed as a destructive regional policy.[49] While prior to 2011, the UAE volunteered its forces to assist US-led missions worldwide, these were always done in coordination with the United States or its regional allies. After the 2011 wave of unrests, however, the UAE's strategy shifted and it doubled down on its efforts to become more assertive in the pursuit of its own interests, including through the projection of hard-power capabilities, even when this put it at odds with its regional allies.[50] Importantly, though, the UAE made it a point to maintain the image of its unity with Saudi Arabia even as these changes occurred[51] – though this public unity was tested by economic and political tensions between the two after 2016.

But what is assertiveness?

Assertiveness refers to the increasingly bold foreign policy decisions made by a country, and a demonstrable willingness to involve itself more forcefully in various international arenas in the pursuit of its own interests, even when this does not align with the interests of its friends and allies. At first sight, this definition might seem straightforward. Yet the concept of assertiveness has been the subject of considerable debate with little consensus on the definition. Some experts believe it represents a 'level of activity in a state's foreign policy', adding that 'It represents the state's willingness to pay the costs, whatever they may be, of following a particular strategy.'[52] This implies the decision is always part of a calculated, longer-term strategy. But at times, the decision to pursue a more forceful policy can be the result of a sudden opportunity. This is because while the decision to become more assertive might form part of a larger strategy, the opportunity to act as such is often sporadic and unplanned.

Assertiveness also encompasses a desire to become self-sufficient, enabling the state to wean itself off its international partners. In other words, self-sufficiency provides the state with the means to pursue greater assertiveness in its foreign policy. It is an effort to equip a state with the necessary means – economic, intellectual, military, policy – to determine its own fate insofar as is possible, which is what a state's pursuit of assertiveness also aims to achieve. Self-sufficiency is not required to adopt a more assertive foreign policy posture, but without it, assertiveness would come with a high level of risk because the state in question would ultimately be bound by its reliance on other states, which would limit the duration, the means and commitment it has to its assertive policymaking. Greater self-sufficiency can therefore translate to greater freedom to pursue a state's own interests.

The existence of an assertive foreign policy can be evidenced through three main indicators: (1) a focused and sustained effort to grow and develop military, political/diplomatic, cultural and economic capabilities – simply put, a state's capabilities determine its strength and influence because they provide it with the means to pursue national objectives; (2) demonstrable intentions to deploy these growing capabilities in the pursuit of foreign policy objectives that reflect national interests, even at the expense of allies and neighbours – because capabilities alone are inadequate if the country in question is not willing to use them; and (3) the success of any deployments, as perceived by the state. This is because change can only gain real momentum and become entrenched if the countries enacting it are confident that the more assertive pursuit of their interests and goals is working. That confidence will only exist if the country's leadership believes its policy is working, which is why their perception is considered, rather than seeking to form or draw upon a more objective, external assessment of success.

This book will explore these dynamics in two parts. First, it will examine why the change has taken place, and second, it will examine what this change looks like. In examining what led to the UAE's greater assertiveness, the focus will be on three key events in the region after 2011: the Arab uprisings, the United States' 'Pivot to Asia' policy statement and the 2015 nuclear deal with Iran, and the impact they had on the UAE's environment and the leadership's psyche. These events either highlighted existing Emirati fears or provided it with opportunities to expand its reach and influence, convincing it to pursue a more assertive foreign policy. Examining the expansion of Emirati capabilities, both military and non-military, coupled with its intention to use these capabilities demonstrates the existence of this assertiveness. Finally, ascertaining the longevity of this new assertiveness can be done through the perception of its success by the UAE itself. The deployment of the capabilities enumerated above may not be judged as 'successful' from an external perspective, but as long as the leadership perceives it as such, this will empower them to continue on their assertive track. And this is how Emirati policymakers view this policy. Finally, the book will conduct an assessment of some of the changes we have seen most recently: with the UAE pulling out its forces from Yemen and closing the base in Eritrea, coupled with the vocal push for a greater focus on soft power starting in 2020. While many view these changes as a new retrenchment after overstretching, it is actually a pragmatic assessment conducted by the leadership that either Emirati goals have been achieved; that the resources are needed elsewhere; or that it is no longer worth pursuing this particular path.

The final chapter will examine what growing Emirati assertiveness means for the Persian Gulf region. To begin with, it will examine the 2017 split among the Gulf Arab states and how this entrenched the trend of assertiveness, especially for Qatar, which was left isolated after a group of states led by Saudi Arabia and the UAE blockaded it. While the January 2021 Al Ula agreement resolved the split in appearance, divisions remain, and are likely to remain, because of the assertiveness of the UAE and now some of the smaller Gulf Arab states. This demonstrates how multiple power centres in the region are likely to make it more unstable.

The UAE exemplifies what seems to be a broader process shaping the region. Decision-making among the Gulf Arabs has become a more complex process, as the smaller Gulf Arab states, led by the UAE, have become bolder in calling for their goals and interests to be considered. It seems they are no longer content to merely follow Riyadh's lead, especially if this does not benefit them or fulfil their interests. Of course, it is possible that the growing confidence and assertiveness of the UAE is not part of a broader pattern in the region. This would mean that what appears to be a current trend is instead a temporary change, and that eventually, the UAE and other smaller Gulf Arab states will default back to their long-standing acquiescence to Saudi leadership, or that it remains limited in scope to the UAE and does not take hold among the rest of the smaller Gulf Arab states. While possible, this seems unlikely, because the forces unleashed can no longer be rolled back. The UAE has invested too many resources in regional conflicts, and its involvement has been too visible for it to simply change course.

The countries experiencing the change, and the UAE in particular, will rapidly learn from instances where they have perhaps overstretched and reassess their stance on specific issues and conflicts, all with a view to attaining their objectives and maintaining the resilience of their drive towards self-sufficiency, even when these conflict with those of its security guarantor or its close allies. To date, the lessons drawn from the UAE's growing assertiveness demonstrate that its policy is fit for purpose – at least in the eyes of decision-makers in Abu Dhabi, and as such, it is likely to be a resilient approach, one which has begun to take hold in other small Gulf States. The UAE will, however, correct course, the ferociousness with which it pursues its interests or the methods it uses,[53] as it sees fit – something witnessed in Yemen in 2019 and Libya in 2020. But it will not abandon this more assertive track.

This trend is altering security dynamics in the Persian Gulf region. As a result, it is vital to understand what caused it, what the changes themselves are and how likely they are to be resilient and spread among other Gulf Arab states. The next chapter will begin the assessment of the regional context that gave rise to this change. It will examine the outbreak of the Arab Spring in 2011, and the impact this had on the region and the Gulf Arab states. Finally, it will examine the UAE's response, showing the start of a more assertive foreign policy.

1 A CRITICAL MOMENT: THE 2011 ARAB SPRING

On 17 December 2010, when Mohammed Bouazizi, a Tunisian street vendor, set himself on fire in protest at the way he was treated after he could not convince police officials to allow him to continue his street vending, he could not have foreseen the changes this would lead to in his region. The so-called 'Arab Spring' began in Tunisia and subsequently spread throughout the Middle East, fundamentally altering the security dynamics of the region. While the protests did topple some of the region's autocrats, it did not change the day-to-day issues that fed the discontent in the region or lead to much change in the way in which they were ruled. But it altered the way states behaved. The revolts left a gaping hole in the region's security dynamics as major regional leaders fell and alternative non-governmental power centres emerged. The United States, considered the traditional security guarantor, did not step in to ensure the survival of US-friendly governments, providing an opportunity for other states to fill the void.

And fill the void they did: most notably the United Arab Emirates (UAE) and to a lesser extent some of the other smaller Gulf Arab states, such as Qatar. They saw the uprisings as 'a rare opportunity to revise the regional order in their favour and establish their control in new ways'.[1] Power shifted from the traditional Arab leaders – such as Egypt and Syria – to the wealthy Gulf Arab states. But the Arab Spring was also perceived as a threat to the Gulf monarchies' domestic political systems and society, as it 'starkly exposed' the 'false stability enjoyed by the autocratic regimes'.[2] The protests were a threat to the political systems in the Gulf Arab states and to their ruling families.[3] Protestors demanded a greater say in decision-making, as well as greater social, political and speech freedoms. But none of these demands fit in with the existing social contract in the Gulf Arab states, which involved lavish government spending on citizens in exchange for an acceptance of the legitimacy of the ruling families. The leadership in the Gulf Arab countries found themselves having to protect their existing political systems not only through token reforms and economic handouts but also by cracking down on the protests. The UAE for its part moved rapidly to crack down on any expression of discontent and desire for change, and combined it with limited elections and further financial assistance, which enabled Abu Dhabi to manage the discontent. Nevertheless, the Arab Spring clearly affected the UAE's perception of international threats and its sense of regime security. This, in turn, impacted the way it conducted foreign policy as Abu Dhabi became more willing to involve itself in the region to increase both its power and influence.

The leadership in the region also saw a weakened Arab world following the outbreak of the protests; a regional central bank official stated that the Arab Spring had weakened regional economies,[4] while regional officials highlighted that the Arab Spring had also created 'major divisions' between countries in the region,[5] allowing countries like Iran to expand their influence. The fear of Iran was heightened by the perception that the United States – the region's traditional security guarantor – was losing interest in the region and in the security and stability of its Gulf Arab partners.[6] The perceived US abandonment of President Hosni Mubarak of Egypt, a long-time partner of the United States, was seen as proof of Washington's new stance on the region.[7] That affected the Gulf Arab states' perception of their security, since their alliances and their relationships with extra-regional powers were, in their view, being upended. This made the UAE all the more focused on independently pursuing its own foreign policy objectives and security.

Why an Arab Spring?

Mohammed Bouazizi set himself on fire on 17 December 2010 to protest the way he had been treated by the authorities. The police in Sidi Bouzid, a small provincial town in Tunisia, had confiscated the vegetable vendor's cart when he refused to pay a bribe, and when he went to the local governmental building to complain, he was not allowed inside.[8] His self-immolation sparked protests in Sidi Bouzid, which rapidly spread to the rest of the country through the use of social media – to the surprise of many.[9] It also spread beyond Tunisia, into Egypt, Libya and the rest of the Middle East. The Arab Spring was a fluid and rapidly evolving social movement that spread across several cultural and national contexts. While the impact of the revolts was different throughout the region, the demonstrators all shared certain grievances, including dissatisfaction with quality of life, poor socio-economic conditions and political discontent with what were perceived by the citizenry as corrupt and overbearing regimes.[10] The demonstrations also

> shared common themes, slogans, modes of action, expectations and hopes. ... Beholden to no government or singular movement and empowered by ubiquitous communications technology, these movements violated the long-standing experiences of Arab politics.[11]

Cognizant that briefly summarizing such a momentous event will not do justice to its complexity, it is important to have a basic understanding of the uprisings' drivers if we are to understand why this event had such a significant impact on the way the leadership in the smaller Gulf Arab states, and the UAE in particular, viewed the region and their ability to influence the course of events.

Protesters in Sidi Bouzid initially wanted to show solidarity with Mr Bouazizi, but underlying anger at the generally poor socio-economic conditions and quality of life, the lack of political freedoms and the corruption of the ruling classes in Tunisia soon emerged as dominant themes.[12] Political representation and the sense of not having a voice was a core driver of discontent, especially as the regime had silenced previous protests.[13] Crucially, these themes were not limited to the Tunisian context, they were felt throughout the region.[14]

In nearby Egypt, labour unrest overlapped with a growing youth movement that was tired of widespread inequality[15] and false promises of reform, and this despite the growth rates achieved in both countries.[16] In Libya and Yemen, the context for the uprisings was not dissimilar: popular discontent over regime corruption, brutality and nepotism,[17] the lack of economic opportunities, both for the youth[18] and for women.[19] In Yemen, however, the political context was also key to the outbreak of demonstrations: there were serious divisions between the north and the south of the country, but the presence of the Houthis – an opposition Islamic political and armed movement that emerged in the 1990s – in the crowds made Yemen's neighbours nervous and, as such, led to the internationalization of its internal troubles.[20] Not too far from Yemen, in

Bahrain, the protests were also the result of dissatisfaction with the ruling family and socio-economic conditions. But this time, they were closely related to sectarian divisions within the country: with the majority Shia population calling for a greater say in the country's political and economic spheres.[21] The sectarian dimension was significant in the Persian Gulf, as differences in socio-economic conditions between the Sunnis and Shias in the Gulf Arab countries and the deliberate marginalization of the Shia[22] exacerbated feelings of disenfranchisement. In Saudi Arabia, the country's minority Shia community, concentrated in the oil-rich Eastern province, had been deliberately marginalized politically and economically for years, and subject to discrimination.[23] Sectarianism meant that the elite's response was calibrated to ensure that perceived Iranian influence over the Shia in their countries was addressed and contained.

Social, economic and political grievances were felt throughout the Middle East, even though the expression of discontent began in Tunisia. Its spread was boosted by pan-Arabism – shared grievances with others of similar backgrounds,[24] as well as the prevalence of technology, television and social media.[25] The existence of shared grievances throughout the region provided organizers of the protests in each country with an opportunity: to tap into those grievances and the momentum that had been initiated. The shared grievances contributed to reducing the geographical distance among each theatre of discontent and provided protestors with a sense of belonging to an immediate community that shared those grievances. As a result, the revolts that began in a small town in Tunisia rapidly spread throughout the region, progressively affecting all Arab countries in one way or another.

The prevalence of technology, television and social media facilitated the spread of discontent, allowing people on the ground to plug into a larger community that shared their grievances and facilitated the coordination of protests and protesters.[26] Protestors became connected to those in neighbouring countries through technology, and as such, while 'the uprisings were overwhelmingly domestic', angry protestors were 'inspired by events abroad to act at home'.[27] Qatar's Al Jazeera network, for example, was key to the revolts: 'It was Al Jazeera's positive and emotional coverage of these revolutionary youth and their ideas, as well as the interactive nature of its platform, that was both unique to the Arab world and captivated viewers across the world.'[28] Social media, for its part, served as a means of transmitting and amplifying common or shared grievances, and unifying protestors across borders.

The general dissatisfaction with the poor quality of life, which resulted from the fragmentation of the social contract that characterized Arab governments, was key in explaining the outbreak of protests. Shared grievances throughout the region and new technologies helped ensure that protesters in each country were not alone and could build on each other's successes.

An Arab Spring in the UAE?

While the root causes of the wave of protests that broke out in 2011 were relatively consistent throughout the region, the impact and consequences of the Arab Spring on those in power were less so. While the 'societies and governments of the Gulf have been immune to neither the message nor the impact of the Arab Spring',[29] in most cases, they weathered the storm more effectively – though it is important to note that these states are by no means a homogeneous group. The UAE escaped the worst of the Arab Spring, for example, but neighbouring Bahrain, Kuwait, Saudi Arabia and Oman felt its effects at varying degrees.

While most of the GCC countries grappled with domestic protests inspired by the Arab Spring in some form or another, the UAE was largely exempt from the uprisings.[30] This exception was explained by the country's religious and sectarian homogeneity – the Shias in the UAE make up only about 5 per cent of the population,[31] and the UAE's great wealth – surpassing the other Gulf Arab states on a per capita basis – enabled it to offset the discontent somewhat.[32] The Emirati ruling bargain was also stronger than those of neighbouring countries because of its smaller indigenous population.[33] The government had successfully connected all Emirati families to state institutions and the ruling family, effectively reducing political pressure.[34] But the discrepancies in wealth and importance between the seven emirates remained a problem.[35] The financial benefits packages to the poorer emirates enabled Abu Dhabi to consolidate its rule over the other emirates but further entrenched the rentier state they had tried to reform. The 2008 financial crisis in the UAE had already shifted power to Abu Dhabi and away from other emirates like Dubai,[36] effectively engraining 'Abu Dhabi's supremacy'.[37] As a result of these discrepancies, the UAE saw small-scale protests over living and labour conditions,[38] and activism, especially through social media, which began before the regional uprisings.[39] The UAE had been grappling with calls for democratization for several years;[40] the Arab Spring, however, emboldened the activists to step up their campaign and lead a peaceful call for reform rather than a change in government or system.[41] In March 2011, among a series of petitions that were circulated online, 133 national figures made of Liberals and Muslim Brotherhood Islamists in the UAE called Al Islah sent a letter to the president of the UAE asking for the Federal National Council (FNC) to be given more legislative powers.[42] According to Emirati professor Abdulkhaleq Abdulla, their demands were reasonable.[43] But Abu Dhabi was too focused on the cooperation between the Liberals and the Islamists to pay attention to the demands in the letter. Abu Dhabi believed that Islamism posed the single biggest threat to its power. Fearing this was Al Islah's attempt to capitalize on the discontent in the region to bring the Arab Spring to the UAE – a likely overreaction and overestimation of Al Islah's actual goals and capabilities – the government moved rapidly to crack down on any expression of discontent and desire for change, taking many Emiratis by surprise.[44] The crackdown combined with limited elections, carefully calibrated rhetoric discrediting those asking for change and further financial assistance enabled Abu Dhabi to skilfully avoid any major outbreak of discontent, and arguably saw its government strengthened as it consolidated its rule over the periphery as a result of the financial assistance packages.

The wave of unrests that swept through the Middle East in 2011 caught the region off guard. The threat to the stability of its political system was felt acutely in Abu Dhabi, even though it was less affected by the protests. The protests led to major changes in the region, changing the UAE's perception of threats inside and outside its borders. The change in threat perception, in turn, affected the UAE's decision-making on foreign policy.

The impact of the Arab Spring on the UAE

The Arab Spring led to several significant changes in the region, which impacted the way the UAE behaved. According to Marc Lynch, the Arab Spring reshaped the region in four ways: it 'challenged America's position in novel ways, exposing all the contradictions in its policies and the limits of its power'; accelerated sectarianism; 'dramatically expanded the intra-Sunni power struggles into a great variety of fractured states, potential allies, and adversaries'; and 'sharply exacerbated the threat perception of the Arab regimes by revealing that popular challengers could actually overthrow them'.[45] For the UAE, the Arab Spring was especially significant in three foreign policy areas: first, the collapse of some noted Arab leaders left a power vacuum in the region; second, fear caused by the opportunity for the rise of Iran; and finally, the muted US response to these changes spearheaded the perception of a US withdrawal from the region. The Arab Spring also sparked an intense internal debate and a reassessment of the UAE's position in the region, with the appearance of some divisions on the topic.[46] While all the smaller Gulf Arab states shared the perceptions described above, the UAE acted on it in the most noticeable way: it demonstrated greater assertiveness and a newfound urgency in the drive towards self-sufficiency.[47]

The collapse of Arab powerhouses

A significant change brought on by the Arab Spring was the collapse of authoritarian Arab leaders such as Mubarak, Muammar Ghaddafi and Zine el Abidine Ben Ali, and chaos in major Arab countries such as Egypt and Syria, which impacted the way the UAE viewed regional and domestic security. Egyptian leadership of Arab countries emerged during Gamal Abdel Nasser's presidency.[48] With strong autocratic leaders, countries like Syria and Libya also became major regional players.[49] As a result, the collapse of both the Egyptian and Libyan leadership and the outbreak of civil war in Syria and Libya meant that several major regional powerbrokers were embroiled in their own domestic turbulence and no longer had the bandwidth to lead in the region. This had a dual effect: it alarmed the UAE and its allies, who were fearful that the same could happen to them, and created a power vacuum in the region: 'The Arab Spring spooked everyone in the region. Most importantly, the royal families of the Gulf realised they are under threat.'[50] An Omani analyst said, 'If something were to happen to a smaller GCC state then all regional order would be gone. There is a real sense of vulnerability among the Gulf Arab states.'[51] Indeed, the leadership in the UAE, while somewhat protected from the full brunt of the Arab Spring protests, worried that the discontent would spill over into its borders.[52] This potentially existential threat to regime security, in turn, affected the UAE's foreign policy decision-making, by infusing it with assertiveness and a sense of urgency in pursuing its own objectives and self-sufficiency.

At the same time, the situation provided an unparalleled opportunity for states in the region who were unaffected or only marginally affected by the regional wave of discontent, including the UAE: those willing to capitalize on developments now had a chance to shape the region more to their liking and 'compete for influence in the power vacuum created by the dislocation of the regional order'.[53] While recognizing the dangers, the UAE saw this as an opportunity to cash in on some of its long-term investments in developing its diplomatic, political and military capabilities, and fulfil its own goals, involving itself overtly in conflicts like Libya and Yemen and pursuing its own agenda, including the containment and rollback of Islamism.[54] Qatar, too, saw a similar opportunity in the outbreak and spread of the Arab Spring. According to Mehran Kamrava, 'During the course of the Arab Spring, Qatar moved away from being a mediator to becoming a more active supporter of change in the Middle East region, deeply involving itself in what it assumed would be new eras first in Libya, then in Syria.'[55] Both countries' foreign policies were impacted by their view of the changes in the region. Qatar, however, unlike the UAE, reassessed its involvement after a series of setbacks. According to Kamrava, it realized 'that perhaps it had overreached, it slowly adapted and adopted a more pragmatic foreign policy'.[56] The UAE, for its part, has consistently increased its involvement in the region since the Arab Spring, including in cases where its goals oppose those of its allies like Saudi Arabia, such as in Yemen.

The perceived rise of Iran

The collapse of Arab stronghold countries was both an opportunity and a problem. It was an opportunity because it allowed the UAE to expand its involvement in regional security. But if it provided an opportunity for the UAE, then it would also provide its regional foes with an opportunity, including Iran. Iran's relations with its Gulf Arab neighbours have been complicated, to say the least. And Iran has been the cause of contention within the GCC states. Threat perceptions – their overinflation or undervaluation – have repeatedly started or entrenched conflicts and rivalries in the Persian Gulf region:[57] 'The most important factor shaping … the UAE's responses to [its] external environment is [its] leaders' perception[s].'[58] To the leadership in the UAE, the Arab Spring led to the weakening of the Arab world, which was now embroiled in its internal discontent and disruptions. This, along with the regional void left by the crumbling of the old Arab leaders, inevitably in their minds, resulted in a rise in Iran's regional power and influence, and its heightening as a security concern both in the region and in its ability to impact domestic security in their country.[59] A senior Emirati government official captured this sentiment in November 2016, when he said, 'The 2011 upheavals created an open space for Iranian intervention and influence,'[60] clearly highlighting how the view of Iran and its rise and reach in the region affected the UAE's perception of regional and domestic regime security, thereby affecting its foreign policy. 'The Arab Spring was the big turning point regarding views of Iran. The region saw Iran in a different light.'[61] Abdulkhaleq Abdulla, a noted Emirati academic, explained that the Arab Spring 'revealed that the fears of the GCC countries regarding Iran are the only constant in Gulf strategic and security thinking.'[62] He underlined that the Arab Spring exacerbated previously held perceptions and views on Iran, adding that 'Iran occasionally attempt[ed] to play on the weak points of the internal Gulf situation, position itself into domestic Gulf affairs, and achieve regional expansion whenever the opportunity presents itself.'[63] Iran's actions following the Arab Spring worsened regional security threats for the UAE, while the internal turmoil felt in the country further exacerbated the fear of Iran's reach into their domestic politics, thereby impacting their foreign policy decision-making.

While Abdulla's assessment was perhaps a little too radical in overestimating Iran's desire to sow conflict and differences within the GCC, it is undeniable that Iran for its part did not help this perception. When the Arab Spring broke out, the leadership in Tehran was quick to capitalize on the protests, hailing them as an 'Islamic liberation movement' and 'awakening', encouraging their spread in the region and pointing to the wave of unrest as the beginning of the end of US presence in the region.[64] By painting them as 'Islamic' protests – and implicitly drawing a link to its own successful revolution in 1979, Iran sought to position itself as a leading voice for change and resistance, in the hope that this would increase its popularity on the Arab street,[65] and to 'glorify the Iranian Revolution and construct it as an exemplary system.'[66] This struck a chord with Iran's Gulf Arab neighbours, who understood that Iran 'as a Persian power cuts its access to Arab countries. So it has to focus on religion.'[67] Iran's stated support for the revolts in the region also served to boost the Islamic Republic's rhetoric of support of the 'oppressed' against the 'oppressors', a long-standing pillar of the system.[68] Framing the protests as 'Islamic' allowed the Islamic Republic to shield itself from their spillover into Iran, which itself had seen a period of discontent following the election of Mahmoud Ahmadinejad in 2009.[69] To Iran's neighbours, its framing of the revolts was proof of its hegemonic intentions for the region.

But Iran's rhetoric was not the only problem: the threat of its growing influence in the context of the fall of Arab strongholds was significant in the minds of its Gulf Arab neighbours.[70] To the Gulf Arabs, this threat became a reality as the Arab Spring wore on and Iran increased its involvement in the region. Indeed, prior to the Arab Spring much of Iran's involvement in the region was limited to soft power projection and leading the resistance against Israel.[71] As a result of the post-2011 recalibration of its power projection in the region, Tehran lost some of its ability to project soft power among the region's Sunnis, but its hard power projection grew.[72] The Gulf Arabs did not see the limits on Iran's powers. Rather, Iran's neighbours saw all of Tehran's regional forays through the prism of a hegemonic strategy to gain influence in the region.[73]

Iran's involvement in the Syrian civil war only served to highlight Gulf Arab fears of Iranian hegemony and was the first public display of the shift from Iranian soft to hard power deployment in the region: 'The real challenge and turning point for how the region viewed Iran was Syria.'[74] Since the outbreak of hostilities in Syria, Iran provided money, weapons, training and advice to the government of Bashar al Assad.[75] The UAE viewed Iran's involvement in the Syrian conflict as a way for it to achieve its hegemonic ambitions. The leadership in the UAE and other Gulf Arab countries 'believe that if Iran and its allies prevail and the current Syrian regime survives unreconstructed it will open the door for further inroads by Tehran into the Arab world and the eventual creation of a Persian mini-empire in the region'.[76] Iran's involvement in Syria heightened the UAE's sense of vulnerability, because it believed that Syria's collapse would put them next on Iran's target list.[77] In fact, some believed that Iran was using Syria as a testing ground for its policy of spreading Shiism in the region, citing unverified allegations of supposed efforts by Lebanon's leading Shia cleric, Grand Ayatollah Mohammad Hussein Fadlallah, to convert Alawis into Shias.[78] As a result, it was seen as imperative to contain Iran in Syria in order to contain it in the whole region.

Iran did not have to be physically present in a country for the Gulf Arab countries to perceive Iranian involvement. When protests broke out in Bahrain on 14 February 2011, the UAE and its allies were seriously alarmed at the prospects of both a collapse of one of their own[79] and the growth of Iranian interventionism in the internal affairs of the Gulf Arab states.[80] The government painted the Bahraini protests as the work of Tehran reaching out to the Shias in the country.[81] This reflected a real fear that Iran would use this as an opportunity to discredit the Sunni leadership and foster instability in Bahrain in order to increase its influence in the country. Both the government in Bahrain as well as its neighbours believed that Iran had real ties with the majority Shia population in the country.[82] It became critical that Iran did not have access and influence in neighbouring Bahrain, perceived as Riyadh's backyard, prompting the Saudi-led intervention by the Peninsula Shield Force in Bahrain, quelling the protests and returning to an uneasy status quo.[83] But in reality, Bahraini Shias were cautious and wary of Tehran.[84] Nevertheless, to this day, Bahraini officials see an Iranian hand in internal tensions. In fact, following the Russian invasion of Ukraine in 2022, a Bahraini official said, 'Countries who are interested in annexing territory will be watching the developments in Ukraine carefully,' alluding to Iran. He added, 'Iran is conducting a continuous aggression of Bahrain.'[85]

The Iranian threat to the UAE and its Gulf Arab neighbours was nothing new, but the Arab Spring heightened it. In the eyes of the leadership in the UAE, the collapse of Arab stronghold states provided Tehran with an opportunity to swoop in and fill the void. And fill the void it did – or tried to at least – with the deployment of a new hard power in the region. The increasing Iranian threat impacted the UAE's regional threat context and posed a potential threat to the domestic stability of its government. It became imperative to increase efforts to contain and push the Islamic Republic back, especially in light of the perceived lack of US intervention in the region to safeguard its allies.

The perception of US influence and power in the region

The opportunity created by the collapse of leading Arab states following the Arab Spring, and the fear that Iran would capitalize on this, was only compounded by growing fears stemming from the Obama administration's perceived desire to disengage from the region, which would have a significant impact on the UAE's security relations and alliances. In his 2009 speech in Cairo, President Obama said, 'No system of government can or should be imposed by one nation.'[86] This was a break from the perception that the United States was a supporter of the autocratic order in the Middle East,[87] though President Obama was careful to assert that this view would not dampen his commitments to governments 'that reflect the will of the people'.[88] This, along with the belief that Obama aimed to turn his attention inwards, established a sense of unease at what the future would hold with regard to their main security guarantor's commitment to them.[89] The Arab Spring was fundamental to the Gulf Arab perception of US presence in the region: 'The greatest impact of the Arab uprising may be to ultimately prove to be the dismantlement of the American Middle East regional order – an outcome which terrifies the regime protected by that order.'[90] President Obama's perceived abandonment of regional friends or disengagement from crises in the region following the outbreak of the Arab Spring had significant repercussions on the UAE's psyche in particular.[91] The perceived change in the UAE's relations with the United States convinced Abu Dhabi that it would have to take greater responsibility in ensuring its own security, through greater assertiveness and self-sufficiency. Key to their perception of US disengagement from the region was President Obama's reaction – or lack thereof – to the outbreak of the protests in Egypt.[92]

The 25 January 2011 'Day of Rage' inspired by events in Tunisia marked the start of large-scale protests in Egypt.[93] Four gruelling days later, on 29 January, the Muslim Brotherhood joined the protests, bringing to it much-needed manpower, organization and experience. Importantly, in Egypt's case, the army refused to shoot at Egyptian protestors after the government ordered it to. The Obama administration was key to this decision, engaging 'in near constant dialogues at all levels up and down the ranks of the Egyptian military, pushing it not to fire, with multiple daily phone calls pressing the case'.[94] The Obama administration decided that Mubarak, a long-time US ally, could no longer remain in place, and only a few days after the outbreak of the protests, on 1 February, President Obama stated that 'an orderly transition must be meaningful, it must be peaceful, and it must begin now'.[95] The problem, however, was that for the United States, 'Mubarak had been one of the good guys …, the epitome of the acquiescent autocrat, the kind of leader with whom America had cut bargains decades earlier'.[96] Egyptian protestors held the symbolic Tahrir

Square until the Mubarak government fell on 11 February 2011, leading to a period of bargaining and transition. The impact of the Obama administration's active call for a transition so rapidly after the beginning of the protests cannot be overstated: 'American allies around the region were aghast that Obama seemed to be abandoning America's long-time Egyptian partner.'[97] The Emiratis, along with the Saudis, 'furious at what they saw as Obama's betrayal', worked hard to keep Mubarak in place, urging him to cling onto power for the foreseeable future, and thus, actively working against American interests.[98] The Obama administration's 'rhetorical embrace of the Arab uprising as the right side of history, his willingness to accept the removal of Mubarak, and his support for Egyptian democracy, even if the Muslim Brotherhood won elections, cut to the very heart of the survival guarantee which Arab regimes wanted from the US'.[99] The Emiratis were 'frustrated with this administration' as a result of this.[100] There was genuine worry that 'if the US would give up on Mubarak so easily, would it stand by them if they faced popular uprisings?'[101] In addition, the US abandonment of Mubarak 'seemed to call into question what remained of US Cold War realpolitik: the implicit US commitment to defend the Gulf monarchies against Iran'.[102] The Emiratis saw unfolding before them the beginning of their worst nightmare:[103] that the United States would no longer be a reliable security partner. The sentiment only worsened as the Arab Spring wore on and new conflicts emerged throughout the region, including in Syria and Libya. In Syria, Washington stayed clear of the conflict despite the images of unparalleled violence committed by President Assad against his own citizens.[104] 'Obama avoided striking Syria because of Iran – he didn't want to rock the boat and confront Iran.'[105] This fed into the Emirati belief that Washington was selling them out in favour of Iran.

To the leadership in the UAE, events in Egypt indicated that President Obama was embarking on a new foreign policy: one of disengagement from the Middle East. This fed their worst fear of being abandoned by their sole security guarantor. But while this sentiment was beginning to get traction among the Emirati policy community, some hoped that it would be an exception rather than the new rule. In discussions in April 2016, Emirati officials not only highlighted the UAE's 'good relations' with the United States 'despite the Arab Spring' but also bemoaned that the United States was too 'legacy driven' and was not 'doing enough' for its friends in the region.[106] Nevertheless, perceived changes in US policy, the new regional void left by the collapse of major Arab states and the perceived rise of Iran contributed to changes in the way the UAE predominantly, but some of its allies as well, conducted foreign policy. While at first the Arab Spring led to a regrouping of the smaller Gulf Arab countries under the leadership of Saudi Arabia, rivalries rapidly emerged, leading the UAE and other small Gulf Arab states to pursue their own agendas in the region.

Changes in the Persian Gulf following the Arab Spring: A regrouping of the GCC?

The immediate effect of the protests in the Middle East was to foster a regrouping of the smaller Gulf Arab states under Saudi Arabia's leadership, thereby increasing the importance of their principal security alliance. The outbreak of the protests in 2011 did exactly that: 'Whatever their disagreements, these regimes first and foremost wanted to survive.'[107]

As established, the 2011 protests posed a challenge to the Gulf Arabs. They made the leadership in the UAE and some of the Gulf Arab countries realize that 'if one was overthrown then all become a target'; it also 'made royal families in the region realise that they needed each other'.[108] When first faced with these threats, and as a result of the sense of vulnerability this created within the Gulf Arab elites, the Gulf Arabs put aside their differences and regrouped under the umbrella of Saudi leadership in order to tackle the perceived threat. Events in the region 'prompted Saudi Arabia to take the initiative and lead. While smaller Gulf Arab states judged it better to align themselves with leaders they know and trust'.[109] 'Even Qatar came back together with Saudi Arabia and the others.'[110] There was a 'unity of views within the GCC, especially on Iran', confirmed several Emirati officials in reference to the post–Arab Spring period.[111] As a unified group, the leadership in the Gulf Arab states put together a $20 billion aid package for Bahrain and Oman, who were experiencing protests of their own.[112] After the deployment of the Peninsula Shield Force in Bahrain and despite their differences on Iran, in April 2011, the GCC foreign ministers issued a statement condemning Iranian involvement in their affairs and calling for Tehran to respect their sovereignty.[113]

But this unity was short-lived. The 'marriage of convenience' that had brought these countries together 'gave way to bitter acrimony'.[114] Cracks developed internally, though these were kept behind closed doors as much as possible. But the divisions between the UAE and Saudi Arabia slowly became more significant. A bureaucrat within the Emirati Ministry of Foreign Affairs confirmed this in 2016: 'Divisions have emerged among the states in the GCC, including most surprisingly between the UAE and Saudi Arabia. This was evident in Yemen, where there are different visions for the way ahead. But the unity of purpose remains, for now.'[115] Familiar rivalries and disagreements on issues like Iran re-emerged: 'A regional order defined by moderate Sunni autocrats united against a radical Shia threat masked considerable internal competition, however. Saudi Arabia aspired to lead a unified Arab world against Iran, but faced multiple challengers.'[116] In addition, the opportunity to drive its own agenda made the UAE more willing to draw on the growing capabilities they amassed over the previous years to defend their individual interests in the region. The UAE and some of its neighbouring Gulf Arab states 'began to aggressively try to mould the direction of the popular uprisings', but rather than work together, their interventions were more 'competitive than cooperative'.[117] In fact, in some instances, the competition further fed into their desire to pursue their own agendas. For example, Emirati interventions in the region following the Arab Spring were at times driven as much by opposing Qatari clients than clear interest or other strategic priorities.[118] This was further worsened by the competing priorities in the region: for example, the UAE focused its efforts on curbing Islamism in the region, whereas Qatar had spent years cultivating a relationship with regional Islamic networks and groups, like the Muslim Brotherhood. Importantly, this put the UAE at odds with Riyadh as well: the UAE, 'far more regionally active than ever before in its history, generally closely aligned itself with Saudi Arabia but had different priorities and a sharply different perspective on Islamist movements', presaging an increasingly problematic point in their relations.[119] While, as established, differences among the GCC states were nothing new, after the Arab Spring, they were no longer pushed aside or quietly dealt with to demonstrate unity.

***

The 2011 Arab Spring posed several problems for the elites in the UAE. First, the regional uprisings highlighted their vulnerability to change and their precarious hold on power. The Arab Spring also left a void in the region following the collapse of countries like Egypt, providing the UAE with an opportunity to step in and fill the power vacuum. But where there was an opportunity for the UAE, there was also an opportunity for Iran, which sought to capitalize on the vacuum by calling for a region-wide 'Islamic Awakening' and deploying its hard power throughout the region. This coincided with the impression that their US ally would no longer blindly defend its partners in the region, affecting their perception of their security relations with the United States, which had provided them with reassurance against threats in the region. The combination of threats and fears the Arab Spring unleashed impacted how the UAE conducted foreign policy, as it increased its involvement in the regional arena, and increasingly did so with little consideration for the interests of its allies and friends.

2 THE US 'PIVOT TO ASIA'

President Obama announced he would be America's 'first Pacific President' during a trip to Japan in the first year of his presidency in November 2009.[1] He believed that his predecessor, President George W. Bush, 'had paid too little attention to Asian regional issues and that the United States should restore and then enhance its traditional level of engagement there'.[2] The slow recovery of the US economy, and the American perception that it need not maintain such a heavy presence in Iraq and Afghanistan, enabled 'America to become more engaged in Asia'.[3]

But the beginning of the Obama presidency seemed to indicate a different path: one where the United States reaffirmed its commitment to the Middle East. Only months after coming to the White House, President Obama delivered a speech entitled 'A New Beginning' during a visit to Cairo in June 2009 to 'Muslims around the world'.[4] In it, he called for a reset in relations between Muslims and the West, based on 'mutual interest and mutual respect'.[5] Arabs believed this signalled a greater US commitment to the region, one that did not involve imposing Western values on the Arab world but, rather, built on a more equal partnership.[6] While President Obama did indeed have the intention of rebuilding ties with Muslim countries following eight years of destructive US foreign policy in the region, his intention was to do so to allow the United States to focus a greater part of its attention on Asia and the growing concern posed by a rising China.[7] Secretary of State Hillary Clinton elaborated on what this 'Pivot' to Asia would entail, presenting it as a reallocation of resources, which had been freed up following the winding down of the conflicts in Iraq and Afghanistan, to the Asia-Pacific.[8]

Ultimately, the Pivot had little real impact on the ground for US partners in the Middle East. Its psychological effect on the region, however, was considerable. Following the events of the Arab Spring and President Obama's perceived abandonment of Mubarak in Egypt, the UAE perceived the statement as proof that the United States was embarking on a long-term strategy of disengagement in the Middle East – at its expense. This highlighted America's unreliability as a security guarantor and partner. The Pivot gave new momentum to the idea that to guarantee its security, the UAE would have to stand on its own two feet.

The United States in the Persian Gulf region

After the Second World War, US presence in the Middle East was dictated by the Cold War and the need to pull Arab countries away from Soviet influence.[9] In the Persian Gulf, however, it was only after the Iraq invasion of Kuwait that US presence in the Gulf Arab states became a permanent presence, marking the beginning of a close security relationship, but one which was not without its complications. The US presence in the Gulf Arab countries was controversial for domestic audiences in those countries – particularly among the religious elites who did not want a more visible and permanent US presence.[10] But this did not prevent America from becoming a major player on the ground.

After the Second World War, the Middle East became a key arena in the struggle against Communism as the US backed Israel against Soviet-backed Arab governments. As such, any intervention in the region was viewed within the context of containing the Soviet Union. When in 1971 the UK withdrew from the region, the Gulf Arabs looked for new partners. The United States did not want to take over the role of the British; instead, it developed a 'Twin Pillar' policy: relying on both Iran and Saudi Arabia to safeguard the United States' local interests and stability in the region. The policy was developed as part of the Richard Nixon Doctrine, which established that while the United States would assist its friends and allies in defending against aggressors, it could not defend all countries in the world.[11] It outlined that the shah's Iran would receive political support and weapons so 'it could act as an American proxy in the region', while Saudi Arabia would be encouraged to expand militarily, but still be viewed as the 'distinctly junior partner in security matters'.[12] This increased existing tensions between Iran and Saudi Arabia as they vied for US support and assistance in the region. The competition for US support was short-lived, however. The 1979 Islamic Revolution led Washington to abandon its Twin Pillars policy and side with Saudi

Arabia and the other Gulf Arab states against an Islamic government that had openly threatened the United States and US persons with the takeover of the embassy in Tehran, which began on 4 November 1979.[13]

The 1979 revolution elevated the Iranian threat in the eyes of the Gulf Arab states. The relatively young Gulf Arab states felt vulnerable even though the United States had abandoned Iran as an ally and had offered them security assurances. In President Jimmy Carter's 1980 State of the Union address, he stated, 'An attempt by any outside force to gain control of the Persian Gulf region will be regarded as an assault on the vital interests of the United States of America, and such an assault will be repelled by any means necessary, including military force.'[14] Yet, the Gulf Arab states maintained a wary eye on US involvement in the region.

The Iraqi invasion of Kuwait further shook the balance of power. It highlighted the weakness and vulnerability of the Gulf Arab states,[15] and helped erase concerns over US presence on their soil. The United States needed access to Saudi bases to help the Gulf countries defend themselves against the Iraqi aggressor.[16] As a result, Saudi Arabia invited US troops to the region, but did so without signing any formal agreement – a testament to the sensitivity of the decision.[17] The Gulf Arab states abandoned the 'myth of self-reliance',[18] and unified to form the Gulf Cooperation Council (GCC).[19] The Clinton administration formalized this step and added a military dimension to it with the development of the 'dual containment' policy, which identified both Iran and Iraq as threats and sought to isolate both countries.[20] Importantly, the relationships with the Gulf Arab states never became an alliance. But this did not stop many in the region from treating it as such. They saw the United States as an ally: 'Yes, the defence relationships aren't formalised, but it's a distinction without a difference because you'll have the tripwire effect,' explained a Gulf analyst during a round table in Dubai in 2016.[21] 'Defence agreements don't have to be worded as an alliance to effectively act as one,' he added. Nevertheless, the move to internationalize regional security contributed to significant domestic political turbulence in these countries, and increased tensions with Iran, which believed in the indigenization of regional security. But ultimately, hosting US troops in the region helped establish an era of relative peace in the 1990s.[22]

A decade later, the attack on the twin towers in New York and targets in Washington DC led to a change in US Middle East policy.[23] President George W. Bush led a new ideological American policy that involved engineering 'social and political change in the Middle East by using force', combating terror by 'toppling the tyrants who supported them' and 'relying on unilateral force to reaffirm US dominance',[24] elements of which were outlined in the 2002 National Security Strategy.[25] President Bush's case for the spread of democracy was not limited to Iraq and Afghanistan – the countries that felt the brunt of the post-9/11 need to take action – it targeted countries like Saudi Arabia, Egypt and Bahrain as well.[26] And that was the crux of the problem: for America's Gulf Arab friends, the US invasion of Iraq in 2003 was considered a 'double betrayal': First, 'the US commitment to regional democratization axiomatically threatened the one-family rule' system in place in the Gulf Arab states. America's ideological foreign policy that aimed to spread democratic values in the Middle East region proved their security partner did not view them as equals. Rather, they saw this as Washington's intention to tell them what to do, including embracing democracy. Second, it led to the 'vast expansion of Iranian influence' in the region because it removed Saddam Hussein as a barrier to the spread of Iranian influence, and in fact, pushed the Sunni country into the Iranian sphere of influence.[27] It was 'guaranteed to stoke resentment'.[28] America's reputation in the Middle East took a severe beating.[29] This set the scene for the perceived change in policy that would come with the election of President Barack Obama.

The election of President Obama was a welcome change, both at home and abroad.[30] Obama openly rejected the Bush doctrine, calling it 'outdated' because it responded to an 'unconventional threat' with 'conventional thinking'.[31] He dismissed the idea of retrenchment and outlined that America would continue to lead in partnership with its allies, but he also believed that foreign policy should be 'driven by national interest' and should aim to establish stability.[32] According to Ben Rhodes, former deputy national security advisor for Strategic Communications and Speechwriting under President Obama, the administration would first have to deal with a number of issues they had inherited from the Bush presidency:

> The project of the first two years has been to effectively deal with the legacy issues that we inherited, particularly the Iraq war, the Afghan war, and the war against Al Qaeda, while rebalancing our resources and our posture in the world ... If you were to boil it all down to a bumper sticker, it's 'wind down these two wars, re-establish American standing and leadership in the world, and focus on a broader set of priorities, from Asia and the global economy to a nuclear-nonproliferation regime'.[33]

The Middle East was intrigued by what this change would mean for them.[34] President Obama conducted extensive outreach to the region, beginning just days after his inauguration with an interview to Al-Arabiya, a Dubai-based Arabic news outlet.[35] He called for immediate engagement with the region, and addressed pressing concerns, including the Israeli-Palestinian issue.[36] Only months after his inauguration, Obama, on his first trip as president, travelled to Muslim-majority Turkey to reiterate the administration's policy of 'broader engagement' of the Muslim world based on 'mutual interest and mutual respect'.[37] Shortly after, he repeated this policy aim in a speech entitled 'A New Beginning' during a visit to Cairo in June 2009 to 'Muslims around the world'.[38] The speech was directed at Arab public opinion and aimed to reset relations between Muslims and the West, based on 'mutual interest and mutual respect'.[39] America's friends in the region thought this might signal a new era of greater US commitment; based on a more equal partnership,[40] it sparked expectations that relations with the United States would be different from now on.[41] But Obama's foreign policy goals were more nuanced than that. He aimed to draw down US presence in the region and widen the focus of America's foreign policy. In fact, Obama's speech in Cairo was not intended to show that the Middle East was a foreign policy priority, but rather 'Obama's outreach strategy reflected less of a sustained commitment and engagement in the region and more of an effort to cut further losses and perform damage control'.[42] American officials, including Thomas E. Donilon, national security advisor to President Obama, made their desire to focus on more pressing concerns clear. According to Ryan Lizza of the *New Yorker*,

> One of Donilon's overriding beliefs, which Obama adopted as his own, was that America needed to rebuild its reputation, extricate itself from the Middle East and Afghanistan, and turn its attention toward Asia and China's unchecked influence in the region. America was 'overweighted' in the former and 'underweighted' in the latter, Donilon told me. 'We've been on a little bit of a Middle East detour over the course of the last ten years,' Kurt Campbell, the Assistant Secretary of State for East Asian and Pacific Affairs, said. 'And our future will be dominated utterly and fundamentally by developments in Asia and the Pacific region.'[43]

As a result, the Obama administration crafted the 'Pivot to Asia' policy.

President Obama's 'Pivot to Asia'

In his 2016 profile of the president entitled 'The Obama Doctrine', Jeffrey Goldberg wrote that Obama was 'fixated on turning America's attention to Asia. For Obama, Asia represents the future'.[44] Aside from a nod towards rebuilding 'ties to (US) allies in Europe and Asia' in his piece in *Foreign Affairs* in 2007,[45] it was only after his inauguration that President Obama highlighted his desire to enact a US Pivot to Asia.[46] During a trip to Japan in his first year in office, President Obama referred to himself as 'America's first Pacific President', stating that 'as an Asia Pacific nation, the United States expects to be involved in the discussions that shape the future of this region'.[47] The Pivot was an ambitious policy that was refined on a number of occasions. But ultimately, the president was forced to scale back his ambitions for US foreign policy in Asia.

Two important international factors enabled and encouraged the roll-out of the policy: the first was China's growing assertiveness in the region beginning in 2010. Initially, the Obama administration did not aim to contain China, rather, to engage Beijing.[48] America's priority was to tackle the effects of the 2008 financial crisis, and in this, the administration 'believed China would be an indispensable partner'.[49] During their first meeting in London on 1 April 2009, President Obama and President Hu Jintao announced the 'US-China Strategic and Economic Dialogue', which was intended to make meetings between senior officials in economics and foreign policy of both countries a regular and structured occurrence.[50] Obama's first visit to China in November 2009 was intended to showcase the beginning of a better relationship with Beijing, but China held firm on a number of issues, leading to media coverage of a 'rising China, more willing to say no to the United States'.[51] Obama's policy of engaging China was not popular with his cabinet, including Secretary Clinton who said, 'I don't want my grandchildren to live in a world dominated by the Chinese',[52] and pushed him to take a tougher stance against Beijing. While China helped the United States out in certain respects, it held firm on others, including helping curb North Korea's bellicose behaviour.[53] In addition, Beijing stepped up its claims to islands in the South China Sea in 2010,[54] leading to Washington's calls for peace talks and urging China to show restraint.[55] Tensions also rose between China and the United States on the economic front.[56] Beijing's growing assertiveness highlighted that President Obama's policy of engagement was not working, instead providing the United States with an opportunity to strengthen ties with its allies and partners in Asia. It also spearheaded the adoption of a 'tougher line', which included filing cases against China at the World Trade Organization and announcing the deployment of a new missile defence system in Japan.[57]

Along with China's growing willingness to assert itself internationally, the drawdown of US troop numbers in Iraq and Afghanistan was an important enabler for this policy shift. US troops had been present in Afghanistan since the first thousand special forces were sent to the country to support US air strikes against Taliban forces following the 9/11 attacks in 2001.[58] Following the 2006 resurgence in violence, President Obama announced a surge in US troops in Afghanistan to tackle the violence,[59] which allowed the start of the drawdown in July 2011. A similar pattern followed in Iraq following the US invasion in March 2003.[60] The US-led coalition ended Saddam Hussein's regime but led to a long era of sectarian violence, lawlessness and political instability. During the campaign, Obama announced he would withdraw US combat brigades from Iraq by the summer of 2010, and the remainder of US troops would leave by the end of 2011. As a result, by 2011, it appeared that the United States would no longer be impeded by its military commitments to Iraq and Afghanistan, enabling it to turn its attention elsewhere. Ultimately though, Obama struggled to fulfil his drawdown plans. Despite his July 2011 target date, American troops remained in Afghanistan until 2012, and it was only in May 2014 that the president announced a timetable for withdrawing US forces from the country by the end of 2016.[61] Nevertheless, the drawing down of the wars in Iraq and Afghanistan – the 'legacy issues' that the Obama administration 'inherited', according to Ben Rhodes[62] – was a factor that enabled the Obama administration to turn its attention to Asia.

What did the Pivot entail?

President Obama outlined his vision for the 'Pivot to Asia' in a speech in November 2011. The speech

articulated an integrated diplomatic, military, and economic strategy that stretches from the Indian subcontinent through Northeast Asia – and one that can profoundly shape the U.S.-China relationship. The core message: America is going to play a leadership role in Asia for decades to come.[63]

President Obama's first stop was the Asia-Pacific Economic Cooperation (APEC) summit, which was hosted in Hawaii, where he stated, 'The United States is a Pacific power and we are here to stay.'[64] In his speech to the Australian parliament on 17 November 2011, President Obama reaffirmed US commitment to its allies in the region, reiterating, 'Our new focus on this region reflects a fundamental truth – the United States has been, and always will be, a Pacific nation.'[65] The president outlined the three areas the rebalance would focus on: security, prosperity and human rights.[66]

President Obama made security in Asia a top priority. During his trip to Australia in November 2011, Obama announced that the United States would base 2,500 marines in Darwin – prompting China to respond that the United States was escalating military tensions in its backyard.[67] President Obama attended the East Asia Summit (EAS) in November 2011, and focused on building the Trans-Pacific Partnership (TPP) so that it would become a 'high-quality trade and investment platform that will include the major economies of the Asia-Pacific', though China did not figure in the initial group of countries negotiating the deal. Following the 2008 economic crisis, the economic angle of the Pivot was also key to its effectiveness. Indeed, 'in 2010, 61 percent of U.S. goods exports and 72 percent of U.S. agricultural exports worldwide went to the Asia-Pacific'.[68] Following the outbreak of the Arab Spring, President Obama also promoted democracy and human rights in Asia. While many of the measures outlined by Obama already existed, including those on pushing back Chinese ambitions, his November 2011 policy statement 'brought disparate elements together in a strategically integrated fashion that explicitly affirms and promises to sustain American leadership throughout Asia for the foreseeable future'.[69] The strategy outlined was complex and multilayered, it involved both simultaneously confronting China and strengthening ties with it.

The Pivot was further clarified by several American officials in the months and years that followed. In October 2011, Secretary of State Hillary Clinton outlined six major pillars of the policy, referring to it as 'forward-deployed diplomacy'.[70] Interestingly, and significant for the Gulf Arab states, Clinton couched it in terms of a move from the Middle East region to Asia, with the headline sentence for her piece stating, 'The future of politics will be decided in Asia, not Afghanistan or Iraq.'[71] Tom Donilon, Obama's national security advisor, regularly engaged with the media and the public to outline the merits of the rebalance to Asia. In

November 2012, he reiterated America's commitment to the rebalance to Asia, and restated the important components of the policy: alliance-building and strengthening, 'forging deeper partnerships with emerging powers', engaging with regional multilateral institutions, strengthening the relationship with China and 'advancing the region's economic architecture'.[72] In 2015, Secretary of Defense Ash Carter outlined the 'next phase' of the Pivot, focusing on three principal issues: investment and development of capabilities 'relevant to the Asia-Pacific's complex and dynamic security environment', deployment of military capabilities 'suited to the Asia-Pacific now and for years to come', adapting America's 'overall defense posture in the region to be geographically distributed, operationally resilient, and politically sustainable', all the while continuing the focus on boosting regional alliances and partnerships, with attention also paid to 'building unprecedented "trilateral" cooperation' – defined as 'networking (America's) relationships'.[73] In 2016, Ambassador Susan Rice, national security advisor to President Obama, assessed that the Pivot was vital to 'renew and redefine U.S. leadership on the world stage' and to boost America's economic recovery.[74] She outlined the policy's success, emphasizing ties to new partners and expanding 'region-wide cooperation' through multilateral institutions, citing US participation in the EAS and The Association of Southeast Asian Nations (ASEAN), and the launch of the Young Southeast Asian Leaders Initiative.[75] But the result was not as clear-cut as she suggested.

The administration was constrained by several other issues. According to Admiral Harry B. Harris, nominated in 2013 to be the commander of the US Pacific Command, 'Continued reductions to meet sequestration-mandated resource levels will diminish our military's size, reach, and margin of technological superiority. All of these factors will impact the U.S. rebalance to the Pacific'.[76] Other international crises also limited the Pivot, including Russia's annexation of Crimea in 2014, which required attention. But it was the unforeseen events in the Middle East that required an enduring commitment to the region: 'The principal challenges likely will emanate from the greater Middle East, a region that is plagued by volatility but inseparable from core U.S. interests'.[77] The region was experiencing 'current' challenges, such as how to stabilize Afghanistan and Iraq, dealing with Iran and the spread of Islamism.[78] Throughout the remainder of his presidency, no matter how much President Obama tried to focus his attention on Asia, consecutive crises in the Middle East made it impossible for him to achieve all that he set out to.

Ultimately, the success of Obama administration's policy of rebalancing towards Asia was mixed. Importantly though, the Pivot had little concrete effect on the United States' commitment to the Middle East. Obama continued to be heavily involved in the unfolding crises in the region. But it was too late. In the UAE, the belief that the United States was disengaging from the region was so predominant that it ignored the numbers pointing towards increasing economic ties,[79] and ever-closer cultural and military relations between Abu Dhabi and Washington.[80] These things no longer mattered, the president had made clear his intention to draw down forces in the Middle East and focus his attention on Asia and that is what America's friends in the region heard.

The impact of the Pivot on the Persian Gulf region

Irrespective of how far the administration got in the implementation of its Pivot policy, it was the message of wanting to draw down America's involvement in conflicts in the Middle East that was heard by leaders in the region.[81] It did not matter that ultimately Obama was not able to disengage from the Middle East as much as he wanted to, the damage had been done by just stating his intention to. The Pivot impacted the region by firmly establishing the perception that US disengagement from the region was not temporary but rather, part of a long-term trend. It made America's partners in the region increasingly nervous about their security, and further added to the unease that had already appeared following the Arab Spring: that the United States could not be trusted to deliver on its security guarantees to the UAE and its neighbours if needed. Importantly, though, while the Arab Spring highlighted Gulf Arab fears of abandonment by the United States, some hoped that Obama's change in foreign policy direction with regard to the region would be an exception rather than the new rule.[82] The statement of the 'Pivot to Asia', however, destroyed that hope. The UAE not only believed that it would be left to fend for itself in case of a crisis, but that it would also face the growing regional threats without US support. This further fed into Abu Dhabi's desire to become increasingly self-sufficient, and its subsequent growing assertiveness.

Long-term US disengagement from the region

President Obama's stated desire to pivot towards Asia erased doubts that his management of the crises during the Arab Spring was a fluke. To the Gulf Arabs, the public statement of a desire to move away from the Middle East towards Asia was the clear announcement of a long-term goal of the United States to lessen involvement in the Middle East. President Obama further fed into this belief with his less-than-complimentary statements on the region's rulers, the lack of democracy in the region and the necessity for regional powers to work together to resolve their differences.[83] In an interview with Jeffrey Goldberg in 2016, he compared the Middle East and Asia, outlining his stark vision of the former and how it compares to Asia's growth potential and prosperity:

> Right now, I don't think that anybody can be feeling good about the situation in the Middle East … You have countries that are failing to provide prosperity and opportunity for their people. You've got a violent, extremist ideology, or ideologies, that are turbocharged through social media. You've got countries that have very few civic traditions, so that as autocratic regimes start fraying, the only organizing principles are sectarian … Contrast that with Southeast Asia, which still has huge problems – enormous poverty, corruption – but is filled with striving, ambitious, energetic people who are every single day scratching and clawing to build businesses and get education and find jobs and build infrastructure. The contrast is pretty stark … They are not thinking about how to kill Americans … What they're thinking about is How do I get a better education? How do I create something of value?[84]

Elites in Gulf Arab states were outraged at the interview. According to a former Emirati military intelligence official, the Pivot, coupled with Obama's language when describing US partners in the Persian Gulf, led to a loss of 'all trust in the US'.[85] In the summer of 2013, the Obama administration conducted a review of the Pivot and their policies in the Middle East. The result of the review was announced by President Obama in a statement to the UN in September 2013, where he was careful to state that the United States would not disengage from the region, but that it would be 'far more likely to invest our energy in those countries that want to work with us, that invest in their people instead of a corrupt few; that embrace a vision of society where everyone can contribute – men and women, Shia or Sunni, Muslim, Christian or Jew' – a contrast to his more positive tone when discussing the Pacific region.[86] A month later, National Security Advisor Susan Rice went one step further and stated, 'We can't just be consumed 24/7 by one region, important as it is … (President Obama) thought it was a good time to step back and reassess, in a very critical and kind of no-holds-barred way, how we conceive the region.'[87] This was jarring to the Gulf Arab states.[88] 'You can't count on the US, it has no vision for the region,' said a prominent regional analyst.[89] Over time, as the policy became clearer and repeated by different parts of the administration, it became clear that pivoting to Asia was something the United States as a whole wanted to focus on.

While some in regional policy circles were reassured that Obama's tenure was nearing an end,[90] others believed that even a Republican president would follow this trend, though the hope was that it would be to a lesser extent than Obama did.[91] An Emirati foreign policy expert referred to this period as a 'new era' characterized by the 'retreat of great powers', clearly seeing a long-term decline of US involvement and power in the region.[92] Others echoed this sentiment: 'Resentment against the US is growing in the region. There won't be a change with the next administration. The Arab public has lost faith in the US. The elites have lost faith. No change of leadership in the US will change this.'[93] Others, including those in the wider GCC, agreed. Experts in Qatar said that the UAE and Saudi Arabia in particular blamed many of the region's woes on the US disengagement from the region, and that they 'don't believe Obama when he says he won't abandon them'.[94] A former Omani member of the Shura council said, 'The US is interested in leaving the region, that much is clear.'[95] A member of the board of Oman's central bank said, 'The region's been taken for a ride by the US. Now it's time for us to be realistic about what we can expect.'[96] During the 2016 presidential race in the United States, the Republican candidate Donald Trump repeated that if he were president, he would be 'making allies pay' for US support,[97] which further unnerved regional leaders.[98] While ultimately President Trump was more vocal in his support of America's Gulf Arab partners during his presidency – in fact, Saudi Arabia was his first state visit as president in May 2017,[99] he did not always deliver in practice, as Gulf Arab states were left to fend for themselves, particularly during the 'maximum pressure' campaign on Iran and the regional tensions this led to throughout 2019–20.[100] And the return of a Democratic administration under President Joe Biden in January 2021 did not help.

The UAE developed a different strategy in its effort not to find itself isolated from future US administrations, especially a Republican one: it chose to cultivate close ties and build influence within the Trump administration, hoping this would help it maintain US interest in its security and engagement in the region.[101] 'We will wait out Obama,' said an Emirati official before the US elections in 2016, displaying confidence in their ability to work with and manage whatever US party came to power after Obama.[102] In fact, while the Emiratis preferred a Republican win, they also believed that a Hillary Clinton presidency, while not ideal, would not be as complicated as an Obama administration.[103] As secretary of state, Clinton demonstrated that she would be tough on Iran and eager to deepen ties with America's Gulf Arab partners. But the UAE's strategy was only partly successful. The United States' policy in the Middle East under President Trump did not go the way Abu Dhabi anticipated. Ultimately, Abu Dhabi came to the view that the perceived US disengagement from the region was a long-term, strategic shift, rather than a change brought about by a single democratic administration.[104]

The United States is not a reliable partner anymore

Irrespective of the impact of the Pivot on the ground, the UAE and its regional allies became convinced that the United States could no longer be relied upon to help them should they require it.[105] In 2016, a regional analyst said, 'The US is not willing to do what is necessary to maintain relations with the Gulf Arabs. It is not in a position to restore confidence.'[106] Obama's dismissive tone towards the Gulf Arab leaders gave momentum to the idea that because he disliked them and their way of governing, he would not necessarily come to their aid unless it was directly in the United States' interests to do so. 'Obama believes the Gulf Arab states are acting like spoiled kids,' said an Omani analyst.[107] He added, 'The Gulf Arab states have no security guarantor anymore.'[108] As a result, whether it was because of President Obama's isolationism, his perceived dislike of the Gulf Arab leadership or the perception that the United States was a waning global power, the result for the UAE and its Gulf Arab neighbours was the same: the United States could no longer be trusted to come to the defence of the Gulf Arab monarchies without hesitation, should it be required to. In Abu Dhabi, it also fostered a sense that the UAE's goals and interests would likely be either ignored or deprioritized by the United States, which meant that Abu Dhabi would have to pursue them itself.

Against this background, it is important to note, however, that during this period US officials were at pains to highlight growing ties between the United States and the UAE and the significant US presence in the region. The UAE and the United States expanded on the 1994 Defense Cooperation Agreement and set up a 'Defense Cooperation Framework', which was intended to improve the integration of United States and Emirati capabilities, and completed the basing of 5,000 US forces at various facilities throughout the UAE, including Jebel Ali port and Al Dhafra airbase.[109] In addition, the UAE also requested to be considered a 'Major Non-NATO Ally', similar to Kuwait and Bahrain, or a 'key U.S. defense partner' in order to expedite the approval of weapon sales to it.[110] Despite the generally negative views of the United States,[111] the UAE continued to do what it could to ensure greater US involvement in regional security matters, and a greater US stake in the UAE's security and military. This, despite the increasing public dislike of the US presence in the region. A 2016 poll showed that disapproval of the United States and its involvement in the Middle East had reached 69 per cent in the UAE, only slightly behind Saudi Arabia's 72 per cent.[112] About 77 per cent of respondents polled disagreed that the United States contributed to peace and stability in the Arab world.[113] But this did not prevent a sizeable 75 per cent of Emiratis polled to state that it was important for them to maintain good ties with the United States.[114] The continued defence cooperation with the United States and Abu Dhabi's continued efforts to court the United States in the security sphere did not, however, change the perspective in Abu Dhabi that in the long run, the United States would not be a reliable partner.

It became clear that the UAE and its neighbours viewed the Pivot as a statement of fact and a long-term change in US foreign policy. This, as the region became increasingly unstable. In other words, as the UAE's threat perception of the region worsened, it also felt less able to address it, given the United States' perceived disengagement from and disinterest in the region.[115] This conferred the UAE with a sense that they would have to take their security into their own hands.

When President Obama announced he would be America's 'first Pacific President' in November 2009,[116] the UAE took relatively little notice because it followed on the heels of the president's speech in Cairo only six months prior, where he reaffirmed America's commitment to the Middle East and its people. The Cairo speech was welcomed as a new era in US relations with the Middle East, one based on 'mutual interest and mutual respect'.[117] But President Obama had another goal in mind: with the gradual recovery of the US economy, and the perception that the United States need not maintain such a heavy presence in Iraq and Afghanistan, America could turn to Asia, a region where 'growth and dynamism' was key because it was linked to US economic growth, and peace and stability would be 'crucial to global progress'.[118] While ultimately the Pivot had little real impact on the ground for US allies and friends in the Middle East, its psychological effect on the region, however, was considerable. The UAE and its allies saw the Pivot – which followed on the footsteps of America's 'abandonment' of Mubarak in Egypt – as further proof of a waning US commitment to the region. As a result, the Gulf Arabs perceived the establishment of a long-term US policy of disengagement from the Middle East, making it an unreliable security partner. This was a major change for the UAE, forcing it to react by becoming increasingly assertive, especially in the pursuit of greater self-sufficiency, including diversifying its security relations and suppliers, and focusing on building indigenous capabilities. It also further fostered a sense that the UAE's goals and interests would likely be either ignored or deprioritized, which meant that Abu Dhabi would have to pursue them itself. The Pivot to Asia was the second catalyst that further entrenched Abu Dhabi's growing desire to become increasingly independent and assertive in the conduct of its foreign policy. But there remained one more major international event that would affect the way the UAE conducted foreign policy: the 2015 nuclear deal with Iran.

3 THE 2015 IRAN NUCLEAR DEAL

On 14 July 2015, after decades of negotiations and a final round of intense talks that lasted nearly three years, the United States, UK, France, China, Russia and Germany (referred to as the P5+1 – the five permanent members of the UN Security Council plus Germany) and Iran finally reached an agreement on Iran's nuclear programme. The negotiations were gruelling and overcame multiple challenges and misunderstandings. The final agreement contained or rolled back parts of Iran's nuclear programme, and extended Iran's 'breakout time' from three months to one year, giving the international community time to react should Iran attempt to dash for the bomb.[1] It was a multilateral victory that put in place a number of unprecedented mechanisms, including intrusive verification procedures, which would provide access and insight into the Iranian nuclear programme.[2] But Iran's Gulf Arab neighbours saw it differently.

It was no secret that the UAE was sceptical of the nuclear negotiations.[3] It resented not being included in them.[4] But the problem ran deeper: to Abu Dhabi, while the 2015 nuclear deal was useful in curbing Iran's nuclear programme, which carried a number of security and environmental risks,[5] it was, in fact, a secondary security concern.[6] The real concern was Iran's regional policy.[7] This was made worse by the difficult regional context, which they viewed as aligning against them, and one which the United States was perceived to be leaving. Abu Dhabi feared the deal would provide Iran with further means to fund its proxies and destabilize the region at its expense and would 'give Iran the green light' to do what it wanted in the region.[8] When the P5+1 finally reached an agreement with Iran, the UAE reacted publicly with caution, but privately prepared itself to contain Iran.[9] It also privately lobbied its allies and friends to ensure that the deal would not diminish the international community's desire to contain Iran and its activities in the region.[10] As a result, while the government publicly supported the deal, it also highlighted the Iran threat at a time when it felt its allies and friends were ignoring its interests and concerns.[11] The events of the Arab Spring combined with the perception of US withdrawal from the region compounded the UAE's fears. The nuclear deal made it seem like Washington was abandoning the UAE in favour of its regional rival, who was now legitimized by the process of negotiations and deal-making with world powers.[12] The deal highlighted Iran as a major security threat for the UAE, and further justified its more assertive foreign policy path.

Iran as a historical threat

It was inevitable that Iran's existence would pose a threat to the UAE and other Gulf Arab neighbours. When he came to power in September 1941 following his father's abdication,[13] Mohammad Reza Shah wanted to ensure his country could become self-reliant, a modern country and a regional, if not international, powerhouse.[14] The shah exploited every opportunity he could to achieve his regional ambitions, which directly affected the security of the Gulf Arab states.[15] After the Islamic Revolution of 1979, the very nature of the new theocratic government in Tehran threatened the UAE and its Gulf Arab allies. The Islamic Republic's desire to spread the Islamic revolution in the region,[16] and Ayatollah Khomeini's repeated challenges to the legitimacy of the Al Saud's reign in Saudi Arabia,[17] did little to help the growing distrust and antagonism the Gulf Arab states felt towards Tehran. Over time, as Iran's system matured, the revolutionary zeal faded,[18] and the Islamic Republic became increasingly pragmatic. As a result, Iran's involvement in the region mainly became a way for it to secure itself and create a buffer zone between its borders and hostile foreign powers,[19] though desires of Iranian regional hegemony and influence remained.[20] As a result, the Islamic Republic and its regional goals have always been one of the most pressing foreign policy concerns for most of Iran's Gulf Arab neighbours.[21] But the Gulf Arab states could not agree on their Iran policy.[22] Oman, for example, repeatedly called for closer relations with Tehran,[23] attracting the ire of some of its more anti-Iran neighbours.[24] At the other end of the spectrum, Saudi Arabia and the UAE are firm on pushing Iran back,[25] while countries like Kuwait and Qatar sit somewhere in the middle: concerned about Iran's regional policies but forced to work with Tehran either because of the sizeable Iranian contingency within their borders (Kuwait) or because of shared gas fields (Qatar).[26] In addition, there were periods where dialogue between the Gulf Arabs and Iran was impossible, and others, where relations were warmer, under Iranian President Akbar Hashemi Rafsanjani or President Mohammad Khatami, for example.[27] As a result, the Gulf Arab states struggled to present a unified front on Iran policy,[28] further limiting their ability to deal with the Iranian threat. This was the context with which the UAE watched the Iranian nuclear crisis unfold.

Iran's nuclear programme

Iran's nuclear programme began under the shah, in coordination with other countries and suppliers.[29] When the Islamic Republic came to power, the United States and its allies, previously content to work with Iran, broke off relations and ceased to supply its nuclear programme and pressured others, including China and Argentina, to do the same.[30] For Iran, pursuing the nuclear path was important because it had devoted too much time, money and effort to walk away from it, and had tied the issue to one of national pride, prestige and innovation.[31] Meanwhile, the United States began the imposition of its multilayered sanctions programme intended to punish Iran for the hostage crisis and its poor human rights record, and eventually, constrain its nuclear programme.[32] In 2002, an Iranian opposition group revealed the existence of two nuclear facilities: an enrichment facility in Natanz and a heavy water reactor at Arak, sparking an international crisis that would last more than a decade.[33]

In June 2003, the foreign ministers from three EU states, France's Dominique de Villepin, Germany's Joschka Fischer and the UK's Jack Straw, engaged Iranian authorities on their nuclear programme, initiating more than a decade of negotiations with the Europeans, which was later expanded to include the other permanent members of the UN Security Council, the United States, China and Russia (known as the P5+1).[34] It was not until the secret talks between the United States and Iran – which had not met bilaterally since the 1979 revolution – in Oman,[35] and the election of President Hassan Rouhani, who brought in a new team of technocrats and made the resolution of this crisis a priority for his administration, that the negotiations were given new impetus. Two months after a phone call between Presidents Obama and Rouhani, the highest official contact between both countries since 1979,[36] negotiators adopted the Joint Plan of Action (JPOA), a roadmap to the final comprehensive agreement, which temporarily froze and even rolled back some parts of the Iranian programme in exchange for a suspension of some sanctions, for the duration of the negotiations.[37] The negotiators renewed the JPOA multiple times, leading to the April 2015 'framework' agreement, which outlined the 'key parameters' of a Joint Comprehensive Plan of Action (JCPOA).[38] After a final painstaking push, the negotiators announced the JCPOA on 14 July 2015.[39]

A good deal?

The JCPOA outlined restrictions on Iran's nuclear programme, and detailed verification and implementation measures, in exchange for comprehensive sanctions relief and peaceful nuclear cooperation. The deal addressed both available routes to a nuclear weapon: enriched uranium and plutonium. Under the terms of the deal, Iran's centrifuges were cut to roughly half the centrifuges Iran had before the agreement for ten years.[40] The deal limits Iranian research and development work, prevents Tehran from enriching above 5 per cent, caps its stockpile of low enriched uranium to three hundred kilograms for fifteen years and extends Iran's breakout time – the time it takes to amass all the raw materials to build a bomb – from two to three months to one year.[41] On the plutonium track, Iran committed to halting construction at the Arak Heavy Water facility,[42] and working with the P5+1 to redesign the reactor. The deal addresses Iran's potential accumulation of fuel at the heavy water plant by requiring Tehran to ship it all out to a P5+1 or third country, where it would be disposed of or treated.[43] Implementation of the deal and potential Iranian cheating would be monitored by the most intrusive and multilayered verification mechanism to date, giving the IAEA access to all of Iran's nuclear facilities for twenty years.[44]

In exchange for these limits, Iran would receive comprehensive sanctions relief. The EU lifted its unilateral sanctions, but the United States could not do the same because of the multilayered and intertwined nature of the US sanctions regime.[45] It did, however, cease to apply all major sanctions on Iran's financial and energy sectors, and gave Iran access to oil revenue held abroad through renewable presidential orders.

Sanctions related to human rights abuses and terrorism remained in place. The EU and the UN agreed to lift their arms embargo and the restrictions on the transfers of ballistic missile technology after several years of implementation. Finally, the JCPOA promoted the establishment of civil nuclear cooperation between Iran and the P5+1 and other foreign nuclear providers.

The nuclear deal was intended to address Iran's nuclear programme: rollback or constrain different parts of it to ensure that it would be a peaceful nuclear energy programme. While this was not the focus, it was hoped that the deal would be the beginning of the end of the Islamic Republic's isolation and lead to the moderation of its other problematic behaviour. Critics focused on the fact that the deal allowed Iran to retain an enrichment programme and that restrictions would be limited in time.[46] Tehran believed that relying on external supplies made it vulnerable, and insisted that it needed to be self-sufficient.[47] In fact, US acceptance of some form of enrichment programme on Iranian soil was instrumental in ensuring the negotiations led to a deal.[48] Critics also criticized the lack of 'anytime, anywhere' inspections of all suspicious facilities,[49] but this would never have been accepted by Iran (or any other country for that matter). While the JCPOA did not completely remove Iran's enrichment capability or close all its nuclear facilities – that kind of agreement was simply not achievable – it effectively constrained and rolled back Iran's nuclear programme. But for the UAE and its neighbours, this was not enough.

The UAE and the Iran nuclear crisis

When the P5+1 and Iran began their negotiations in earnest, the UAE was both dismayed and fearful. First, it felt isolated as the world powers negotiated a regional security crisis without any GCC country represented. More importantly, it felt betrayed as its security guarantor and friend – the United States – chose to talk to the UAE's greatest rival: Iran. Finally, to Abu Dhabi, the nuclear negotiations and subsequent deal not only elevated the Islamic Republic by giving it legitimacy from its interaction with the world powers but also gave it the financial means to pursue its expansionist foreign policy agenda, making it an even greater concern. The UAE's views and fears were shared by some of the other Gulf Arab states too.

Beginning in 2005, the Gulf Arab states loudly expressed their fears of the Iranian nuclear programme. In 2006, the then secretary general of the GCC stated that Iran's nuclear programme 'totally turns over the balance of power, and makes Iran the master of the region'.[50] The Arab public was broadly in favour of an Iranian nuclear programme – especially in the context of Iranian popularity on the Arab street following the presidency of Mahmoud Ahmadinejad – which they viewed as a way to balance against Israeli hegemony and US presence in the region.[51] Their leaders, however, felt differently. A civilian nuclear programme would provide Iran with a path towards becoming nuclear-capable, and while Gulf Arab fears 'do not necessarily stem from the threat of a direct nuclear attack from Iran', they do fear the 'ripple effects' a nuclear-capable Iran would cause throughout the region,[52] and the potential for a conflict drawing in other players like the United States and Israel. Such fears were compounded by the possibility they would be caught in the crossfires: facing retaliation by Tehran or by Iranian proxies.[53] They were also afraid that Iranian leaders believed a nuclear programme 'afforded them a degree of insulation against a retaliatory attack', paving the way for Tehran to 'more aggressively intervene and influence the broader region'.[54] This involved boosting support to Hezbollah, and other Shia groups in the region, most notably in neighbouring Iraq, where the fall of Saddam Hussein had left a power vacuum, providing Iran with an opportunity to significantly increase its influence.[55]

While a lesser concern, the leadership in the Gulf Arab states also feared the civilian nuclear programme itself. Several Gulf Arab capitals and major cities sit just across from Iran's Bushehr nuclear power plant – closer than to Tehran.[56] If there was an accident, winds in the Persian Gulf, which blow from east to west, would make the Gulf States vulnerable to radiation leaks, while water supplies would be disrupted because coastal currents circle counterclockwise.[57] Abu Dhabi was particularly concerned as it believed the UAE would be the first to feel the effects of a nuclear accident in Iran.[58] These worries were compounded by the fact that Iran was the only country with a civilian nuclear programme and a fully functioning nuclear power plant that was not party to the Nuclear Safety Convention – the international treaty that established fundamental safety principles to which states that operate nuclear plants subscribed to.[59]

Despite their concerns, the Gulf Arab states remained largely quiet when the nuclear crisis first broke out in 2002 and for a few years after that. Preoccupied with Iran's involvement in neighbouring Iraq,[60] they were also 'constrained by two powerful and convergent forces: their own public opinions and resilient pan-Arab norms'.[61] As a result, responses to the nuclear programme were not unified. Their response to the crisis and the subsequent negotiations followed a three-pronged strategy – one which typified Gulf Arab foreign policy more generally: 'keep the discussion away from the public arena, placate Iran to avoid antagonizing a powerful neighbour and rely on EU diplomacy and American military forces to constrain and deter Iran'.[62] As a result, the UAE and its allies remained on the sidelines as the Europeans negotiated with Iran on its nuclear programme.

After his inauguration in January 2009, President Obama recorded a message directly to the Iranian people in March 2009 on the occasion of *Nowruz* – the Persian New Year – calling for a US engagement of Iran that is 'honest and grounded in mutual respect'.[63] This, along with President Obama's direct outreach to Supreme Leader Ayatollah Ali Khamenei,[64] set the tone for the new US administration's goals with regard to Iran. But it was not until the Sultanate of Oman offered to broker talks between Iran and the United States directly that the negotiations began in earnest. Once these negotiations seemed serious, the UAE and its Gulf Arab neighbours claimed to want to participate.[65] But they could not agree what form their participation would take, who they would send as their representative, whether the GCC or an individual state and, if the latter, then which country – something interviews with officials across the region confirmed.[66] They judged that not only would their contribution to the negotiations be marginal but there was not much they could offer Iran to entice it to give up its programme or enrichment, while others believed that nothing could entice Iran to give up its nuclear programme. The lack of GCC unity on Iran complicated matters. Oman and Qatar, for example, have a long history of economic and diplomatic exchanges with Iran, while Saudi Arabia competes for regional hegemony with Iran. Differences even exist within countries: the emirates in the UAE had different views and policies on Iran.[67] Abu Dhabi harboured real antagonism towards Iran, Ras Al Khaimah was directly affected by the islands dispute and, as such, was also tougher on Iran, while the emirates of Dubai and Sharjah did not want confrontation with it.[68] Some Arab governments believed ambiguity on Iran 'served their interests well', but that, in fact, it left them at the mercy of the United States and its allies, reduced their ability to 'shape the future of their own region'[69] and allowed Iran to exploit these differences.[70] Finally, the Gulf Arab states believed they could not be seen as 'leading the charge against Iran', because of the backlash they would face from Tehran.[71] Rather, they opted to use whatever diplomatic leverage they had on the United States and its allies to push Iran harder in the negotiations.[72] This would allow them to simultaneously continue to deal with Iran on the issue that mattered to them most: regional security, while they continued to lobby the negotiators and were kept informed of the negotiations on the nuclear programme by their allies.

The UAE and its neighbours continued to fear the outcome of the negotiations but nevertheless publicly supported them because they had the potential to resolve a long-standing international concern. Behind the scenes, however, they made it no secret that the negotiations and a potential final nuclear deal with Iran would not resolve their main concern: Iran's regional meddling.[73] In 2016, the UAE's ambassador to the United States, Youssef Al Otaiba, stated that the nuclear deal 'would only be good if it addressed the way Iran behaved in the region'.[74] To them, the international focus on Iran's nuclear programme was too narrow, ignoring the main reason why Iran was a problem. The UAE pointed to Iran's 'multi-decade investment into its proxies'[75] and feared the deal would provide Iran with further means to increase this funding, increase its meddling in the internal affairs of Arab states and destabilize the region at their expense. Officials in Abu Dhabi said they believed the deal would 'give Iran the green light' to do what they wanted in the region,[76] and 'free its hand to provide additional funding to Hezbollah, the Houthis and the Shias in Iraq'.[77] The UAE and some of its Gulf Arab allies called for a 'grand bargain' type of agreement that would help contain Iran's regional endeavours. But negotiators on both sides agreed that such an agreement was beyond reach. In fact, in private, a US negotiator stated that the United States would 'not make the discussion about regional issues because the Arabs were not in the room, and the US could not decide for the region'.[78] In addition, the UAE believed the negotiations were legitimizing the Islamic Republic as a major international player because it was negotiating with the world powers. The interim deal announced in November 2014 confirmed these fears: to them, it officially 'normalised' Iran, and demonstrated the lengths to which the Western negotiators would go to ensure that Iran would agree to a deal. As a result, opposition to the last stretch of negotiations increased, as did efforts to lobby the United States to ensure that the deal would not become an end in itself.[79]

The Obama administration tried to assuage Emirati and Gulf Arab fears by keeping them informed of the outcome of the talks. In May 2015, President Obama invited the leaders of the GCC states to Camp David to show unity and reassure its Gulf Arab friends. The Gulf Arabs wanted to draw attention to the challenges a post-deal Middle East would pose: 'We are not wasting time confronting that agreement. We don't want to be seen as going against a close ally. ... Instead, we are bracing ourselves for the post-agreement world.'[80] They aimed to reach a clear agreement on the plan for containing Iran after a nuclear deal.[81] Secretary of State John Kerry seemed to indicate this was in reach when he said, 'We are fleshing out a series of new commitments that will create between the United States and the GCC a new security understanding, a new set of security initiatives. That will take us beyond anything that we have had before.'[82] But the summit ended in disappointment; only two of the six GCC members sent their heads of state, and the United States was unable to provide the types of security assurances that Kerry had promised.[83] It was far less than what the UAE and its Gulf Arab neighbours wanted.[84] While their strategy of remaining in the background and lobbying their allies to get what they wanted worked for the UAE during previous rounds of negotiations, it did not for the final round, where instead, it felt its interests were ignored by the Obama administration.

When the final agreement was announced, the UAE expressed cautious support for it publicly but continued to focus its efforts on addressing the Iranian threat to the region.[85] Abu Dhabi nevertheless found the agreement limiting because it narrowly tackled one issue and feared it would provide Iran the means to further destabilize the region.[86]

The impact of the 2015 nuclear deal on the UAE

When the negotiators reached the final deal in July 2015, the UAE cautiously expressed support for it, while drawing attention to Iran's role in the region. Abu Dhabi recognized that the agreement was a significant achievement, but that it would only worsen its security. For the UAE, the nuclear deal provided Iran with a boost in standing and capability, making it stronger in the region, and more capable of threatening the UAE directly.[87] This was made worse by the belief that the world powers led by the United States were likely to look the other way if Iran increased its nefarious activities in the region so the deal's implementation would not be jeopardized. As a result, the UAE felt compelled not only to show support for the deal but also to oppose it. The nuclear deal further entrenched the prevailing belief that the UAE would have to become self-sufficient in the pursuit of its own security and well-being, and firmly highlighted the need to stand up to and contain Iran in any way and arena possible.

Freeing Iran

When the nuclear deal was announced, Iran's neighbours reacted sceptically: cautiously supporting the deal but highlighting that it would not be good for the region.[88] The ruler of the UAE, Sheikh Khalifa, was the first Gulf Arab ruler to send a congratulatory telegram to President Rouhani, expressing hope for regional security.[89] But the UAE was fearful of what the deal would do to Iran's regional ambitions. An Emirati official said, 'Iran feels vindicated by the deal to continue its role as a regional hegemon using its proxies. The deal worsened regional relations.'[90] For Abu Dhabi, the nuclear deal was problematic on several levels. First, the leadership in the UAE firmly believed that the nuclear deal would strengthen Iran in the region.[91] The Emirati news wire that reported the congratulatory note sent by the ruler of the UAE to Rouhani after the deal also quoted an 'official source' calling on Iran to roll back its regional activities now that the nuclear deal was done: 'Iran could play a (significant) role in the region if it revises its policy and stops interfering in the internal affairs of countries like Iraq, Syria, Lebanon and Yemen. ... Accompanying (efforts) would be for Iran to demonstrate a genuine desire to help extinguish fires devouring the region.'[92] But the deal 'didn't lead to the moderation of Iranian behaviour', explained several Emirati officials.[93] As a result of the deal, 'Iran is less isolated and stronger', said an Emirati official.[94] The UAE believed the agreement would result in a more confident Iran, boosted by its decades-long negotiations with world powers and the 'acceptance' of its controversial nuclear programme. 'Iran is more confident to interfere, and blunter in its violations in the region. The deal gave Iran the green light to do what it wanted', explained an Emirati official.[95] A foreign ministry staff member added, 'the deal made Iran more aggressive. It has displayed the worst behaviour in the region since.'[96]

Second, much like its regional allies, Abu Dhabi believed the deal would give Iran the means to pursue its active foreign policy in the region through the release of Tehran's blocked funds abroad and sanctions relief.[97] To them, this would result in a bolder and more active Iran in the region, one that would not hesitate to challenge the Gulf Arab states if it needed to. Iran would be 'more free to give money to Hezbollah, the Houthis, and the Shias in Iraq.'[98] The deal released Iranian assets and oil revenues held in restricted accounts in the United States. Combined with the release in sanctions pressure that the deal would provide, the Emiratis (as well as its neighbours and many in the West)[99] believed that Iran would use the approximate $100 billion it would receive towards boosting its regional forces and proxies to destabilize the region at their expense.[100] The perceived rise of Iran and the perceived development of its capabilities posed a direct threat to the UAE, both in the region and domestically. In the immediate term, they were proven right as Iran steadily increased its involvement either qualitatively or quantitatively in the region. While most of that was a function of events on the ground in the region, such as the rise of ISIS, and occurring before Iran received its sanctions relief in January 2016, the UAE and its allies perceived it as a direct result of the JCPOA.

Third, in the UAE's eyes, the entire process of negotiations and the final agreement also legitimized the leadership of the Islamic Republic.[101] Indeed, for the better part of two decades the leadership of the Islamic Republic was in negotiations with the five permanent members of the UN Security Council and Germany – some of the most powerful states on the international stage. While this was difficult enough to accept for the UAE and its allies, to them, it was the final deal that provided the Islamic Republic with real legitimacy, both for the government itself and for what they considered to be an illegitimate nuclear programme.[102] The deal sent the 'wrong message' because 'Iran gets an endorsement' of its nuclear programme.[103] The UAE's commitment to non-proliferation and its 123 agreement with the United States – an approach it was 'trying to promote' in the region – was 'undermined' by the Iran deal.[104] As a result, to them, the nuclear deal made Iran stronger, more capable, legitimate and bolder, and allowed it to pursue its regional ambitions unchecked.[105]

Iran for its part had already been involved actively in the region even when under sanctions,[106] but as we saw above, it did not help itself vis-à-vis its Gulf Arab neighbours, as it continued its nefarious activities in the region and, in some cases, intensified them.[107] In Syria, after the death of a senior Islamic Revolutionary Guard Corps (IRGC) commander, in October 2015, Brigadier General Hossein Salami, deputy commander of the IRGC, announced that Iran would increase its presence in Syria, both in quality and quantity, and provide both tactical and general advisory help and weapons.[108] In Iraq, ISIS' takeover presented a real problem for Iran because of Iraq's importance in Iranian thinking, the porous border and the shared political, economic and religious ties between the two countries.[109] As a result, Tehran increased its involvement in the country, in particular through the deployment of hard power.[110] In Yemen too, Iran increased its involvement in the conflict and ties with the Houthis in the aftermath of the nuclear deal.[111] Importantly, though, the correlation with the JCPOA was tenuous at times – facts on the ground, such as the rise of ISIS, were a major factor in Iran's behaviour. But the UAE could not help but predominantly view the changes in the region in the context of the nuclear deal and the confidence it gave Iran. Privately, some Emirati officials hoped the deal would provide 'wind in the sails of the moderates' – though they were sceptical this would happen, because they believed the moderates were not really in charge in Iran, based on their past experience with the Khatami administration.[112] They wanted evidence of a shift in Iranian policy before they considered engagement.[113]

The US factor

The fear of Iran's expansionist agenda for the region was made worse by the timing of the nuclear deal: occurring at the moment when the UAE's trust in the United States was at its lowest,[114] and the fear of US abandonment was at its highest – perceptions that the JCPOA only strengthened.[115] Confidence in the Obama administration and the United States as a security guarantor was at an all-time low in the Gulf Arab countries following the Arab Spring and the abandonment of Mubarak, and the announcement of the US Pivot to Asia.[116] The JCPOA exacerbated these fears in two ways: it further highlighted that the United States – the UAE's primary security guarantor – was abandoning it, in favour of dealing with Iran. Second, the United States would appease Tehran to ensure the success of the JCPOA.

To the UAE, the JCPOA negotiations and the final nuclear deal was proof that not only was the United States seemingly less engaged in the region but what little interest it had in the Middle East was focused away from the Gulf Arabs and towards Iran. For the leadership in the UAE, this was a real blow to their efforts to tighten their relations with the United States and highlight that they were America's indispensable partner in the region.[117] President Obama further fed into this perception, as his administration believed the best way to curb conflicts in the region was to adopt a more nuanced policy vis-à-vis US support of its Gulf allies and begin to resolve America's problems with Iran. In an interview with Jeffrey Goldberg in the Atlantic in April 2016, President Obama called Saudi Arabia and Iran to 'share' the region:

> The competition between the Saudis and the Iranians – which has helped to feed proxy wars and chaos in Syria and Iraq and Yemen – requires us to say to our friends as well as to the Iranians that they need to find an effective way to share the neighborhood and institute some sort of cold peace. An approach that said to our friends 'You are right, Iran is the source of all problems, and we will support you in dealing with Iran' would essentially mean that as these sectarian conflicts continue to rage and our Gulf partners, our traditional friends, do not have the ability to put out the flames on their own or decisively win on their own, and would mean that we have to start coming in and using our military power to settle scores. And that would be in the interest neither of the United States nor of the Middle East.[118]

This led to frustration and anger within the elites in the UAE who felt that the United States had betrayed them even though they had been useful security partners in the region.[119] This frustration was amplified because the UAE saw this not just as US abandonment but a pivot towards their regional rival, Iran.[120] As a result, no matter what President Obama did to reassure them, it fell on deaf ears. In fact, President Obama found himself acquiescing to Gulf Arab interventionism in the region in order to appease fears of abandonment, including in Yemen.[121]

Second, the UAE feared the United States would no longer help contain Iran, because the Obama administration now had a stake in the successful implementation of the JCPOA so they would not work as actively to ensure Iran's regional containment.[122] Instead, Washington would appease Tehran to ensure the success of the nuclear deal. An Emirati official summarized the perception, saying that there was a lack of desire to confront Iran in Washington, because they did not want to 'risk the deal. They're held hostage by it.'[123] An Emirati-based think tank expert stated that President Obama refused to take action in Syria 'because of Iran', he 'didn't want to confront Iran', especially during the negotiations and after the final deal.[124] Senior Emirati foreign ministry officials lamented that now that the deal had been reached, the United States was 'not doing enough' to 'stand up to Iran', blaming it on President Obama's 'legacy driven' foreign policy.[125] Another Emirati official said there was 'no political motivation to criticise Iran, to make sure the deal could succeed'.[126] With the deal, the United States had demonstrated that it was prepared 'to live with a more reactive Iran in the region' and it 'recognised Iran's growth', and that US policy on Iran would no longer be limited to just containment, thus continuing the reversal of twenty years of American foreign policy in the Middle East.[127] Finally, officials in the UAE believed that the United States was acting weak on Iran in Syria, and that Obama's unwillingness to defend the red line on the use of chemical weapons in Syria by the government was the result of a desire not to jeopardize the negotiations with Iran.[128] The Emiratis clearly viewed US withdrawal from the region and the pivot to Iran as a fait accompli.

The nuclear deal further proved to the Emiratis that the United States could no longer be counted as a security guarantor, entrenching the idea that the UAE would have to pursue self-sufficiency and its own foreign policy objectives independently of the United States. The UAE's fears were not limited to Iran and the perception of US retrenchment; however, concerns over Saudi hegemony and the decisions of the young Crown Prince of Saudi Arabia Mohammed bin Salman (MBS) were also significant.

The Saudi factor

The nuclear deal exacerbated Emirati fears of Iranian hegemony and US abandonment. While publicly, previous events in the region encouraged the Gulf Arab states to unify in the face of a growing external threat, including a closer public stance between Saudi Arabia and the UAE, behind closed doors, the succession of events in the region that culminated with the nuclear deal reinvigorated fears of a potential Saudi reassertion of its leadership over the smaller Gulf Arab states.[129]

The UAE was concerned that Saudi Arabia would seek to counter emerging threats by first asserting its leadership over the smaller Gulf Arab states, and dragging them into conflicts they were not prepared to engage in.[130] Fears of Saudi hegemony among the smaller Gulf Arab states, including the UAE, were not new. Such fears were behind the lack of full military integration within the GCC in the years after its formation.[131] And even when GCC military integration came five years later with the establishment of the Peninsula Shield Force (PSF) in 1986, the smaller Gulf Arab states wanted to guard against Saudi overreach and hegemony, as well as the possibility of being dragged into a conflict that did not concern them, insisting that when the PSF 'enters a member's territory, the command structure reverts from Saudi Arabia to that of the host country'.[132] More recently, prior to the final round of nuclear negotiations, such fears reappeared: an Emirati official outlined his fear of the 'hegemonic overreaction' of Saudi Arabia, in which Riyadh would exploit the threat from Tehran to win Washington's recognition of Saudi pre-eminence in the Sunni Arab world.[133]

The 2015 nuclear deal exacerbated this fear for the UAE, though it was careful not to show this publicly. Abu Dhabi believed that the heightening of the Iran threat following the deal could open the door to Saudi reassertion of its leadership within the GCC in order to stand up to Iran more effectively.[134] This would place Abu Dhabi at the mercy of Saudi ambitions and interests. Saudi assertion of its hegemony and using levers to exert influence and pressure over its smaller neighbours was already evident in the pre- and post-JCPOA period: According to a Saudi policy analyst, Riyadh did not hesitate to 'shame' Kuwaiti counterparts, including by cutting off ties between tribal families, over what was considered to be overly 'positive' views of Iran.[135] It was particularly difficult for those in Kuwait to remain accepting of Tehran's regional position following the uncovering of a Hezbollah cell in the country,[136] and the debate over whether this should be exposed in the media or kept quiet.[137] For the UAE, Saudi hegemony was evident in Yemen: Riyadh expected its GCC allies to contribute to efforts to push Iran back in Yemen,[138] but Riyadh's efforts, including relying on groups affiliated with the Muslim Brotherhood,[139] directly conflicted with the UAE's goals in the country.[140] These differences with Riyadh in Yemen highlighted the feeling in Abu Dhabi that its allies and partners were ignoring or minimizing the UAE's interests and policy objectives. In addition, MBS's ruling 'style' concerned the Emiratis.[141] The Emiratis believed that the Saudis were not paying enough attention to their international image and making rash decisions, particularly after the murder of Jamal Khashoggi, and subsequent crisis such as the leaked hacking of Amazon CEO Jeff Bezos in January 2020.[142] Saudi Arabia's growing disregard for international norms and their indiscriminate campaign in Yemen had already begun to impact their influence in Washington, DC. For the UAE – a country hyper-concerned with its image in the West – Saudi actions could negatively affect their image too, given the two were at pains to highlight their close ties and were therefore viewed by many as two sides of the same coin.[143] A more overbearing Saudi ally could impact Emirati security, for example, by dragging Abu Dhabi into a war that it had no interest in fighting. Growing Saudi recklessness, embodied by MBS, also risked dragging the UAE into unwanted tensions or tarnishing its reputation internationally. In the years that followed, Riyadh also began to confront the UAE's regional economic leadership, and did not hesitate to up the ante in order to show its displeasure at its ally. In July 2021, under the guise of reacting to the Covid-19 pandemic, Saudi Arabia momentarily banned flights from the UAE specifically. A few months after, it announced that all companies wishing to do business in Saudi Arabia would have to establish their regional headquarters in the country, posing a threat to Dubai, a well-known regional hub. The tensions and economic tit-for-tat between the UAE and Saudi Arabia further fed into the prevailing perception that self-sufficiency had to be achieved rapidly, so that the UAE could secure its own interests, especially when these did not coincide with those of its closest ally, Saudi Arabia.

When the world powers and Iran announced the nuclear deal on 14 July 2015, the UAE expressed support for the deal but cautioned that it would worsen regional tensions. The deal had a significant impact on the psyche of the leadership in Abu Dhabi: it further highlighted the immediacy and importance of the Iran threat in the context of the post–Arab Spring era and the announcement of a US Pivot to Asia, it was seen as proof of Washington's intention to abandon its Gulf Arab allies in favour of Iran and it revived existing fears of Saudi hegemony. As a result, the UAE believed it would have to increase its individual efforts to counter and manage the Iranian threat. Second, given that, in their eyes, the United States could no longer be trusted as primary security guarantor, this intensified the UAE's prevailing desire to become increasingly independent and self-sufficient.

4 THE UAE'S GROWING ASSERTIVENESS

n the years following the Arab Spring, regional events, including the uprisings themselves, the statement of a waning US commitment to the Middle East and the 2015 nuclear deal with Iran, prompted the UAE to develop a more assertive foreign policy. But what does greater assertiveness look like? As previously established, it includes a focused and sustained effort to grow and develop military, political/ diplomatic, cultural and economic capabilities, giving it the means to pursue national objectives; and demonstrable intentions to deploy these growing capabilities in the pursuit of foreign policy objectives that reflect national interests, even at the expense of allies and neighbours – because capabilities alone are inadequate if the country in question is not willing to use them. This chapter will assess the UAE's capabilities and examine its willingness to deploy those capabilities.

Growing capabilities

Assessing changes in capabilities is an important indicator of a change in policy and objectives, because no country can be assertive if it does not have the means to do so. The UAE already devoted time and money to developing its capabilities prior to 2011, for example, developing a relationship with the United States after the First Gulf War that included US provision of hardware, training, dialogue, basing and joint exercises.[1] On the political/diplomatic and economic front, several economic setbacks related to the UAE's image following the 9/11 attacks[2] helped Abu Dhabi realize how much refining of its image could increase its influence, particularly among Western countries. Diplomatic efforts in the West were complemented by Emirati investment in areas ranging from real estate and sports teams, to aid to neighbouring countries,[3] all of which was intended to generate influence through multiple channels. Crucially, however, these efforts were all quite limited when compared to the UAE's endeavours following 2011. After the Arab Spring, the UAE's strategy changed: Abu Dhabi used economic diplomacy far more proactively to achieve the outcomes it wanted,[4] and intensified public relations efforts to improve its image. Militarily, Abu Dhabi increased its demand for military equipment, diversified its suppliers significantly and doubled down on its efforts to develop an indigenous military–industrial complex.

Military capabilities

Military capabilities have long been considered to be among the principal means allowing a state to acquire power and influence. Prior to 2011, the UAE had already undertaken some efforts to develop its military capabilities. The bilateral Defense Cooperation Agreement (DCA) of July 1994 formed the basis for UAE-US military cooperation.[5] The UAE participated in US-led military operations throughout the world, including in Bosnia during and after the Bosnian war (1992–5) and in 1992 in Somalia, for example.[6] To Abu Dhabi, this was important because it allowed it to gain valuable experience on the ground while demonstrating that it could be a dependable and necessary ally to the United States, its main security guarantor. But none of these deployments were conducted alone or in the pursuit of Abu Dhabi's own objectives. In its procurement, Abu Dhabi focused on air power,[7] purchasing eighty F-16 Block 60 aircrafts (with a contract eventually signed in 2000) from the United States for $6.4 billion.[8] The aircraft's design gives it a greater fuel capacity over the base model, allowing them to be flown for longer and over greater distances. These purchases suggested that the UAE had decided on the need for a national power projection capability in the mid-1990s, and the focus on air power suggested that Iran was the main target. The UAE continued to expand its military purchases in the 2000s, with a focus on air power, anti-missile systems and ground launched strike capabilities – intended to counter the Iranian ballistic missile threat. But in 2006, Anthony Cordesman and Khalid Al Rodhan judged that while the UAE had invested heavily in developing its air power, 'in practice, the GCC has invested in what is little more than an expensive façade, and internal rivalries preclude the development of well-trained and integrated forces. This makes the UAE Air Force heavily dependent on the United States for any large-scale operation against Iran.[9] In addition, Washington's continued insistence on interoperability and compatibility of systems, aiming to ensure the continued dependency of the UAE and its allies on the United States and its military–industrial complex,[10] made it difficult for countries like the UAE to develop independent doctrine on the deployment of their military capabilities in the pursuit or defence of their own interests.

But the situation changed significantly after the outbreak of the Arab Spring in 2011. While the UAE has had high levels of military imports since 2001, these increased by 63 per cent in 2012–16.[11] According to a UAE-based analyst, in the aftermath of 2011, Abu Dhabi was intent on building a military capability that was qualitatively and technologically superior to others in the region, which would, along with the growth of its soft power, help the UAE project power in the region.[12] The UAE's military build-up seemed primarily geared towards showcasing strength,[13] replicating key US military capabilities on a smaller scale, addressing the perceived growing Iranian threat and ensuring that despite its international procurement efforts, the UAE would increasingly pursue the establishment of an indigenous military–industrial complex. But as the UAE increased its involvement in regional fora, the requirements of active combat operations also drove some of their purchases, as did 'defence diplomacy': investing large sums of money into the US military–industrial complex as a means to buy loyalty and support.[14] Three clear trends emerged from the UAE's greater assertiveness in the military capabilities sphere: the first was the general urgency with which UAE weapons procurements increased in the years following 2011, the second is Abu Dhabi's effort to diversify its sources of security and its military procurements following the growing perception of US disengagement from the region and third is the newfound desire to build its own military–industrial complex.

Increase in weapons purchases

Despite the UAE's greater willingness to break with its allies and partners, the United States continued to be a key security partner. According to SIPRI, the UAE was the United States' second largest client for weapons sales, at 7.4 per cent of total US exports between 2013 and 2017.[15] The perceived growth in the Iranian threat after 2011 led Abu Dhabi to focus its efforts on missile defence systems, space and air-based intelligence and reconnaissance platforms, which are essential to an effective targeting programme against Iranian missiles, and project power in the region.[16] In 2011, the UAE purchased two THAAD missile defence batteries from Lockheed Martin to counter Iranian ballistic missiles,[17] followed by an order of twelve more M142 HIMARS launchers and ATACMS from Lockheed Martin in 2015 – doubling their fleet,[18] an upgrade contract for the UAE's existing F-16E/F combat aircraft – though details of the upgrade were not made public.[19] Requirements of deployment to regional conflict areas have also led the UAE to purchase additional Patriot missiles,[20] as well as the Air Tractor and Archangel counter-insurgency aircraft.[21] In February 2022, following the Houthi attacks on the UAE, the US State Department approved $65 million worth of spare and repair parts for its Hawk, Patriot and THAAD missile defence systems.[22]

Along with greater procurement, the UAE also aimed to ensure that it could continue to benefit from the United States' security umbrella and superior technical, training and deployment expertise.[23] While Abu Dhabi was fearful of a US withdrawal from the region, it also wanted to ensure that insofar as the United States was interested in remaining a significant security partner, it could. This would enable it to continue to benefit from US-provided security, assistance, training and weapons, while it used the time to develop its capabilities through other means – either with other partners or indigenously. The UAE and the United States established a Joint Strategic Military Dialogue allowing military officials to meet regularly to improve integration between their armed forces, and General Martin Dempsey chaired the first session in May 2014.[24] The United States continued to train Emirati armed forces through the US Foreign Military Sales programme, through which the UAE buys its US-made weapons and military kit.[25] Finally, the UAE continued to participate in international US-led military operations, though 'some experts say the UAE has joined U.S.-led operations to further invest the United States in UAE security, to prepare its forces for potential combat, and to increase UAE influence over U.S. regional policy'.[26] Through its increased weapons purchases, the UAE aimed to counter the perceived growing Iranian threat, continue to build ties with its primary security guarantor and continue to demonstrate its value as a political and military partner in the region.[27]

Greater diversification

Relying solely on the United States seemed unreasonable given its perceived disengagement from the region: it 'isn't doing enough', said an Emirati official in April 2016.[28] As a result, while the UAE increased its efforts to become increasingly self-sufficient in this field, it knew it would still need to rely on external providers in the meantime, and as such, sought to broaden its defence relations.[29]

France was already a prominent security partner for the UAE following the 2008 agreement establishing a French military base in the UAE and giving the French navy and air force access to Emirati ports and airbases,[30] key to France's ability to project power in the Asia Pacific.[31] But cooperation between the two increased significantly in the years following 2012, with France becoming the UAE's most important security relationship after the United States.[32] Regular visits by France's then Defence Minister Jean-Yves Le Drian, including visits to Abu Dhabi's defence forum,[33] and closer cooperation to tackle the threat of terrorism – perceived as a key threat by the UAE – are examples.[34] Both countries also conducted joint military exercises, including in May 2012[35] and November 2016.[36] France was the source of surveillance platforms with the sale of two Falcon Eye reconnaissance satellites from Airbus/Thales to the UAE in 2014. According to Theodore Karasik, a UAE-based analyst, 'From the UAE's point of view, France is eclipsing other western countries in terms of the counter-terrorism agenda.' Importantly, he points to the provision of intelligence, surveillance and reconnaissance by France on efforts to fight ISIS in particular, 'that other allies, such as the United States, do not. Paris and Abu Dhabi see eye to eye on requirements for countries such as Libya and Egypt, as well as to Jordan, in the fight against ISIL.'[37] This view was shared by several other interviewees.[38]

The UAE also boosted military cooperation with the UK, with whom it has a Defence Cooperation Agreement dating to 1996. In November 2012, the UAE and the UK announced a joint defence partnership, which would serve as a basis for greater weapons sales to the region from the UK, including the Typhoon fighters.[39] But relations between the two countries were not without complications, as the UAE believed London to be too supportive of the wave of uprisings that swept through the Middle East region in 2011. As a result, it ultimately refused to purchase Typhoon fighters and ceased using British officers to train the Emirati military.[40] The UAE also bought two GlobalEye airborne early warning radar aircraft (based on a Bombardier Global 6000 frame) from Saab in 2015 and exercised an option on a third aircraft in 2017[41] and two more Bombardier Global 6000 aircrafts modified by Marshall Aerospace for electronic and signals intelligence gathering.[42]

Importantly, in its quest for greater diversity, Abu Dhabi did not want to limit itself to Western security guarantors, especially when these partners refused to sell them certain weapons systems. It increasingly turned its attention to other major players, including China and Russia. The UAE's desire to purchase armed drones became more urgent following the deployment of its capabilities in Yemen and Libya. After the United States refused to sell it armed drones,[43] Abu Dhabi turned to China. In 2016, it acquired the Chinese-made Wing Loong drone,[44] which it upgraded with the purchase of the Wing Loong II in 2018.[45] It has used them in operations in Yemen, Libya and Eritrea. It is noteworthy that the Chinese approval process for weapons exports is faster and does not come with many of the constraints that Washington builds into its deals, making it easier for buyers, including the UAE, to use them in any way they see fit, including in their campaign in Yemen.[46] But they also pose a problem because the United States – the main provider of military platforms for the UAE and its allies – considers Chinese technology a security risk, and does not allow data gathered from Chinese drones to be integrated into US command chains.[47] Turning to China for drones may be an effort to convince the United States to sell the UAE the more sophisticated MQ-9 Reaper and MQ-1B Predator UAVs,[48] which are more advanced and could be better integrated into the UAE's military planning. This would be in line with the overall Emirati desire 'to maintain the strongest link with the US military sphere',[49] especially for the time being as it sees no other viable alternative to obtain the best quality equipment – China's drones do not have the reputation of being of high quality[50] – and while it continues to develop its indigenous capabilities. Notably though, the weapons procurements from China represent just an acquisition of capability.[51] China cannot and does not want to provide the same level of security the United States provides the UAE for now, 'making the relationship an operational, not strategic, one'.[52]

Russia has also been an important source of weapons and equipment for the UAE. Some of this activity occurred prior to the period under study – in 1998 for example, the UAE was 'the fourth biggest Russian arms customer after China, India and Iran'.[53] But after 2011, the UAE continued its efforts to diversify its procurements by further building ties with Russia and doing so with greater urgency, viewing Moscow as an 'alternative supplier or as a second option whose presence might increase regional buyers' leverage with U.S. officials and exporters'.[54] UAE interest in the purchase of other military equipment, such as anti-tank missiles and surface-to-air missiles, led to further sales in the years that followed.[55]

Greater self-sufficiency: Developing its own military–industrial complex

For the UAE, working with non-Western security providers such as Russia was an attractive option because Moscow did not object to moving the assembly of its military equipment to the UAE, or to assisting the UAE build its own equipment.[56] Abu Dhabi's long-term goal of becoming self-sufficient became all the more urgent following the perceived US abandonment of the region, the growing security threat posed by Iran and the UAE's involvement in regional conflicts.[57] This resulted in an Emirati push for joint production or assembly,[58] or even requiring that sellers invest in the UAE and share technology through offset agreements, which 'compel foreign suppliers to invest in local industrial projects so that the recipient country can offset the typically significant cost of defense procurement. Such programs have allowed the [UAE] to connect their domestic defense sectors with global defense producers and acquire advanced defense industrial knowledge and technology'.[59] While its indigenous defence industry remains modest, the UAE was characterized as 'the most promising of the Arab candidates seeking to gain emerging arms producer status',[60] and aiming to become a net exporter 'over the next five to ten years'.[61] This goal was facilitated by the UAE's more advanced knowledge-based economy, and its advanced investments into R&D, as well as the motivation to both diversify the economy and become self-sufficient.[62] Given that the UAE is generally unforthcoming about defence priorities and achievements, observation of its International Defence Exhibition and Conference (IDEX) shows – a biennial IDEX for the region – is revealing.[63] In 2014, the UAE established the Emirates Defense Industries Company (EDIC) through the merger of a number of state-controlled defence companies and focused on expanding its production of components for the platforms imported from foreign suppliers.[64] This raises a question for foreign suppliers about whether these components will 'eventually replace – rather than duplicate – capabilities mastered by more advanced defence industries'.[65] In 2019, the UAE went a step further, announcing the formation of 'EDGE', a government-owned company that consolidated a number of other entities in the sector and absorbed EDIC, with the 'mandate to disrupt an antiquated military industry'.[66]

Nevertheless, Abu Dhabi knew it would still have to rely on foreign suppliers to continue to build military capabilities, while it boosted its indigenous capabilities. In 2017, Russia announced the signing of 'an agreement on industrial cooperation in the field of military engineering' with Abu Dhabi, which outlined a joint effort to develop a light fifth-generation jet for the UAE.[67] The UAE also pursued a number of ad hoc deals with international firms to help build new indigenous systems. For example, in 2013, it worked with Yogoimport, a Serbian firm, to jointly develop an Advanced Light Attack System (ALAS) cruise missile, which evaded international export control restrictions and was simple to manufacture.[68] Gaub and Stanley-Lockman enumerated other Emirati foreign partners, ranging from well-known first-tier weapons and military equipment suppliers, such as France and Germany, to smaller producers such as Estonia, Malaysia and South Africa, and to partners in the region.[69]

Following 2011, the UAE's desire to increase its military capabilities became more urgent. The outbreak of the Arab Spring, the announced US Pivot to Asia and the Iran nuclear deal led to fears of US unreliability as a security guarantor and the perception that regional threats were growing. It became imperative for the UAE to become increasingly assertive in the pursuit of its security. But military capabilities were not the only area the UAE focused on; it also expanded other capabilities in the years following 2011.

Other capabilities

Political and diplomatic clout

In the years that followed 2011, new fears and opportunities highlighted the importance of greater international influence in order for the UAE to pursue its interests more effectively.[70] The failure of a deal to take over the operation of several US ports by DP World in 2006 first brought this to light for the UAE. In March 2006, the British High Court gave Dubai Ports World (DP World) – a state-owned terminal management company – approval to acquire Peninsular and Oriental Steam Navigation Company (P&O), a British-owned company that also operated twenty-one ports in the United States. But in the United States, the idea that a state-owned Middle Eastern company could control US infrastructure drew ire from politicians across the political spectrum.[71] Fear of terrorism led Congress to threaten to block the sale and the-then Democratic governor of New Jersey Jon Corzine went so far as to say, 'This transaction fails the basic test of common sense with regard to our nation's homeland security. … Dangerous men, tainted blood money and nuclear technology have moved across UAE borders.'[72] As a result, DP World announced they would drop out of the deal shortly after.[73] Emirati officials were surprised at the level of vitriol directed at them; one stated, 'What we learned is that Congress does not know very much about us.'[74] This first major setback was a wake-up call for the UAE, and a reminder that their image needed work.[75] But it was only after the Arab Spring that the UAE's efforts to build its international influence and image as a forward-looking, modern state took on a sense of urgency.

In the aftermath of 2011, the UAE increased its efforts to build its political and diplomatic capabilities, including embarking on a spending spree in the countries where it aimed to improve its image, or when it wanted to obtain a particular policy outcome. In 2013, the UAE reportedly spent $14.1 million in lobbying and influencing in the United States, citing 'illicit finance issues' – likely referring to terror financing and sanctions on Iran – as the goal,[76] which was an increase of 40 per cent compared to its spending in 2009.[77] This period also saw the UAE target countries other than the United States, including in Europe, where the Emiratis were accused of similar efforts.[78] The UAE seemed to firmly believe in the value of drawing on Western PR firms to sway opinions in target countries, so much so that it funded a campaign by Glover Park Group – an American communications consulting firm – to counter negative press on Egyptian President Abdel Fattah el Sisi, as Ambassador Al Otaiba reportedly stepped in personally to ensure that US media coverage of events in Egypt was not overly harsh or critical.[79] This was intended to secure the UAE's candidate of choice in Egypt after the loss of Mubarak during the Arab Spring. The spending was coupled with continued outreach on the part of an effective diplomatic corps in key countries to improve the UAE's image and, more importantly, help steer policymakers in target countries towards decisions that were favourable to the UAE. This was most notable in Washington, DC, where the UAE ambassador maintained his posting despite a damning series of emails leaked by *The Intercept* outlining his 'sordid life',[80] expanding on the extensive contacts between UAE officials and the Trump campaign leading up to the 2016 US elections,[81] and detailing his links to international businessmen, including Jho Low, reportedly involved in a global corruption scandal.[82] By the time the Qatar crisis broke out in the summer of 2017, the UAE's PR effort had taken on gargantuan proportions, and had become increasingly bold, including a battle between the UAE and Qatar to discredit and tarnish each other's reputations,[83] and an Emirati effort to involve itself directly in US domestic politics, by encouraging the dismissal of US Secretary of State Rex Tillerson for being 'weak'.[84] This reportedly advanced the Emirati agenda with the US officials.[85] The UAE's involvement in US domestic affairs was a direct result of the growing sense of abandonment it felt following President Obama's lack of support to Mubarak in Egypt during the Arab Spring, the aforementioned Pivot to Asia and the Iranian nuclear deal. These all cultivated the idea that the United States was no longer interested in maintaining its presence in the region and securing its Gulf Arab allies.[86] Interestingly, despite the realization that a change in US engagement in the region was inevitable,[87] the UAE still devoted considerable resources into fostering good relations with the man who would become president of the United States in 2016, Donald Trump, in order to delay or, better yet, reverse the perceived disengagement.[88]

In the years following 2011, Abu Dhabi also developed an active PR campaign to promote its image as a forward-looking, modern, progressive Muslim society, in the hopes that this would increase its influence abroad and demonstrate what a 'reasonable' partner it could be.[89] Ambassador Al Otaiba penned several opinion pieces in foreign media on a range on topics, including on tolerance,[90] shoring up support for the battle against ISIS[91] and the rights of women.[92] One component of this campaign was to promote the idea that women in the UAE, despite living in a Muslim nation, enjoyed expansive rights and improved working conditions. For example, in 2014, the UAE conducted a media blitz to promote pictures of female army pilot Major Mariam Al Mansouri, who led the UAE's air strikes campaign against the Islamic State in Syria.[93] The country also regularly holds major events to commemorate International Women's Day and touts its efforts to promote the employment of Emirati women in senior positions both in government and in the private sector.[94] These efforts complemented the development of the UAE's check-book diplomacy and leveraging economic and financial assistance in the pursuit of its interests.

Economic and cultural influence

Using the dispensation of aid or money to attain political goals was not new for the oil-rich Gulf Arabs.[95] But in the years following 2011, the UAE's economic assertiveness – both by investing abroad and willing to make that investment conditional upon following the UAE's conditions – gained in momentum. It also sought to portray itself as a cultural hub in the region. The UAE diversified its economy by investing in various sectors abroad, from real estate to sports teams.[96] While this was primarily intended to diversify the economy and the UAE's investments, it was also intended to give the Emiratis more reach across sectors and influence internationally. Importantly, though, the Emiratis were 'careful to keep their stakes in western companies and multinationals relatively small in order to assuage fears that their investments are being used to gain political influence, and to avoid future xenophobic backlashes' of the type they witnessed with the DP World crisis.[97]

After 2011, the UAE further developed its influence through the cultural scene as well as the dispensation of aid.[98] It developed a cultural infrastructure in the country, which would showcase the UAE as a forward-thinking, educational and cultural centre in the region. Efforts included attracting prestigious foreign universities and museums, including France's *Louvre*,[99] to set up satellites in the UAE. For Abu Dhabi, international aid and disaster relief has also been key to expanding its international influence. From funds sent to the United States in response to hurricanes Katrina and Irma, to financial assistance to Syrian refugee resettlement programmes,[100] and building hospitals in the United States,[101] these efforts helped boost the country's image.

The UAE also developed a more elaborate strategy for financial assistance, one which included more active involvement in the recipient state's political and economic management. This was intended to secure influence and greater say in decision-making in target countries. Financial assistance from the UAE included 'demands for domestic spending, including welfare benefits and infrastructure investment', often 'at moments of incremental public concern for fiscal deficits and sustained lower energy prices', all in support of the UAE and its allies' 'own set of norms and priorities'.[102] In other words, the 'return on investment' – not always calculated in pure monetary terms – became key.[103] Rather, this involved advancing its foreign policy objectives, including limiting 'competition, especially political space that is tolerant to activist religious political organization, or political Islam', and not hesitating to challenge 'Western advice and hegemony'.[104] The 'proactive use of economic diplomacy' by the UAE,[105] while not new, shifted in nature and became a tool to increase influence and affect change in areas where the UAE has ideological and political goals.[106] The lack of economic conditionality, like those of the IMF and World Bank lending programmes that require states to enact reforms to receive the money, made Emirati funding attractive. But that funding came with a different type of condition, greater Emirati say and influence in the internal political space of target countries. It was also more nimble than international organizations, and could easily switch off the tap if the target county was not complying with Emirati requirements.[107] The UAE used economic assistance in this manner to shape the course of events in Egypt.

During Mohamed Morsi's tenure, the UAE allegedly plotted the Islamist government's demise in coordination with the Defence Ministry in Egypt, sending financial assistance to mount protests against the Muslim Brotherhood government.[108] It was only after the collapse of Morsi's government that Abu Dhabi pledged $3 billion in aid to the new government.[109] The UAE allocated approximately $1.56 billion to developing infrastructure, healthcare and education in the country.[110] In total, a UAE brochure on aid to Egypt outlined that Abu Dhabi had allocated $10 billion for the country.[111] The UAE also developed a 'wide-ranging developmental strategy' for Egypt, demonstrating its commitment to the country 'in the quantity and diversity of its aid and investments, as well as its interest in localizing aid through direct investment in construction and industry'.[112] Its financial support was complemented by the establishment of a UAE–Egypt Task Force to 'speed up legislation, reforms, and other measures meant to attract more investments'.[113] This was coupled with an Emirati branding strategy at the Egypt Economic Development Conference that aimed to portray the meeting as an effort to help the Egyptian people, and showcase the UAE's assistance as collaborative rather than as a patron.[114] This demonstrated the UAE's heightened sense of the importance of framing and image in ensuring its success in increasing its influence and sway in Egyptian decision-making. The UAE's added edge was that it mimicked its own model of

state-led capitalism, fuelled by real-estate projects and centered on a political orientation that is informed by Islam, but secular in presentation. In this secular vision, business sense and value for money describe the aid and strategic partnership ethos, rather than cultural or religious obligation.[115]

But the UAE's assistance to Egypt would increasingly come with strings attached. It expected 'the Egyptian government to implement administrative and economic reforms', demonstrating Abu Dhabi's commitment to the political system that replaced the Islamist government and discouraged 'political steps such as a reconciliation with the Muslim Brotherhood'.[116] The Egyptian case demonstrates that following 2011, the UAE decided to take matters into its own hands by using financial assistance and trade as a way of securing influence and achieving its policy objective of curtailing Islamism, which was on the rise in Egypt. This was demonstrably more assertive than the way the UAE used cheque-book diplomacy and aid in the past.

Curtailing Islamism was only one Emirati foreign policy objective, the rise of Iran was another.[117] As a result, the UAE used its economic sway to contain Iran as best as it could. One area in which it did this was in disrupting Iran's relations with China. The UAE, along with its regional allies, was alarmed at the military, political and economic ties between China and Iran,[118] and as a result, 'enacted a plan – at times jointly, other times individually – in the 2000s to reach out to China in a robust manner to bring a balance to Beijing's Iran policy through economic engagement'.[119] This coincided with China's desire to become a more active player in the Middle East.[120] For the emirate of Dubai the shift eastward came out of necessity following the 2009 crisis,[121] but for the UAE in general, it was in part in response to its fears of a growing Iran and the perception that the United States was no longer a reliable partner. The real effort to court Beijing and create lasting links in multiple sectors began in earnest with the announcement of a 'strategic partnership' in January 2012,[122] which was expanded to a 'comprehensive strategic partnership' following President Xi Jinping's visit to the UAE in July 2018.[123] In 2015, the UAE was the regional host for the Asian Infrastructure Bank, and this despite 'an appeal from the United States to its allies not to do so',[124] demonstrating once again that it was not afraid to pursue its own interests, even when these did not coincide with those of its partners and allies. Further, the UAE was critical of the 'internationalisation of the Chinese renminbi' when Emirate NBD became the first bank in the region to issue a yuan 'dim sum' bond in 2012.[125] These efforts were built on a $10 billion

UAE–China joint strategic investment fund that was created in 2015 to help support and deepen economic relations between the two.[126] The entire process has been accompanied by a growing institutionalization of their relations in all spheres.[127] These efforts were also conducted in the context of the UAE's economic diversification and its desire to 'build a corridor of trade from China to Europe',[128] and were not limited to China. The UAE also built a 'robust economic relationship', ranging from trade in commodities to tourism, with Russia,[129] and looked to other countries such as India, Japan, the Philippines and South Korea, just to name a few.[130]

Intent

The inherent uncertainty of intentions is what makes them so important to gauge – because doing so adequately will speak volumes about a state's likely trajectory. Following 2011, the UAE became 'serious about using its defence industry to enhance its operational capabilities',[131] increasing its strategic depth and in the pursuit of its own interests. As the Arab Spring protests spread, Abu Dhabi involved itself in various regional arenas, including Egypt, Libya and Syria, to change the outcome of certain events, increase its influence in various countries or build new relationships with stakeholders.[132] It did so by drawing on its military capabilities; political, diplomatic and economic levers; and existing networks of contacts and international businesses which gave it additional sway.[133] The UAE's involvement in Yemen and Libya represents recent examples – though there are several more – of the UAE's willingness to draw on all its capabilities to pursue its foreign policy objectives.

Yemen

Of the countries engaged in the Saudi-led coalition in Yemen, the UAE made the most significant contribution. It initially joined the coalition alongside Saudi Arabia, and in support of Riyadh's goals to push back the Houthis in Yemen and, importantly for the UAE, contain Iran.[134] For the UAE, given the regional context, it was important to show support and contribute to the Saudi-led endeavour to contain a rising Iran in the region in 2014 when the Houthis took over the Yemeni capital, because it was clear that the United States would not do it.[135] But gradually, Emirati objectives in the conflict differed from those of its ally, and Abu Dhabi pursued them despite the fact they were at times in opposition to Saudi Arabia's aims. The UAE's contribution to the conflict in Yemen is an example of Abu Dhabi's willingness to use its growing capabilities in the pursuit of its own objectives.

After the initial public show of support from Saudi Arabia's allies for Riyadh's efforts to lead a coalition to contain Iran, the Yemen conflict began to expose and deepen existing underlying tensions. When the Houthis took over Sana'a, Abu Dhabi was first to pledge its commitment to the Saudi-led coalition, committing troops – 'the largest and most experienced contingent of ground troops',[136] intelligence and firepower to conduct counter-insurgency, provide ground and air support, and clear landmines.[137] These efforts were supplemented with significant economic assistance and investment, including $4 billion of aid over the course of three years according to the UAE's minister of state for international cooperation.[138] The UAE's contribution to the coalition and operational command on some frontlines helped curb Houthi advances in the southern and eastern governorates, including from Aden and Mukalla in 2015 and 2016. Such operations were conceived and conducted by the US Special Forces and the Emirati Presidential Guard. The UAE's efforts in the Red Sea coast in 2017–18 were also notable, and an example of its assertiveness. The UAE identified and developed local forces 'who were disciplined and strong willed enough to operate alongside close air support to take coastal areas, the Houthis' major Achilles' heel'.[139] They made significant advances until they had to move inland and take Hodeida, then they stalled. In public, the UAE's efforts in Yemen were intended to display a unified front with Saudi Arabia and the other members of the coalition in the battle against the Houthis and Iran. Foreign Minister Anwar Gargash stated, 'The Emirati political and military stand in supporting Saudi and Gulf security is progressive … Our goal is to succeed in returning security to Yemen and to protect the security of the Gulf through Yemen'.[140]

The alignment with Saudi Arabia was short-lived, though the two rekindled their efforts to work together in Yemen down the line. Yemen was complicated because Abu Dhabi and Riyadh had 'different visions for the way ahead, but wanted to stay together'.[141] While the UAE and Saudi Arabia shared the goal of pushing back the perceived Iranian influence in Yemen, the UAE also had a number of interests it aimed to secure. Along with containing Islamic extremism, which it conflated with Islah and the Muslim Brotherhood, 'reconstruction, commercial interests and maritime security concerns', particularly in the south and east, drove the UAE's involvement in Yemen, as did anti-terrorism efforts.[142] The UAE also wanted to ensure access to the Red Sea, the Indian Ocean and extend control over the Bab al Mandab straits to strengthen its position as a global trading hub. As a result, the UAE drove the coalition's efforts in the south and east, and built partnerships with, paying, arming and training local ground forces, including 'Southern Resistance' forces, some of which are loyal to the UAE rather than Yemeni officials.[143] The UAE then looked east, and with the help of American troops, Emirati soldiers captured the ports of Mukalla and Shihr, and islands in the Bab al Mandab straits, through which most of the world's oil passes,[144] helping its anti-piracy efforts.

Abu Dhabi also focused on counterterrorism efforts in Yemen. For Abu Dhabi that involved pushing back the growth of al Qaeda in the Arabian Peninsula (AQAP) in Yemen, but more significantly containing Al Islah,[145] Yemen's main Islamist political party with close ties to the Muslim Brotherhood – which the UAE saw as a major threat. After 2016, much of its counterterror efforts were directed at Islah, which the UAE saw the Abdrabbuh Mansur Hadi government as being in league with. The Yemeni civil war and the coalition's efforts against the Houthis helped foster fertile grounds for the expansion of AQAP.[146] In fact, as the conflict wore on, the UAE's priority shifted to focusing on fighting Islamic extremism and terrorism in the south, including in Mukalla, an AQAP base.[147] After the Houthis were largely driven away from the south[148] – the UAE's area of focus – Abu Dhabi's objectives became twofold: to draw down its efforts in the fight against the Houthis and hand over to its allies,[149] and focus on the fight against extremism. But the UAE's focus on Islah and counterterrorism put it at odds with its Saudi ally. Indeed, Riyadh turned to Islamic leaders to help its fight against the Houthis, including backing Al Islah – perceived as a long-running threat in the UAE. Abu Dhabi encouraged Riyadh to abandon its Islamist allies and advocated working with former President Ali Abdullah Saleh (before he was killed in 2017), arguing he would have been more reliable than Saudi-backed Abdrabbuh Mansur Hadi, whose presidency was rejected by the Houthis.[150] Significant tensions emerged as Riyadh worried that Abu Dhabi was creating pockets of influence for itself,[151] and even resulted in conflict among their local allies when in February 2017, UAE-backed allies fought forces loyal to Saudi Arabia.[152] The situation worsened as the UAE increased its assistance to separatist groups in the south, which seized control of the port city of Aden, previously the temporary base for President Hadi's government, in August 2019.[153] This marked a break in the uneasy alliance between the UAE-backed Southern Transitional Council (STC) and the pro-government forces backed by the Saudi-led coalition. While the UAE initially pledged its support to Saudi Arabia in pushing back the Houthis in Yemen, it rapidly developed its own objectives, which it pursued even when these did not align with Riyadh's objectives, demonstrating that Abu Dhabi did not hesitate to deploy its growing capabilities in the pursuit of its own interests. And only when Abu Dhabi believed its objectives had been achieved, including building influence on the ground, did it revert back to working closely with Saudi Arabia to secure a truce in 2022.

Libya

In Libya, the UAE also displayed a willingness to draw on its growing capabilities in the pursuit of its own interests. Its objectives in the country changed as the reality on the ground shifted, affecting its intervention. Its initial intervention can broadly be categorized into three parts: collaboration with NATO for the intervention in 2011, changes on the ground in 2012–14 and growing concern over the growing Islamist influence and instability in eastern Libya, and the post-2014 elections phase, where Abu Dhabi started actively supporting General Haftar.

The UAE involved itself in Libya following the outbreak of the protests and Muammar Ghaddafi's excessive use of force to quell them.[154] It seemed odd that the UAE would intervene in favour of an Arab Spring uprising – that was the opposite of the status quo it sought to maintain in the region. But Libya presented them with an opportunity to secure its legitimacy within Libya,[155] and, importantly, to demonstrate what an invaluable partner the UAE could be to the United States and its allies in the region. The UAE also believed that if it participated in the coalition, it could influence US and Western policy in arenas that concerned it. For example, Emirati officials reportedly leveraged their involvement in the coalition efforts in Libya to ensure that the United States and its allies would not call for action to support the protestors in Bahrain.[156] The UAE took on a leadership role within the GCC in coordinating intervention, taking on much of the lobbying efforts within the Arab

League and conducting a diplomatic push to provide intervention with a UN mandate.[157] The UAE declared its intention to take part in the NATO-led mission on 24 March, deployed to implement UN Security Council resolution 1973, and deployed six Mirage and F-16 fighter jets.[158] The 'UAE forces also provided NATO a high level of area knowledge in addition to their air fighting capabilities. At the political level, they provided the operation with much-needed legitimacy within the Arab world'.[159] The operation was conducted in collaboration with other Arab countries, including Qatar,[160] and included financial assistance to the rebels and a flurry of diplomatic activity to add pressure to the Qaddafi government.[161] Some read these deployments as part of a UAE effort to increase ties with the United States, and increase US interest and stake in Emirati security.[162] But when observed with further deployments in Libya in the following years, ones that were not always in alignment with US objectives, it became clear that Abu Dhabi joined the NATO-led strikes in an effort to increase its visibility and military practice in this arena, and to pursue its own objectives down the line. In 2016, Riad Kahwaji, director of a prominent military think tank, emphasized that it was key for the UAE to join 'international coalition efforts like those led by the US or NATO' so that the United States and its allies would view Abu Dhabi as a 'competent military power in a coalition'.[163]

As the conflict dragged on, Libya became an arena for GCC competition, and importantly, events on the ground changed Emirati objectives. The Qataris significantly ramped up their involvement both with the coalition, working closely with the French, and with the rebels and the National Transitional Council (NTC), providing funding and assistance in light of the freezing of Libyan assets.[164] Qatar also led the effort to arm the rebels, despite the sensitivity of the issue and the arms embargo that was in place, and sent humanitarian assistance.[165] But Qatar's involvement with Muslim Brotherhood affiliates posed a problem for the UAE, which was concerned about the growing influence of Islamism inside the country, despite the initial results of the first elections in 2012 where Islamist groups lost ground.[166] The UAE was also concerned with the growing instability in eastern Libya, which posed a threat to Egypt. But Abu Dhabi did not initially change the nature of intervention in the country. It continued to support the militias it had been working with since 2011.

Eventually, though, the NATO-led mission was no longer enough to meet the UAE's goals, since the Muslim Brotherhood were still active in

Libya and Islamist ideology was thriving. The UAE initially established links with a 'conglomeration of predominantly anti-Islamist actors like the Zintan Brigades militia and the Libyan National Army under the command of General [and since, Field Marshal] Khalifa Haftar', placing it in direct opposition to Qatar.[167] In the spring of 2014, General Haftar opened a front against the Islamists in eastern Libya, spurring the state to call elections in June 2014 as a way to strengthen its authority. But the elections effectively split Libya in two: the coalition of Islamist militias from Misrata referred to as 'Libya Dawn' established itself in Tripoli,[168] establishing the New General National Congress – an alternative administration, and pushing out the UN-recognized government to the city of Tobruk in the east.[169] This new rival power centre presented a challenge for the international community which sought to support state institutions. As a result, the UAE and Egypt launched air strikes on Islamist targets in Tripoli in August 2014.[170] Importantly, UAE and Egyptian airstrikes were conducted without notifying the Obama administration, demonstrating their resolve in taking matters into their own hands, once again. The lack of notification to the United States here was key: it highlighted an Emirati desire to pursue their own interests without support or acquiescence from Washington. Fahmy Howeidi, a moderate Islamic intellectual, highlighted the significance of the UAE air strikes: 'The UAE strike in Libya must be read as something else entirely because it represents a shift from indirect intervention to direct military intervention, and it is not to help a friendly state but to support one faction against another factions.'[171] The UAE also increased military transfers and deployments to Libya, and this despite the arms embargo.[172] The SIPRI Arms Transfer Database estimated that Libya received 750 Spartan APC/APVs between 2012 and 2013, 50 Typhoon APCs in 2012, 38 Typhoon GSS-300s, 103 Panthera T6 APVs between 2015 and 2016 and 10 N35 APCs in 2017.[173] This was confirmed by a 2017 UN Panel of Experts report on Libya,[174] and a 2018 report which indicated that this type of support was ongoing.[175]

After 2014, given facts on the ground, the UAE's objectives widened. Not only was Abu Dhabi focused on ensuring the rollback of Islamism in the country, but it was also concerned by the threat of instability in the east posed to Egypt and focused on confronting terrorism. As a result, after 2014, the UAE unapologetically increased its support to General Haftar, who was recognized by eastern-based authorities and was handpicked by Egypt as their counterterrorism counterpart in Libya. The

UAE did so, even after reports of his brutality,[176] his unwillingness to back the Government of National Accord and work with other groups in the country[177] and his alleged provision of free passage to ISIS fighters from Derna to Sirte.[178] In 2016, the UAE provided him with air support from the Al Khadim airbase. Reports also emerged that the UAE-run military base in eastern Libya had undergone significant development between March and November 2017.[179] This was key to the war effort as the base saw 6,200 tons of weapons and ammunition land there from Al-Sweihan in the emirate of Abu Dhabi and Assab base in Eritrea.[180] In summer 2018, the UAE lent its support to General Haftar to begin exporting Libyan oil under his control outside the channels approved by the UN.[181] Abu Dhabi believed that with enough support, General Haftar could capture the capital and gain enough legitimacy to become head of state. While the UAE was reportedly surprised by Haftar's assault on Tripoli in 2019, it jumped at the opportunity to ensure his success, especially after the US change of heart in April 2019, when the Trump administration threw its weight behind Haftar.[182] Abu Dhabi reportedly provided him with Chinese-made drones used to conduct air strikes on Tripoli in 2019,[183] and itself conducted more than 850 drone and jet strikes in the country between April 2019 and 2020.[184]

All the UAE's efforts indicated a growing commitment to supporting the anti-Islamist forces in Libya and increasing its presence in the country. Importantly, it showed the UAE's intention and willingness to draw on the range of capabilities that it had acquired to attain its objectives. It also showed growing disregard for international processes, fora and the interests of other, including friendly, states in its policymaking – what mattered to it above all was securing its interests and objectives. While the UAE displayed a desire for self-sufficiency prior to 2011, it was only after this date that Abu Dhabi significantly increased its political, diplomatic, military and economic activities in the region and beyond, and pursued its interests unilaterally.

5 THE PERCEPTION OF SUCCESS

The UAE devoted significant time and effort in developing its capabilities – both military and non-military – and demonstrated a clear willingness to deploy those capabilities in the region and beyond since 2011. While this helps to establish a greater Emirati desire to act assertively in its foreign policy at specific times, it does not establish a long-lasting trend. In order to determine the existence and longevity of the UAE's growing assertiveness, it is imperative to examine how Abu Dhabi views the outcomes of its foreign policy decisions because the focus on capability and intent only presents a partial picture. For the UAE to be aware of its growing clout and to continue the drive towards greater assertiveness, it must regard the use of its capabilities as acceptable, and even successful in achieving its objectives. Only then will the leadership decide to continue on the path they are on. Naturally, if every deployment of political or military capability were unsuccessful in securing a state's interests in the eyes of that state, it would not contribute to a growing confidence in its influence and might. It might even lead to a sense of restraint, with the state in question taking time to reassess and address obstacles to the effective deployment of its capabilities in the pursuit of its interests. Moreover, for the changes in Emirati foreign policymaking to endure, they must be conducted in a manner that does not lead to Emirati overreach, which could involve getting bogged down in multiple conflicts and arenas, and spreading itself too thin, thereby affecting its ability to achieve its objectives. In other words, the perceived successful employment of these growing capabilities should continue to provide Abu Dhabi with confidence in its abilities and decisions, and instil a desire to continue the current path to developing its international clout. Since 2011, the UAE has continued on its assertive drive, albeit with varying momentum, reflecting continued reassessment of the value of assertiveness and adjustment of the policy.

Effectively determining the success of a policy itself is challenging, and can be based on several factors, including whether it achieves the state's objectives.[1] The leadership's assessment of the success of their foreign policy endeavours may be different than the assessment of an impartial third party. But it is the perception of the country's leadership that matters when it comes to a country's foreign policy decision-making, which is why we consider the state's perspective of the success of the policy it is deploying, rather than seeking to form or draw upon a more objective, external assessment of success. This chapter will examine how the Emirati elite view their policy of greater assertiveness, believing it has achieved several of their objectives, and giving the policy greater endurance, despite adjustments along the way. It will also examine the UAE's contribution to the war in Yemen and in Libya. While it will be difficult to offer a complete assessment of the UAE's mission in both countries because the conflicts are ongoing – despite Abu Dhabi's claims that it would withdraw most of its forces from Yemen in July 2019[2] – it is vital to examine practical examples of Emirati assertiveness playing out in the region and how they are viewed by the country's leadership.

A successful policy?

The UAE put its increasing capabilities to use in various fora. The result has been mixed, but the UAE has made some gains: its image has broadly improved internationally – though its ambivalent stance in the Ukraine conflict that erupted in 2022 has affected this – as has its ability to influence foreign powers and secure its interests. The country learnt the hard way from its experience in 2006 with DP World that without improving its image, it would not be able to build a wide-ranging relationship – not limited to government ties – with the West. Through their efforts, the Emiratis were able to improve their image significantly: despite the poor perception of the UAE in the West following the involvement of some of its nationals in the 9/11 attacks in 2001, in the years following the Arab uprisings it was no longer seen as a harbinger of extremism. A former Emirati military official explained that the UAE had developed a great deal of soft power it could use in its favour; the UAE 'looks more measured, has more clout. We have a good image', he said[3] – a sentiment that was shared by many officials and experts in the UAE.[4] He contrasted this with the UAE's neighbour and ally Saudi Arabia, and said he believed that the UAE looks measured and has greater influence in the United States.[5] Abdulkhaleq Abdulla, a noted UAE-based academic and regional specialist, stated, 'It has dawned on [the UAE] that they have lots of [levers] and they can cash them in.'[6] A few years later, he highlighted the UAE's confidence in its regional endeavours, when he said that 'the UAE was the heart of decision-making in the Arab world.'[7] 'The UAE is confident because its policies are working. We are able to adapt to changing circumstances fast,' he said in the winter of 2021 in the context of the UAE's public campaign to focus on soft power, rather than military deployments.[8] Back in 2014, the US ambassador designate to the UAE claimed that the country 'is a strong military partner and a reliable contributor to coalition operations, participating in five major such efforts with the US since Operation Desert Storm.'[9] This, despite some of the capacity problems faced by the UAE.[10] Another UAE-based analyst with deep knowledge and experience of regional issues explained that despite the country's success in amassing hard and soft power, Abu Dhabi was aware of its limitations and recognized that it was not a regional power yet.[11] Rather, he believed, Abu Dhabi was intent on building up a military capability that was qualitatively and technologically superior to others in the region, which would, along with its growth of soft power, help the UAE project power in the region.[12] Importantly, though, it would also help the UAE be perceived as a serious international power. He went on to state his belief that the US perception of the UAE as a serious military power, and as such, a valuable partner, in the context of military coalitions was not limited to the United States, extending to Europe and the NATO alliance.[13] Over time, however, as it deployed its hard and soft capabilities and grew increasingly confident in its abilities, Emirati officials began to view themselves differently, no longer focusing on the country's limitations, but rather focusing on what it had achieved and how it was a force to be reckoned with internationally. In 2021, an Emirati official said that thanks to the tools it has developed, both hard and soft, the UAE was 'in a position to lead and break barriers.'[14] For him, the UAE was now playing in the big leagues, 'we are partners with big powers, not followers.'[15] He added, 'we need to take the lead in the Arab world, we have to be number one.'[16] Another official highlighted how nimble the UAE had become, 'the adaptability of our foreign policy is what makes our strength. Our foreign policy principles stay the same, such as tolerance, but we adapt to changing circumstances, and changing administrations, successfully.'[17]

Diversification

The UAE has also succeeded in diversifying its security partners. 'We are diversifying our partners,' explained an Emirati official, 'we have different interests with different countries. We don't have to choose sides, but we will always be transparent. The US will remain one of our main allies, but we will now rely on different partners for different issues.'[18] In an effort to hedge its position, the UAE sought closer partnerships with smaller regional states, including building ties with Egypt, which became increasingly dependent on the UAE. It also increased exchanges with larger players. 'The UAE's strategy became to talk to Russia and China directly,' explained a Gulf official in 2016, referring to a new bilateral engagement rather than through the GCC.[19] The UAE 'aimed to diversify its risks by going to Russia and China and others for deals and weapons. And it succeeded,' said a former Emirati military intelligence official in 2016.[20] 'We have, and will continue to have strategic relations with the US, but we will also build and maintain strategic relations with China, Russia, the EU and others,' said an Emirati official in early 2022.[21] 'We can't put all our eggs in one basket,' said an Emirati foreign policy expert,[22] as a military official explained that for Mohammad bin Zayed, Russia and China were 'up', as the United States was 'down'.[23]

Prior to a summer 2018 visit to Abu Dhabi, President Xi Jinping called for 'a blueprint for China-UAE cooperation so as to unlock its full potentials and advance China-UAE relations at a higher level and speed, and build a China-UAE community of shared future in Belt and Road cooperation'.[24] In July 2019, during a visit to China by MBZ, the two upgraded their 'strategic partnership' to a 'comprehensive strategic partnership' that involved new deals in various sectors.[25] As the relationship with China continued to grow, the UAE succeeded in getting access to technologies that Western powers were loath to share with it, including in the military sphere.[26] Throughout 2020–1, the two continued building their ties: China is expected to build the UAE's 5G network and was quick to supply the UAE (and other Gulf Arab states) with their Covid-19 vaccine after the outbreak of the virus, and even allowed the UAE to be the first country to produce it outside China.[27]

Emirati officials expressed appreciation for China's help,[28] but this came at a cost to the Gulf Arab states later on as questions emerged on the efficacy of the Chinese vaccine.[29] The relationship garnered greater local and international attention as the Chinese ambassador to the UAE penned a piece in *The National,* the UAE's national newspaper, highlighting the 'brotherly' nature of Emirati-Chinese ties,[30] and the *Financial Times* conducted a deep dive on the nature of their ties.[31] It also added to tensions with the United States, as Washington – increasingly nervous about the UAE's ties to China – was more forceful in pushing the UAE to call off Chinese-led projects in the country. In 2021, the *Wall Street Journal* reported that the UAE had called off the construction of what the United States believed to be a Chinese military facility inside Khalifa port following intense US pressure.[32] Prior to the UAE calling it off, a US official said of the construction work, as well as the UAE's deal with Huawei to build the country's 5G network: 'Obviously the Emiratis know exactly how serious we think this is, and we have explained very clearly what this would mean for the relationship. If this were to go forward it would fundamentally alter the relationship and change what we could provide to the UAE.'[33] While in this instance, the UAE halted the project, Abu Dhabi continued to highlight and expand its relations with Beijing.[34]

The UAE also sought to improve relations with Russia, despite the initial differences between them in Syria. The two signed a 'Declaration of Strategic Partnership' in June 2018, which served as a basis for the expansion of their political, security and economic ties.[35] Russia and the UAE had built extensive trade ties with trade volume growing from $200 million to $1.6 billion between 2000 and 2017, with the UAE becoming Russia's biggest trading partner in the region.[36] The declaration also outlined regular meetings and consultations between both sides, cooperation on oil market stability and combating terrorism, and increasing foreign direct investment.[37] Over time, differences between the UAE and Russia on crises in the region diminished. In fact, the Russian and Emirati positions became closer, as the UAE resumed dialogue with Bashar al Assad following a change in course on Syria,[38] Russia and the UAE coordinated their support to General Haftar in Libya (before shifting their focus),[39] and Moscow began a diplomatic engagement of the UAE-backed Southern Transitional Council (STC) in Yemen.[40]

But the relationship was not without its difficulties, especially following the Russian invasion of Ukraine in 2022, which created difficulties for the UAE with its Western partners. The UAE's Western partners firmly backed Ukraine, asking their international partners to take a stance against Russia – a move that was poorly perceived in the UAE. 'This is a new Cold War: we're being asked to pick a side. Instead, the US should be approaching their allies and working with them,' said an Emirati official shortly after the Russian invasion.[41] The UAE played a delicate balancing act – one that became increasingly difficult to maintain – where it refused to side with Russia or the United States, but also did not want to be seen as backing the Russian invasion. The UAE's voting record at the UN during the crisis attracted the ire of its partners. It abstained in the first UN Security Council vote condemning the invasion by Russia on 26 February 2022, in an apparent quid pro quo where the UAE secured Russia's support in a vote on labelling the Houthis a terrorist organization.[42] As a result, the United States undertook a significant lobbying effort to bring the UAE on board for the UN General Assembly vote on the same topic, which then it secured, along with a vote shortly after on the humanitarian impact of the invasion on 23 March.[43] But in an expression of frustration felt in many countries in the Middle East over the West's response to the crisis, the UAE, along with all other Gulf Arab states, voted against expelling Russia from the UN Human Rights Council on 7 April 2022. The UAE's response to the crisis developed against the backdrop of growing frustration with the United States. Given the rapid Western mobilization in favour of Ukraine, the UAE's unwillingness to take a firm stance against Russia will undoubtedly leave a mark on the image it spent so long building.

The UAE also became bolder in its pursuit of new partnerships, including dealing with countries it did not have relations with, or even with rogue nations. In late 2021, one Emirati official referred to this as the UAE's new 'zero enemy' foreign policy.[44] As part of this policy, the UAE normalized ties with Israel, re-engaged with Syria's Assad and established rapidly growing ties with Turkey under President Recep Tayyip Erdogan despite a decade of enmity. On 13 August 2020, the United States, the UAE and Israel announced a normalization agreement, officially the Abraham Accords Peace Agreement: Treaty of Peace, Diplomatic Relations and Full Normalization Between the United Arab Emirates and the State of Israel. The UAE and Israel had already been working together behind the scenes for several years, but their dealings were always behind closed doors because public opinion in the UAE, and in other Gulf Arab states, did not seem to be ready for public normalization.[45] Official, public normalization was risky, especially as domestic opposition to it remained significant and required a strong hand to quell it.[46] Nevertheless, the UAE went through with it, both demonstrating its assertiveness and risk tolerance. In May 2021, another round of violence broke out between Israel and the Palestinians, leading to an eleven-day-long conflict that saw airstrikes by the Israeli Air Force inside Gaza and rocket fire by Hamas and the Palestinian Islamic Jihad into Israel, and brought the long-forgotten Israeli-Palestinian conflict back to the forefront of international affairs. The countries that had engaged in normalization with Israel found themselves in a difficult situation, and some sought to downplay their new relations with Israel. But the UAE did not feel the need to do the same. It continued brandishing its ties with Israel: shortly after the ceasefire took hold in Gaza, the Israeli ambassador to the UAE attended an event establishing a joint venture between an Israeli and Emirati company, followed by a ceremony celebrating the region's first permanent exhibition commemorating the Holocaust.[47] This demonstrated the level of confidence Emirati officials had in their assertive foreign policy. When violence broke out again during Ramadan in April 2022, the UAE publicly rebuked Israel by summoning the new ambassador,[48] but no set-back to-date has conferred the UAE with a sense of restraint in its desire to expand ties with Israel. The only area in which cooperation is expanding at a slower pace is in the military sphere: 'The military sphere will be the last dimension of the relationship with Israel, we have to be careful with how we progress there,' explained a general in the armed forces.[49]

After the outbreak of the Arab Spring and the start of the uprising in Syria, the UAE recalled its ambassador. Seven years later, in December 2018, it reopened its embassy in Damascus as part of an effort to mend ties with Syria and rehabilitate the disgraced Syrian president, including by supporting Syria's reintegration into the Arab League.[50] The Syrian regime had regained control of much of the country, and talk of reconstruction began to emerge within circles in the Middle East, providing an economic opportunity for the UAE, as well as a chance to contain Iran's presence in Syria. For the UAE, Syria was also about balancing their relations with Russia, 'it was intended to appease Russia,' explained a regional expert based in the UAE.[51] In a short space of time, the UAE became one of Syria's most significant trading partners, accounting for 14 per cent of Syria's foreign trade.[52] In November 2021, the UAE's foreign minister, Abdullah bin Zayed al Nahyan, went to Damascus to meet Bashar al Assad, while the UAE received Assad in Abu Dhabi on 19 March 2022, in a move that surprised and frustrated US officials: 'We are profoundly disappointed and troubled by this apparent attempt to legitimise Bashar Assad,' said Ned Price, the US State Department spokesperson, following the visit.[53] Receiving Assad, without notifying the United States, seemed like a deliberate snub at a time of growing frustrations with the United States.

But Syria was not the only state that the UAE pursued better relations with, Abu Dhabi decided that after over ten years of animosity with Turkey, it was time to mend ties beginning in 2021. The Arab Spring pitted the two countries against each other when Turkey emerged as a staunch supporter of the Muslim Brotherhood and the protests in the region. The two countries engaged in an intense rivalry visible throughout the region, with, at its worst, a Turkish accusation that the UAE helped fund the coup against Turkish President Erdogan in 2016.[54] But rising economic difficulties in Turkey, Ankara's 'efforts to distance itself from the Brotherhood',[55] a stalemate in Libya and a change of heart in Abu Dhabi on minimizing tensions with neighbours contributed to a change in policy and the beginning of a dialogue between the two. In April 2021, Turkey named a new ambassador to the UAE, allowing for diplomatic interactions between the two countries. In August, the UAE's national security advisor, Sheikh Tahnoon bin Zayed al Nahyan, visited Ankara to meet with Erdogan to discuss bilateral ties, including investment opportunities, and regional issues.[56] This was followed by a visit to Ankara by Abu Dhabi Crown Prince Mohammed bin Zayed in November 2021 and one by President Erdogan to Abu Dhabi in February 2022.[57] Once the high-level diplomatic visits began, ties between the two rapidly improved, and the money began to flow. In November 2021, the UAE announced it would set up a $10 billion investment fund for strategic investments in Turkey; in January 2022, the UAE's central bank agreed on a nearly $5 billion currency swap agreement with Turkey's central bank;[58] and in February,[59] the two signed agreements in several sectors, including defence and trade.[60] Significantly, many of the reasons for the animosity between the two countries have been rendered moot – the Muslim Brotherhood and many of Turkey's (and Qatar's) partners in the region have lost ground, while the impetus for expanding their ties continues.

Despite the occasional setback and the different methods and pace of engagement, these new diversified partnerships demonstrate the success the UAE has had in being more assertive in its foreign policy, and building greater self-sufficiency by diversifying its security, political, military and economic partners – a success that Emiratis are aware of and do not shy away from highlighting.[61] The UAE's efforts to increase its political influence both within the region and beyond has also paid off, further boosting its ability to diversify its economic, political and security partners.

Economic success

In the economic sphere, the UAE found it easier to conduct business deals in Europe and the United States with minimal or no opposition, in part, due to its improved image. The Emirati ambassador to Washington, DC, Youssef Al Otaiba, drew parallels between the Emirati and American outlook on business interests in 2016: 'The US and the UAE have a lot in common when it comes to how we view business. ... The UAE has one of the most open and innovative economies in the world, and over the years, we've demonstrated that the UAE is a dependable and significant economic partner of the US.'[62] One example of the relative ease with which the UAE was able to secure economic deals abroad was the successful purchase of aerospace companies working on US airports by government-owned Dubai Aerospace Enterprises without any protest from Congress, even though earlier, Congress had questioned allowing Dubai Port World a series of acquisitions in the maritime and port sector.[63] In 2017, Aerospace Enterprises bought Dublin-based AWAS, a major aircraft lessor in a deal that attracted little negative attention.[64] In fact, the UAE as a whole, with Dubai in the lead, became a key business and trade partner for many companies within and outside the region. This followed extensive efforts to diversify the country's economy – a successful endeavour as 'the proportion of UAE GDP accounted for by hydrocarbons has fallen from as high as 90 percent in the 1979s to about 28.2 percent in 2013',[65] build the UAE as a regional financial hub[66] and draw on each Emirate's strength in expanding its economic activities – focusing, for example, on heavy manufacturing in Ras Al Khaimah and infrastructure and financial services in Dubai.[67] This success in establishing itself as a regional – seen by some locals as an established global – business hub was touted by Emirati officials and experts alike,[68] and was often the subject of op-eds in the media. 'The UAE is already a global trade and communication hub ... This means that from the economic point of view, the UAE should no longer think of itself as a Gulf state with a global role, but needs a rethink of itself as a global state that is positioned in the Gulf,' read a *Gulf News* article in 2015.[69] But success inevitably attracted attention, and others, including

Saudi Arabia, also wanted a piece of the pie, dictating new policies in 2021 that challenged the UAE's economic dominance.[70]

The UAE's economic efforts abroad were not focused just on the West, they went 'hand in hand with a major expansion of investments by *Khaleeji* (Gulf Arab) companies, private investors, and GCC sovereign wealth funds in North Africa and the wider Arab world'.[71] The UAE's new economic 'interventionism' was key to linking together the country's multiple foreign policy objectives. Many of the UAE's regional investment strategies were not economically profitable, but they made 'sense when political, military, diplomatic, symbolic, and economic influences are combined and seen as complementing each other'.[72] In other words, greater economic assertiveness occurred in the context of greater military and diplomatic assertiveness, and each served and reinforced the other, making the trend a more entrenched and longer-lasting one. Indeed, in Egypt, its economic strategy aimed to buy Abu Dhabi leverage, which it used to obtain political gains.[73] The UAE pledged to assist the interim government in Egypt after the ouster of Mubarak, but suspended the payouts while the Muslim Brotherhood were in power, only resuming a wide-ranging assistance programme after the Egyptian military took over. This demonstrated that Abu Dhabi was not afraid to pursue the outcome it wanted for the country – even when this was in direct opposition to what its partners were pushing for: the United States, for example, while reticent to deal with a Muslim Brotherhood government, did not condone this type of intervention to change the government. But the UAE was successful in helping bring about the changes it sought for Egypt, naturally bolstering it in its new approach. And importantly, the leadership in the UAE saw it as such, further bolstering their interventions in the region. In a *New York Times* profile of Mohammed bin Zayed, Robert Worth, the journalist who interviewed the Emirati leader, stated, 'The overthrow of Morsi was the first great success of M.B.Z.'s counterrevolutionary campaign, and it seems to have supercharged his confidence about what could be done without American constraints.'[74]

The perceived success of the UAE's military assertiveness

In the years that followed 2011, the UAE assertively pursued the development of its military, diplomatic, political and economic capabilities, and, importantly, deployed military capabilities on its own for the first time. Aware that the UAE's regional involvements went beyond just these arenas, this section will briefly examine how Abu Dhabi viewed its deployment in Yemen and Libya.

Yemen

While the impact of the UAE's deployment in Yemen will continue to be felt for the foreseeable future, it has seen success in Yemen on several fronts: expanding its influence, increasing its land and naval presence in and around the country in strategically significant areas and waterways, and regaining some of the territory lost to the Houthis and to Islamic extremists. But most importantly, the leadership in the UAE believes the deployment in Yemen achieved several of their objectives.

The UAE succeeded in pushing the Houthis back and recapturing some parts of the country as part of the Saudi-led coalition. Abu Dhabi led the operational planning and the execution of several combat operations, demonstrating to its allies and partners that despite its small size, it could plan for and execute military operations successfully. In addition, the UAE's ability to identify local partners and build auxiliary forces, which they trained and sent equipment to, made it a key partner in counterterrorism efforts in Yemen. The UAE's operations in Yemen became an additional pretext for it to expand its activities, basing and influence in the Horn of Africa.[75] It also succeeded in building influence in and around Yemen, projecting power across the Bab al Mandab and into eastern Africa. Its cooperation with and successful training of local forces provided it with potential proxy forces that it could draw on in the future. In the south, it backed the STC – a 'self-styled southern government-in-waiting' formed in April 2017, which along with its allies 'hold most of Yemen's four southern governorates',[76] as well as other groups, such as the Giants Brigades, a group of about 15,000 fighters, part of the Yemeni National Resistance Coalition. In addition, the expansion of UAE naval bases contested Iranian regional naval expansion, and 'could contribute to the United Arab Emirates' strategic depth in an eventual clash with Iran … (providing) depth that might allow a reserve force of Emirati surface combatants, aircraft, and even submarines to remain active and able to interdict Iran's coastline and shipping during an extended war'.[77] But as the conflict in Yemen continued, Emirati deaths increased and the coalition's reputation was affected by their indiscriminate bombing campaigns and the humanitarian crisis unfolding in Yemen.[78] The UAE's relationships, whether with its allies, including Saudi Arabia, or its partners on the ground began to suffer, as objectives diverged and the conflict dragged on. In addition, while the new relationships the UAE had built with groups on the ground were invaluable, these groups were not as organized and disciplined as the UAE painted them out to be, partly explaining their failure in Hodeida in 2018, after a relatively successful campaign along the coast.[79] All this diminished the UAE's successes and tarnished its reputation. None of these, however, prevented the Emiratis from believing their intervention in Yemen was a success.

Officials in the UAE believed that the country had achieved its objectives in Yemen: it contained regional Iranian influence and pushed back the Houthis, it increased its influence and military presence inside and outside the country, and it built its ability to project force in the region.[80] This despite what they perceived to be less-than-promised US involvement; according to a former Emirati national security advisor, the UAE 'was expecting a lot from America in Yemen, surveillance, target selection, but none of that came'.[81] 'The US was reluctant to help,' explained an Emirati official.[82] Importantly, the UAE believed it had successfully demonstrated to its Western security partners that it was an invaluable and competent ally, one that spoke Arabic, and could help coordinate with groups on the ground and its US ally. Abu Dhabi had also developed relationships with partners on the ground which would allow it to have lasting influence in Yemen, all the while lessening its physical presence in the country. Abdulkhaleq Abdulla explained that the UAE was confident it could rely on 'local forces to continue confronting the Houthis on their own. The UAE has already trained a total of 90,000 Yemeni forces who are capable of filling the vacuum and supporting the legitimate Yemeni government. They can do the job and are well-trained, well-equipped, and battle tested.'[83]

While some of this was true, it was not the whole truth: the battle for Hodeida in 2018 presented the UAE with several problems, and ended up not going in the direction Abu Dhabi hoped. 'The UAE did great PR for the campaign [in Hodeida], but most people who spent time on the coast in 2018 know that the main fighting force was a contingent of Salafi-aligned fighters who looked very different from the disciplined military force the UAE represented their Yemeni allies as being.'[84] Emirati officials, meanwhile, believed that the Red Sea coast campaign demonstrated their ability to manage both the military and the political side of the conflict. They felt that had they been allowed to proceed with their campaign, they would have been able to turn the tide of war: 'If we had gone into Hodeida, the war would have been over.'[85] In reality, they failed to sell the campaign to the United States, who sought to prevent a battle for Hodeida, and convince international organizations, including the UN, that such a campaign would not lead to a humanitarian disaster. Instead, the United States helped broker the 2018 Stockholm Agreement, which prevented the battle. This helped the UAE's decision to change track and draw down its efforts in the area: 'In a clear demonstration of the speed with which UAE decision-makers can adjust strategy, by mid-2019 the Emirati forces had begun dismantling their presence on the Red Sea coast.'[86] While to some this may be seen as an admission that they failed because they could not capture Hodeida, Emirati officials explain the change in their policy as necessary given that most of their objectives were attained, and proof of their nimbleness. 'Whereas when the demilitarization was first proposed Abu Dhabi had been against it, six months later it would claim that the drawdown was in support of the Stockholm Agreement.'[87] Ultimately, for the Emiratis, the UAE's successes on the ground demonstrated that it was able to project force and use its extensive foreign-bought arsenal in the pursuit of its goals. In an interview in 2016 – only two years into the conflict – the head of an Emirati think tank explained that the UAE had been 'smart about building itself a military capability with large airpower and qualitative support that helps it effectively project power in an arena like Yemen.'[88]

Abu Dhabi judged its intervention in Yemen a success in achieving its objectives of containing Iran, and by extension the Houthis, in the areas it was concerned with, including rolling back extremism in southern Yemen and increasing its influence inside and outside the country. The Emirati elite believed they did so, all the while demonstrating their ability to conduct such operations on their own. And when their efforts on the ground stalled, including in the lead up to the siege of Hodeida, to them, their rapid change of direction in response to events on the ground was proof of their nimbleness, pragmatism and realism. From the perspective of the country's leadership, all this meant that it could draw down its presence in the country because most of its objectives had been achieved: the intervention in Yemen had been a success. To them, the drawdown or 'strategic redeployment'[89] announced in July 2019 was a result of this success. While to those watching from the outside it may seem that the UAE reduced its presence in Yemen because it was overstretched, the Emirati leadership did not see it that way.[90] To them, the country had achieved its objectives; it no longer needed such a heavy-handed presence on the ground and could turn its attention elsewhere. Rather, they believed they could delegate to the forces they had built relations with, and help them without too great a cost. It also became clear that while the UAE had achieved several objectives, the drawdown from Yemen was also the result of growing frustrations within Emirati decision-makers and MBZ in particular, over the internationally recognized government in Yemen and how they were 'flouting any leg up the UAE gave them' – clearly believing the main push in the war came from the UAE, and not from other members of the coalition.[91] Nevertheless, in the autumn of 2021, the UAE began to highlight its 'reassessment' and 'new approach' to regional conflicts,[92] one which involved greater soft power and less emphasis on military strength, including in Yemen. But this effort to showcase their regional endeavours as non-military was short-lived. In January 2022, the UAE-backed Giants Brigades regained Shebwa in the south and districts in southern Marib in the space of a week.[93] Emirati-backed groups were again empowered, as Emirati influence increased, including with the establishment of a UAE-aligned governor in Shebwa in December 2021.

But the UAE's success will also be measured against the durability and the sustainability of the relationships it has in Yemen, along with its ability to continue to influence events without attracting the ire of the Houthis. Initially, UAE-backed groups were able to maintain a degree of cohesion as splits emerged within the remainder of southern forces. But as the conflict continued, these divisions expanded, and frustration at the UAE and its involvement grew,[94] leading to concern in Abu Dhabi. In addition, the gains by the Emirati-backed groups in Yemen invited countermeasures by the Houthis targeting the UAE in January 2022, the first since 2018. Following several weeks of threatening attacks on the UAE, on 17 January, the Houthis claimed a missile and drone attack on an industrial area outside of Abu Dhabi and an area near the airport, which left three dead and six injured.[95] A week later, another missile strike targeting Abu Dhabi and al-Dhafra airbase in Abu Dhabi where US and French military personnel are stationed was intercepted and destroyed by the UAE and the United States using Patriot missiles,[96] and a week later still, the UAE intercepted another ballistic missile fired at the UAE, just as the Israeli President Isaac Herzog was visiting.[97] The attacks tainted the UAE's image as a safe and prosperous country in an unstable neighbourhood – they very thing the Emirati leadership is so keen to safeguard. 'We warn foreign companies and investors to leave the Emirates. This has become an unsafe country,' said the Houthi spokesperson Yahya Saree.[98] The attacks frightened the leadership in the UAE: 'They are a real threat,' explained an Emirati official shortly after they happened.[99] The UAE was also frustrated with the US response, believing Washington was not doing enough to safeguard them in the face of this threat, despite additional US security guarantees and sending the USS *Cole* and a squadron of advanced F-22 fighters to the UAE.[100] Emiratis 'discounted what the US did', said an Emirati analyst referring to the sending of the frigate, 'because they know the US won't and can't do anything against the Houthis. We'll have to tackle it ourselves.'[101] 'We are aware that escalation happens fast, and that it will affect us and our neighbours first. So, we continue to engage and de-escalate with Iran despite these attacks,' explained an Emirati official.[102] 'The UAE made it clear to Iran that the Houthis didn't have these weapons, and we know where the weapons come from,' he added in reference to the UAE blaming Iran for the attacks.[103] The two countries were careful to compartmentalize their dialogue and use it to avoid escalation, and the UAE did this as it firmly highlighted its ability to defend itself and participated in targeting Houthi positions in Yemen. From Abu Dhabi's perspective, the attacks presented a problem, especially in terms of the country's image as a safe haven in an unstable region – one which external analysts could view as a consequence of overstretch – but it firmly believed that security-wise, it could tackle such threats and its response to the crisis demonstrated its strength and its nimbleness.[104] In fact, a few months later, the UAE's footprint in helping establish a truce among the warring parties in Yemen was visible. The break in hostilities that began in April 2022 would not have been possible without the UAE's involvement. While Saudi Arabia and Oman were instrumental in organizing the technical aspects of the truce, and incentivizing conflict parties to fulfil its confidence-building measures, the UAE helped select members of the new Presidential Council that replaced President Hadi. Council members Tareq Saleh, Abdulrahmen Abu Zara'a and Ayderous al-Zubaidi have strong connections to the UAE, including financially. Despite the ups and downs in the UAE's involvement in Yemen, the country's leadership believed its assertive policy was paying off, indicating it was likely to last.

Libya

By 2022, the UAE remained involved in Libya, and despite changes on the ground, it continued to believe that it was successful in several areas. It established a foothold, including by building links to, and a dependence of, local actors, including with General Haftar and his troops.[105] While ultimately Haftar was not as successful as Abu Dhabi had hoped, the UAE succeeded in other areas. It demonstrated its worth as a partner and ally to Western countries, both diplomatically, in coordinating Arab support for the coalition, and militarily, with its contribution to the campaign in Libya.[106] It has also increased its influence within the NATO-led coalition: 'The UAE's contribution to NATO's Operation Unified Protector and its wider role in Libya should be seen as an attempt to maintain the regional stability of the Gulf while at the same time shaping perceptions as a reliable partner with NATO'.[107] The UAE was instrumental in gathering and coordinating Arab support for intervention in Libya[108] – a testament to its growing regional influence. In addition, 'participation in the NATO-led coalition also gave the UAE increased leverage over the (re)shaping of Western policy toward the Arab Spring once the initial shock of the Arab Spring wore off'.[109] Indeed, Emirati officials reportedly leveraged their involvement in the coalition efforts in Libya to 'influence the US position towards the uprising in Bahrain', and ensure that the United States pursued a policy that was in line with what Abu Dhabi – and in this case, Saudi Arabia – wanted for this small country.[110] Importantly, the UAE is now a significant player in Libya; no resolution of the conflict can be envisaged without some coordination with it, which is why it was invited to participate in the Berlin Conference on Libya in January 2020.[111] An Arab Gulf analyst noted in 2016 that the UAE was a small country with limited resources, but that its effort in Libya was an example of 'successful Emirati power projection'.[112]

It is notable that the UAE failed in reducing instability in the country or ridding it completely of Islamism, though Haftar made significant advances in this in eastern Libya. In addition, Haftar was not able to capture Tripoli in 2019. But the lead up to his incursion demonstrated how rapidly the UAE could capitalize on an opportunity. Abu Dhabi was reportedly not aware of Haftar's assault on Tripoli initially, but moved quickly to ensure it would be a success. According to a Western diplomat quoted in a 2019 Crisis Group briefing, 'the UAE was initially surprised by Haftar's push. But once Washington green-lighted it, they said "OK, let's take advantage of this opportunity"'.[113] The UAE funnelled weapons to Haftar to help, they saw 'it as a low-cost investment that could yield disproportionate returns for their interests'.[114] The UAE was also able to obtain a US change of position on Libya in April 2019, with the administration moving to support Haftar. This made it difficult to end the offensive on Tripoli and left the UN powerless, while the Europeans could only muster a tepid response, with little effect.[115] But it still was not enough for Haftar to capture the city, especially once Turkey intervened openly on behalf of UN-backed Tripoli government of Prime Minister Faiez Serraj in January 2020, following a year of covert weapons shipments to the government. In fact, Turkey's intervention in the conflict in Libya – in part to oppose the UAE and its allies in what it perceived as an effort to contain it in the region[116] – was a failure for the UAE. It added an unforeseen but significant dimension to the conflict: the UAE, Egypt and Haftar would now have to contend with Turkish military presence in the country, protracting the conflict and risking escalation or, alternatively, pushing it in favour of the government in Tripoli. Importantly, the UAE's involvement in Libya on Haftar's side garnered greater international scrutiny for its blatant disregard of international norms and the UN arms embargo.[117] This prompted further scrutiny of Emirati activities in Libya and beyond. In November 2020, the Pentagon's inspector general accused the UAE of funding the Russian mercenary Wagner Group in Libya.[118] In February 2021, a new UN report alleged that the UAE had direct ties to armed Sudanese groups fighting with Haftar. These allegations complicated the country's relationship with the United States and affected the image it spent so long refining. A former Emirati government advisor referred to it as a 'morass' but highlighted that this was not a view that was shared by others in government.[119]

The UAE demonstrated its nimbleness in Libya when facts on the ground changed. Recognizing that it would likely not achieve its objectives through Haftar given the trajectory Libya was on, the UAE shifted its policy. In 2020, the UAE was alarmed by General Haftar's losses on the ground, fearing that if they continued supporting him amid these failures, it could find its influence curbed in Libya.[120] In addition, frustrations were growing with the way Haftar was conducting his campaign: in June 2020, the UAE Foreign Minister Anwar Gargash said, '[Some of] Abu Dhabi's friends had taken their own unilateral decisions. A lot of these unilateral calculations have proven wrong.'[121] The growing realization was that it would be unwise to put all their eggs in the Haftar basket, which was confirmed by events on the ground. First, the other actors the UAE was coordinating with in Libya, from France to Russia, began to pursue diverging goals, potentially squandering the Emirati role in a post-war reconstruction phase. In addition, in early 2021, the Libyan political and peace process made a significant leap forward: on 5 February, UN-backed negotiations in Geneva led to the nomination of Abdul Hamid Dabaiba as prime minister-designate and Mohamed al-Mnefi as the leader of a new three-man presidency council, effectively establishing an interim government until elections.[122] They were not General Haftar's chosen candidates, but in a move that was 'nothing short of a U-turn', the General stated he would be willing to work with them.[123] In addition, in April, Libya's new interim leaders received the endorsement of the country's divided parliament and took office in Tripoli. This was the final push the Emiratis needed to embark on a new direction in Libya and engage with the new Libyan interim government. In early April 2021, the UAE Foreign Minister Abdullah bin Zayed al Nahyan received Jan Kubis, the UN Special Envoy on Libya, and affirmed Emirati support for the Libya Government of National Unity and the UN process. Around the same time, Dabaiba travelled to Abu Dhabi to solicit Emirati support for Libya's interim government, which he secured with a June 2021 meeting with Crown Prince Mohammed bin Zayed who pledged to upgrade UAE–Libya diplomatic relations.

From the outside, the shift from openly supporting General Haftar to engaging with the interim government would seem to indicate a realization that the UAE's initial efforts and strategy in Libya failed. But in the UAE, the reassessment and change in course was seen as proof of the country's nimbleness and pragmatism: that it is capable of noticing when a particular policy has not paid off, and change course fast, to ensure it minimizes losses and maximizes its potential gains.[124] That it is able to do so independently of other countries and partners is seen as a testament to the strength of its policy of assertiveness. Aside from not wanting to be left behind as the political winds shifted in Libya, the UAE aimed to secure its role in the reconstruction phase, and it could not do so if it remained a steadfast supporter of General Haftar without any room for engagement of other parties. It remains to be seen whether it can be a significant player in the reconstruction phase, as some Libyans resent the Emirati role in the conflict and incidents with Emirati counterparts damaged the country's reputation in Libya.[125] This would only leave it with the option of playing a diplomatic role – a far cry from the influential role it seemed to be growing into at the outset of the conflict. What's more, the UAE's ability to play a diplomatic role itself is in question: their steadfast support of one side over the other has hampered their ability to play mediator, and while they were able to open channels of dialogue with opposing parties to the conflict, their savoir faire in dealing with political actors remains to be seen.[126]

Abu Dhabi saw its regional interventions as achieving outcomes that were successful or, at the very least, acceptable.[127] And when the interventions were not as successful as hoped, then the UAE's ability to rapidly change course was a success. This provided it with the confidence to continue its assertiveness in the region and beyond, rather than reassess the usefulness of this policy. The fact that the UAE could involve itself in these arenas, sometimes openly against the objectives of its allies and partners, and still not suffer any significant adverse consequences, meant that it stood to gain from the continuation of its assertiveness.

6 WHAT THIS MEANS FOR THE PERSIAN GULF

In the years following the 2011 Arab uprisings, the UAE's drive towards independence and assertiveness increased in pace and intensity. Over time, the UAE's neighbours sought to mimic Emirati assertiveness because of the perceived gains this brought Abu Dhabi. This resulted in other smaller Gulf Arab states also pursuing a more assertive foreign policy in the region. Others, though, did not pursue it with the same intensity and commitment as the Emiratis did. Qatar, for example, demonstrated assertiveness in its regional policies, including in Libya during the Arab Spring. But Doha scaled back some of its activities, 'gradually realising that perhaps it had overreached'.[1] Doha remained cautious following setbacks after the Arab Spring for several years[2] but gradually increased the intensity with which it pursued its interests assertively again following the outbreak of the 2017 split between the Gulf Arabs.

The result of the increasing number of small states pursuing their interests irrespective of what allies and partners want is that multiple centres of decision-making emerged in the region. This made the regional context more unpredictable because it was no longer possible to attribute decision-making to the two regional hegemons, Iran and Saudi Arabia. In addition to the new regional unpredictability, incidents of tension could no longer be pigeonholed into the rivalry between Iran and Saudi Arabia. Rather, public disagreements and competition erupted between players within the GCC as well, such as between the UAE and Qatar. When such disagreements occurred in the past, they were firmly dealt with behind closed doors. In the years following the Arab Uprisings, however, splits between the GCC states became increasingly public, as the UAE and some of its small neighbours no longer wanted to simply defer to Saudi Arabia for foreign policy decision-making, and were no longer afraid to voice their disagreements with each other. This culminated in the very public split within the GCC in the summer of 2017, where Saudi Arabia, the UAE and Bahrain blockaded Qatar after it refused to comply with a list of demands issued by the three states. Public disagreements between close allies were also not unheard of, despite efforts to highlight brotherly ties between the GCC states. For example, Saudi Arabia – the UAE's closest ally – was not afraid to take on the UAE's economic dominance in the region in 2021. The growing assertiveness displayed by the smaller Gulf Arab states, and the UAE in particular, has altered security relations in the region. First, at the very least, it has given the UAE greater sway over regional security – a victory in itself for Abu Dhabi. Importantly, it has also led to more decision-makers on foreign policy, each pursuing their own interests and no longer aligning themselves systemically with one of the two regional hegemons. The UAE's greater foreign policy assertiveness, sporadically mimicked by other small Gulf Arab states, opens the door to more frequent tensions as these countries compete with one another and with the two regional hegemons, Iran and Saudi Arabia. This chapter will examine some of the key dynamics at play in a region characterized by the growing independence of the states within it, and the impact this will have on security relations in the future.

The broader impact of the change

Since 2011, the UAE has displayed a consistent forward momentum as it continues to expand its involvement and influence both in the region and beyond. As a result, at the very least, the UAE will exert significantly more influence on regional affairs going forward, which will affect the normal order of business in the region. But beyond the UAE, the trend of greater assertiveness seems to extend to other smaller Gulf Arab states as well. For example, while Oman has always led a relatively independent foreign policy, it has become increasingly assertive in the pursuit of this independence following 2011, although it remains to be seen if this will continue under the rule of Sultan Haitham bin Tariq, sworn in January 2020. Qatar for its part experimented with assertiveness in the past, but more fitfully than its Emirati neighbour, though it became increasingly assertive following the 2017 split. Certainly, the increasing number of decision-shapers and makers, as a result of the bolder stance taken by the smaller Gulf Arab states, and the weight of their decisions carries the potential for greater friction in the region. Clearly, if the region is no longer dominated by the rivalry between Iran and Saudi Arabia as the dominant forces in the Gulf but a more complex one involving a series of multiple forceful actors – or, indeed, if this traditional rivalry is overlaid with another layer of antagonism, this time among the traditionally compliant Gulf Arab states themselves – then the likelihood for greater tensions increases.

Tensions within the GCC

The greater willingness to pursue national interests, even when they conflict with those of allies and partners, has already had a significant impact on regional security, including on the interstate trust within the GCC and its ability to work as a unit. 'There is no GCC today', said a former member of the Shura council in Oman in 2016.[3] The UAE's greater assertiveness 'further contributed to the undermining of the smaller GCC states' alliance model', increasing tensions and rivalries within the group.[4] While some of this has been long-standing – for example, Oman's willingness to engage with Iran has always been a source of contention within the GCC – the differences among the GCC states have become increasingly visible since 2011. When Saudi Arabia proposed to upgrade the GCC to form a union in 2011,[5] Oman opposed it and in 2013 threatened to walk away from the GCC if it became a union.[6] In 2014, the region experienced the prelude to the 2017 GCC split. In March, Saudi Arabia, the UAE and Bahrain withdrew their ambassadors from Doha in protest at Qatar's 'interference' in their domestic affairs and support of 'any party aiming to threaten security and stability of any GCC members' – referring to the Muslim Brotherhood.[7] This followed tense discussions between the Emiratis and the Qataris over Sheikh Yusuf al Qaradawi, the spiritual leader of the Muslim Brotherhood, who delivered an inflammatory speech calling out the UAE for not supporting Islamic government on Qatari national television a month prior.[8] This diplomatic crisis lasted until November of the same year, when the three countries announced they would return their ambassadors to Doha after an emergency meeting of the GCC in Riyadh. But the differences that lead to the crisis remained.[9] Other instances of this type of intra-GCC disagreements have been rife since 2011, but none as visible and drastic as the summer 2017 split with Qatar.

In June 2017, Saudi Arabia, Egypt, the UAE and Bahrain cut air, sea and land transport links with Qatar. Led by Saudi Arabia and the UAE, the blockading states once again accused Qatar of sponsoring Islamist groups in the region, including the Muslim Brotherhood, and maintaining close ties with Iran. Why then? A few months prior, in April 2017, Qatar reportedly paid up to $1 billion to secure the release of a party of twenty-six Qataris hunters, including members of the royal family, who had travelled to Southern Iraq and been kidnapped in December 2015 by Shia militant group Kataeb Hezbollah. The funds were reportedly sent to Shia militant groups and Iranians, as well as Tahrir al Sham, an al Qaeda affiliate in Syria, though Qatar denied this.[10] From the UAE, Saudi Arabia, Bahrain and Egypt's perspective, Qatar was funnelling cash to their main regional rival and helping it achieve its objectives in Syria. Shortly after, in June, the emir of Qatar reportedly made pro-Iran and anti-Trump statements that appeared on the Qatari news agency and television. To the four blockading states, this was the last straw. It did not matter that the United States believed the reports were the result of a potential hack by the Russians (and subsequently, rumours emerged that it could have been the Emiratis), the damage had been done.[11] Saudi Arabia, the UAE, Bahrain and Egypt cuts all ties to Qatar and issued a list of thirteen demands, including shutting down *Al Jazeera* and other Qatari regional news outlets, and severing ties with Iran and Turkey. Qatar stood firm, refusing to give in to their demands, instead, further building its ties with Iran, leading to a crisis that lasted over three years and left lasting scars on the region.

The 2017 rift is an example of the UAE's growing assertiveness and willingness to pursue its own interests, even when this opposes those of its partners, or may carry a significant cost to it. Abu Dhabi drove the idea of blockading Qatar as it pursued its efforts to contain the spread of Islamism – including the Muslim Brotherhood – in the region. From Abu Dhabi's perspective, Doha's relationship with unsavoury groups in the region was a real problem, which had to be addressed. Clearly, recalling ambassadors from Doha in 2014 in a very public manner had done little to dim Qatar's resolve in its foreign policy. The 'point of view of the Abu Dhabi leadership, therefore, is not just about differences over foreign policy with Qatar: its position is that Qatar was complicit in a serious and possibly existential threat to its rule'[12] – a position that is not necessarily shared at the same threat level by Riyadh. Saudi Arabia is known to work with Islamist groups, including in countries like Yemen where it worked with Islamist groups in the fight against the Houthis.[13] To Abu Dhabi, though, it did not matter that Saudi Arabia did not share the same threat perception, all that mattered was that it could convince Riyadh to come on board to apply pressure to Qatar, which it did.

The UAE's policy was also a reason for the rift's entrenchment.[14] Towards the end of 2019, Saudi Arabia and Qatar began discussions on mending their ties. From Saudi Arabia's perspective, the rift no longer made sense. It was a public relations nightmare, as the blockading states looked like they were losing the battle because Qatar's policies were not changing; President Trump had left the White House, paving the way for a more critical American president, more determined to avoid American embroilment in Middle Eastern affairs; and the Covid-19 pandemic broke out, further entrenching economic problems in the country and beyond. In November 2019, Qatar's foreign minister Sheikh Mohammed bin Abdulrahman al Thani travelled to Saudi Arabia for discussions on ending the rift – the highest-level meeting between the two since June 2017. But Abu Dhabi was not on board. It was not ready to forgive Qatar for its transgressions, and believed the blockade could still work if given time. Mending ties with Qatar was akin to giving up since nothing had changed in Qatar's foreign policy since the outbreak of the rift. Abu Dhabi reportedly actively sought to block progress in initial conversations between Saudi Arabia and Qatar.[15] According to Qatari officials, 'every attempt to fix the talks with or without the UAE has been spoiled by the UAE'.[16] Ultimately, however, the UAE resigned itself to the idea that Saudi Arabia wanted to end the blockade.

In January 2021, the Gulf states announced the Al Ula agreement, ending – at least on paper – the rift between the blockading states and Qatar.[17] They resumed diplomatic ties and promised to reinstate trade ties. In return, Qatar promised to freeze the lawsuits it had launched against the blockading states in various international fora including the World Trade Organization and the International Civil Aviation organization. But the agreement did little to really mend ties between some of the countries concerned. The Emiratis were cautious in their assessment of the agreement, referring to it as the start of a new dialogue, not the end. UAE Minister of State for Foreign Affairs Anwar Gargash indicated the need to rebuild trust: 'We need to be realistic about the need to restore confidence and cohesion.'[18] Indeed, many of the core areas of friction were not addressed, including elements that had driven the Emiratis to push for the blockade, such as Qatar's relationship with

Islamist groups in the region, including the Muslim Brotherhood. Anwar Gargash brought attention to some of these, asking what Qatar was going to do about them:

> One of the big things will be the geostrategic dimensions, how do we see regional threats, how do we see the Turkish presence? The issue comes to the same fundamental questions ... how is Qatar going to deal [with] vis-à-vis interfering in our affairs through support of political Islam? Is Turkey's presence in the Gulf going to be permanent?[19]

Other remaining points of friction include battles between the different media networks in the region, including anger at continued *Al Jazeera* coverage of events inside other Gulf Arab states. Bahrain and Qatar were unable to resolve their differences in the immediate aftermath of Al Ula, instead increasing their attacks on one another through national media platforms.[20] While the Emiratis and the Qataris continued bilateral engagement to work towards resolving these differences, progress was slow. But the PR machine was in full motion, as pictures of Saudi Crown Prince MBS, Qatar's Emir Sheikh Tamim bin Hamad al Thani and the UAE's National Security Advisor Sheikh Tahnoon bin Zayed smiling and looking relaxed in a Red Sea resort emerged in September 2021, intending to highlight that the Gulf countries' brotherly relations were back on track. Behind the scenes, though, differences continued to simmer. The rift had left a real mark on the Gulf Arab states, and Qatar in particular, never before had it been ostracized and isolated in such a public manner by its closest allies. The rift 'hurt Qatar. Qataris felt the UAE had gone too far both in insulting the Qatari leadership and in the way they dealt with Qatari nationals. It will be hard to get over all this with the UAE,' explained an expert based in Doha.[21] And importantly, never before had its citizens been affected so profoundly. Many Qataris lived in neighbouring Gulf countries, and an estimated 5–10 per cent of marriages are between Qataris and other Gulf Arab citizens, meaning the measures split up entire families.[22] The crisis 'disrupted supply chains, affected the flow of goods and services, and wreaked havoc among companies in the region'.[23] For Qatar, erasing the memory and impact of the rift will be difficult.

In addition to the rift being an example of greater Emirati assertiveness, it is also a case study in the effects of that Emirati assertiveness on countries in the region. Qatar also felt the impact of events in the region since 2011.

It too saw an opportunity in the Arab Spring to expand its influence and a 'chance to step up to the big league',[24] felt the fear of US withdrawal from the region[25] and, despite its better relations with Iran, also looked at the nuclear deal with apprehension, especially regarding the possible effect it would have on Iran's regional relations.[26] But Qatar's resort to greater assertiveness was irregular compared to the UAE. Without the confidence or the perceived success that the UAE had, Qatar witnessed several setbacks as a result of its greater assertiveness, which imbued it with a sense of restraint.[27] Its foreign policy-making was more subtle:

> During the course of the Arab Spring, Qatar moved away from being a mediator to becoming a more active supporter of change in the Middle East region, deeply involving itself in what it assumed would be a new era first in Libya, then in Syria. Gradually realizing that perhaps it had overreached, it slowly adapted and adopted a more pragmatic foreign policy.[28]

In other words, Doha believed that its interventionist stance had begun to take its toll on its ability to achieve its foreign policy objectives and its reputation. Qatar pragmatically changed tack when it realized that it could not sustain the assertiveness it had displayed in the region after the Arab Spring. This demonstrates that if a state does not perceive its policy as successful and without costs, then it is likely to change track. But the rift with its neighbours introduced a new dynamic in the equation for Qatar.

The split with its GCC allies left Qatar isolated from its closest partners, and eager to build bilateral relations with several countries both within and outside the region. Doha had already increased the build-up of its military capabilities with greater momentum following the Arab Spring, and had invested considerably into developing its political and diplomatic influence abroad – much like the UAE. But following the split it was forced to further build political and diplomatic capabilities, and boost economic and political relations with several countries. As a result of the blockade, Qatar lost air, sea and road access to neighbouring countries and some of its trade partners. Importantly, Qatar relies almost exclusively on food from abroad for its small population – it imported 90 per cent of its food from over one hundred countries in the years leading to 2017.[29] While Qatar effectively diversified its sources of food, 27.4 per cent of its total food imports came from Saudi Arabia and the UAE, and importantly, over 40 per cent arrived through the land border with Saudi Arabia, making this crossing a significant choke point for Qatari food imports.[30] During the blockade, Saudi Arabia's food exports to Qatar dropped by a significant 99.3 per cent in the second half of 2017.[31] This meant that Qatar had to either look elsewhere for some of its core imports or invest in its own capabilities – it did both. In the immediate aftermath of the blockade, Tehran assisted the newly blockaded Qatar by sending food and supplies,[32] as did Turkey, which also sent a contingent of troops to help protect Qatar.[33] In the months that followed, Qatar further built ties with both countries. Turkish exports to Qatar increased by 90 per cent in the first four months of the blockade,[34] while Iranian exports increased by 181 per cent in the period between 2016 and 2017.[35] Doha also re-sent its ambassador back to Tehran after recalling him in 2016 in solidarity with the Saudis following the assassination of Sheikh Nimr al Nimr and the storming of the Saudi embassy in Iran. Along with finding alternative supply routes and partners, Qatar invested in its own capabilities. It expanded its Hamad Sea Port by opening five new shipping lines,[36] and organized an official inauguration to highlight how helpful the port's expansion had been in circumventing the blockade. 'The port ... will break the shackles of any restrictions imposed on our economy,' said Qatari Transport Minister Jassim bin Saif al-Sulaiti at the inauguration.[37] Doha also invested in building its own food production capacity, reportedly growing it by 400 per cent in the two years that followed the blockade.[38] A Chatham House report on food security in Qatar stated, 'Perhaps even more remarkably, the country is now self-sufficient in dairy, having previously relied on imports for 72 per cent of its supply.'[39] Qatari dairy company Baladna, founded by Syrian-Qatari brothers, grew significantly following the blockade as it airlifted cows into Qatar to make up for the shortages and established a large dairy farm. Only two years later, the company was producing all the milk Qatar needed and exporting to several other countries.[40]

As a result of the blockade, Qatar developed a more diverse and more resilient web of relationships in several sectors. In fact, it strengthened its relationships with the very countries the blockading countries wanted to split it from: Iran and Turkey. Qatar's pursuit of these new relationships, combined with efforts to increase its self-sufficiency in response to its isolation provided it with a greater capability to pursue its foreign policy objectives,[41] which in turn will further feed into the conduct of its foreign policy in the future. In the years that followed the rift, Qatar once again pursued a more assertive foreign policy, both in the region and beyond, including in Africa, often in direct opposition to the policies of its supposed allies. 'Even if the rift is fixed,' said a Qatari official in 2020, 'Qatar will continue to pursue bilateral relations with other countries.'[42] The official further explained that not only had Qatar gone through the trouble of building these bilateral relationships now, it also made sense to maintain them. In fact, after the Al Ula agreement, Qatar's Foreign Minister Sheikh Mohammed bin Abdulrahman al Thani explained that 'bilateral relationships are mainly driven by a sovereign decision of the country … [and] the national interest', cautioning that as a result, the Al Ula agreement would have 'no effect on our relationship with any other country.'[43] Qatar had also learnt the lesson that even its closest allies could not be counted on, so it would have to chart its own path in the future.[44] 'The blockade taught Qatar that it needed to be as independent as possible,' explained a Qatari academic.[45] This indicates that the rift – in part, a result of growing Emirati assertiveness – has led to a growing Qatari willingness to pursue its interests and, thereby, display greater assertiveness, irrespective of whether it conflicts with those of its partners or not. This will likely lead to further animosity and competition as Qatar's foreign policy objectives may conflict with those of the UAE – as they have in the past – and Doha pursues them more vigorously.

One example of Qatari assertiveness was the links it established with the Taliban in Afghanistan – despite it being a source of contention with the UAE and Saudi Arabia – and its efforts to mediate between the group and the United States. When US President Trump came to power, he made it clear he wanted his country out of Afghanistan as soon as possible. Qatar saw this as an opportunity to position itself as an indispensable mediator. The Afghan government of Ashraf Ghani offered unconditional talks with the Taliban to end the war in February 2018, leading to a mutual ceasefire during the Eid al Fitr celebrations in June. But the ceasefire collapsed following the end of the holiday. Qatar secretly hosted talks between American officials and the Taliban's political commission in July 2018,[46] and shortly after, in September, President Trump appointed Zalmay Khalilzad as special advisor on Afghanistan to facilitate the peace process. Several rounds of talks were held in Doha throughout 2018–20, culminating in the 29 February 2020 peace deal between the United States and Afghanistan, signed in Doha. The 'Doha Agreement', as it became known, outlined the withdrawal of US and NATO troops, included a pledge from the Taliban to curb terrorist groups in the areas it controlled and another to hold talks with the Afghan government.[47] But the deal had no provisions for its enforcement, and it involved trusting the Taliban to fulfil its obligations.

Almost immediately, cracks emerged in the deal as the Taliban resumed its insurgency. The United States continued its withdrawal from the country, even when Biden became president. Unsurprisingly, in August 2021, the Taliban took over Afghanistan, just as the last remaining US troops left the country. The withdrawal and its aftermath were catastrophic. But Qatar was able to draw on its links with the Taliban to position itself as an indispensable actor in the days following the Taliban takeover of the country, as it helped the international community evacuate their citizens, while raising its stature with its most significant partner, the United States. During a trip to Doha in September 2021, US Secretary of State Anthony Blinken heaped praise and thanks on Qatar:

> Many countries have stepped up to help the evacuation and relocation efforts in Afghanistan – in Afghanistan, but no country has done more than Qatar … For years, at our request, you facilitated diplomacy between the Taliban and the Afghan government to try to bring the conflict to a peaceful resolution … The strongest relationship that we have and that we and Qatar have built through this evacuation and relocation effort I know is going to pay continued dividends across these and so many other key areas in the months and years ahead. What Qatar has done here for Americans, for Afghans, for citizens of many other countries will be remembered for a long, long time. And so, on behalf of the American people, thank you.[48]

To Qatar, this was a significant victory. It had succeeded in making itself indispensable to the international community in this instance. But its influence over the Taliban remained limited, making the relationship a potential liability down the line. For example, in September 2021, the Taliban refused to allow Afghan girls in secondary school to resume their studies, a ban they expanded in March 2022 to all young girls. Qatar called the move 'a step backwards' and 'very disappointing'.[49] As a result, the Qatari government was growing increasingly frustrated with the Taliban, especially after the group began to consider moving their office from Doha to the UAE or Saudi in early 2022.[50] In addition, Qatar's recognition as a mediator in complicated conflicts, or with actors that no one else wants to talk to, began to pose capacity problems for the little country, and this will be difficult for it to overcome.[51] Nevertheless, from Qatar's perspective, its assertiveness and willingness to build ties with the Taliban, despite the opposition and the tensions with the UAE and Saudi Arabia, paid off.

Differences also emerged with countries the UAE saw as close allies. While differences between the UAE and Saudi Arabia were not unheard of, the direct and open competition between the two was new. After the Covid-19 pandemic and its significant economic effects on the region, Riyadh began to target the UAE's economic dominance in the region. In February 2021, it called on all companies that wanted to operate in Saudi Arabia to set up their regional hubs in the country and offered tax breaks and other incentives for them to move, affecting several businesses that had set up regional headquarters in Dubai.[52] In July, Riyadh changed import rules for the GCC countries to exclude goods produced in free trade areas or using Israeli-produced components – directly affecting the UAE.[53] Such efforts tarnished the UAE's ability to flaunt its economic credentials as a regional hub for business, but for the UAE, they were only minor setbacks.[54]

Events such as these point to the potential for smaller Gulf Arab states to follow in Abu Dhabi's footsteps, and the impact of more decision-makers in the region. Some of the smaller Gulf Arab states have dabbled with greater assertiveness since 2011, but as time goes by, and Abu Dhabi continues on its current path, this may well prompt them to pursue their own assertive foreign policy with greater conviction, either because of Abu Dhabi's perceived success in its foreign policy or because its greater assertiveness will have affected its neighbours in a negative manner, and contributed to the breakdown in GCC relations. Even if they do not go to the same lengths as Abu Dhabi, their efforts will still change the nature of regional security and policymaking – as demonstrated by the UAE's role in conflicts in the region, either in opposition to Saudi Arabia, such as in Yemen or on its own, without its allies, such as in Libya. If they do not follow suit, or only sporadically display assertiveness in the region and beyond in the way that Qatar has in the past, it still impacts regional relations because it erodes the ability of the Gulf Arab states to work together as a group under the umbrella of the GCC, something we have begun to witness in a lasting fashion following the summer 2017 GCC rift, and which continues despite the Al Ula agreement of 2021.

Tensions with Iran

Iran's existence, especially after the 1979 revolution, posed a foreign policy difficulty for the Gulf Arab states. But the Gulf Arab states could not agree on their Iran policy: 'The GCC's stance on Iran is not clear or organised. The GCC can't act together,' said an Emirati researcher.[55] The GCC 'doesn't even have a minimum definition on Iran: is it a threat? A challenge? There's no consistency', explained a Qatar-based regional analyst.[56] This created tensions within the GCC and made Iran's policy erratic. Despite the rivalry between both sides of the Persian Gulf, prior to 2011, Iran engaged the GCC countries both as a group and on a bilateral level when it became too difficult to engage the group together. For example, after the tensions sparked by the 1979 revolution in Iran and Oman's mediation efforts between Iran and the remaining GCC countries failed, Tehran wished to reassure all states of the GCC of its policies in the region, and dispatched officials to all countries.[57] Iran wanted to build relations with GCC states as part of a concerted effort to build regional security, but 'it proved … easier to establish bilateral cooperation with the smaller countries than with Saudi Arabia which in general distrusted Iran more'.[58]

The growing assertiveness displayed by the UAE, and to a lesser extent some of its Gulf Arab allies, is increasing the differences between the countries of the GCC. The rising and increasing public tensions within the GCC provided an opportunity for Tehran to improve its standing in the region, weaken the GCC and deal with each Gulf Arab country separately, thereby increasing its chances of improving relations with those who are willing to deal with it. 'Iran is benefitting from the differences within the GCC,' explained a Qatari academic.[59] Iran watched the increasing differences between the GCC closely, and believed that 'the splits within the GCC will get worse: not all are on board with Riyadh's policies, and they are not all viewed as equally important', according to an Iranian official.[60] In 2017, another Iranian official stated that 'Saudi Arabia is not interested in de-escalation, but rather, wants to escalate' with Iran.[61] In 2019, during a small round table with some Iranian officials, one of them separated Saudi Arabia and the UAE from the rest of the GCC countries, stating that neither wanted to resolve their differences with Iran, believing that 'Iran's nose should become bloody before either country talks to it', adding that 'there is no GCC anymore'.[62] As a result, even before the summer 2017 GCC crisis, Iran's policy was to actively engage the countries of the GCC individually.[63] It aimed to build ties with those who were more willing to engage with it to offset the heightening of tensions with Saudi Arabia and the UAE.[64] For Tehran, the 2017 GCC split with Qatar was a welcome opportunity to expand on this policy and demonstrate that it would happily assist a neighbour in need. Following the announcement of the split in June 2017, Tehran assisted the newly blockaded Qatar by sending food and supplies,[65] while delivering a message of solidarity with Foreign Minister Javad Zarif tweeting, 'Neighbours are permanent; geography can't be changed. Coercion is never the solution. Dialogue is imperative, especially during blessed Ramadan.'[66] Individuals in the region also believed that Iran was actively trying to break the GCC apart. 'Iran's actions were to isolate Saudi Arabia from the GCC and to get rest of the GCC to turn to towards it.'[67] Nevertheless, Tehran responded positively to mediation efforts by countries like Kuwait on behalf of the GCC as a whole, including in Spring 2017, but it did so believing that they would not lead to anything concrete, given the tensions between Iran on the one hand, and Saudi Arabia and the UAE on the other.[68]

The situation changed considerably followed President Trump's 'maximum pressure' campaign and the outbreak of the Covid-19 pandemic in 2019, both of which upended regional security dynamics and led to a flurry of diplomatic activity. In 2018, President Trump withdrew the United States from the Iran nuclear deal and established a policy of 'maximum pressure' on Iran. The campaign saw the reimposition of wide-ranging sanctions on Iran, along with an increase in bellicose rhetoric and military posturing from the United States and its allies. The policy flopped though: Iran did not return to the negotiating table, its nuclear and missile programmes grew exponentially and it became more aggressive in the region and more repressive at home. The UAE and its GCC allies were supportive of 'maximum pressure' initially, believing the United States was finally doing what was needed to contain Iran. The UAE hoped that the campaign would lead to policy change in Iran. But Iran responded to the policy by lashing out extensively in the region, and targeting Gulf Arab infrastructure and interests where it could not target the United States directly. In September 2019, two key Saudi Aramco-owned oil installations – Abquaiq and Khurais – were attacked by drones, forcing the country to suspend over half of the country's oil production.[69] Yemen's Houthi rebels claimed the attack, but the United States blamed Iran – an accusation it reiterated following an investigation into the attack.[70] The Gulf Arabs were aghast at the lack of US response to the attack, further feeding into their perception that the United States could no longer be relied on. 'It didn't take long for MBZ to realise that Trump was fickle,' explained a military official in the UAE.[71] Along with the aftermath of 'maximum pressure', the rapid spread of Covid-19 through the region served as a reminder to both sides of the Gulf that geography means shared destiny. The pandemic highlighted that a virus knows no borders, and that if a country manages a public health crisis poorly, then it is likely to affect neighbours too. 'Covid showed us we could not deal with it in isolation from others. The policies of our allies, as well as those we compete with, mattered,' said an Emirati official in 2021.[72] As a result, some of Iran's Gulf Arab neighbours helped it battle the virus early on as the pandemic ravaged the country. Oman and Qatar sent multiple cargoes of medical aid to Iran,[73] while Kuwait donated $10 million in humanitarian support.[74] Perhaps more surprising was the UAE's decision to send two aircraft loaded with medical supplies and technical equipment to Iran in March 2020.[75]

The fear of Iranian reprisals for 'maximum pressure' and the perception that the United States was unreliable, coupled with the outbreak of the pandemic led to a change. As early as 2019, the UAE began to adopt a more pragmatic approach to the Iranian threat as it grappled with the need to secure itself, rather than rely on its security guarantor, the United States. It feared that the Trump administration might lead the region to war and that Dubai would be the first port of retaliation for Iran, after Iran's Revolutionary Guards threatened it.[76] As a result, Abu Dhabi conducted limited outreach and de-escalation vis-à-vis Iran. In July, Iranian officials announced that the UAE had sent a delegation to Tehran for discussions on maritime issues. The Emiratis downplayed the meeting, stating that it was part of a series of meetings between the coast guards of the two countries, but following months of crises in the Persian Gulf waters, it seems discussions focused on broader de-escalation.[77] In August 2020, the UAE's Minister of Foreign Affairs Sheikh Abdullah bin Zayed al Nahyan and his Iranian counterpart Javad Zarif exchanged greetings for Eid al Adha and discussed strengthening cooperation on Covid-19.[78] Most significant was the continuation of the dialogue during and in the aftermath of the Houthi missile and drone strikes targeting the UAE in early 2022.[79] Emirati officials made clear to their Iranian interlocutors that they believed Iran had a hand in the attacks, but they continued the dialogue nevertheless.[80] While the tone in Abu Dhabi with respect to Iran had changed – 'Iran will not disappear and will not change, our population has roots there and we can't just isolate it,' explained an Emirati official in a pragmatic manner in 2021[81] – some of the beliefs on Iran did not: 'We continue to watch the division of power inside Iran and how this shifts,' explained an Emirati official referring to the fluid nature of politics inside Iran and the lack of certainty over whether negotiating partners in Iran will be able to deliver on their promises.[82] 'Iran will need to show good faith in talks,' he added[83] – a sentiment that was shared by many in the UAE and within the Gulf Arab states.[84] Abu Dhabi was not alone in conducting limited, de-escalatory talks with Iran – Saudi Arabia followed suit in April 2021. The talks were limited in nature, covering the conflict in Yemen, which had been ongoing since 2015, and they were conducted fitfully, as Iran suspended them for several months in the autumn of 2021, before they resumed again in April 2022.

For Tehran, the growing assertiveness of the smaller Gulf Arab countries, and the UAE in particular, has been a welcome development as it creates more centres of power and spreads decision-making among the states in the region. This inevitably results in diverging views of Tehran, traditionally seen as the main regional aggressor, and provides Tehran with an opportunity to build relations with countries that are more willing to engage with it, to offset any escalation in tensions with the others.

As the trend of growing assertiveness firmly established itself within the UAE, others in the region began to take note. After all, if the UAE could do it, why not them? Qatar was most notable in this regard. While the small Gulf Arab state had spearheaded a more assertive foreign policy in the immediate aftermath of the Arab Spring, it gradually realized it had overstretched itself and reigned in some of its foreign interventions. The 2017 Saudi-led blockade of Qatar firmly established the need for Doha to become self-sufficient, something it has pursued vigorously since.

The result of the spread of assertiveness and independence among the Gulf Arab states is the increasing number of small states pursuing their interests irrespective of what allies and partners want. This means multiple centres of decision-making emerged in the region, making matters more unpredictable. It also increased the fault lines in the region, opening up the possibility of disagreements and tensions between more states. Public disagreements and competition erupted between players within the GCC, as well as with the region's traditional rival, further complicating security relations in the region.

CONCLUSION

Prior to the outbreak of the Arab Spring in 2011, security relations in the Persian Gulf were largely determined by the competition for regional hegemony between Iran and Saudi Arabia, and the different layers of this rivalry.[1] Today, the region is changing. While Saudi Arabia and Iran remain major regional powers, a growing assertiveness has taken shape within the UAE and, to a lesser extent, some of the smaller Gulf Arab countries, particularly since 2011. While the UAE displayed elements of this trend prior to then, it was a series of significant events after 2011 – the Arab Spring, President Obama's announcement of a planned 'Pivot to Asia' and the 2015 nuclear deal with Iran – that unleashed new fears and opportunities, acting as additional external constraints on the foreign policy decision-making of the UAE and its neighbours, making increased assertiveness a more tangible and seemingly lasting trend.

The UAE embodies this trend most visibly today. A constellation of internal and external factors has enabled it to act more independently and assertively in its foreign policy since 2011 in particular, and this small Gulf state has become the most prominent and resilient manifestation of this trend. In the conflict in Yemen, for example, the UAE pursued its own interests rather than merely supporting Saudi Arabia in its pushback of the Houthi rebels and containment of Tehran. For the UAE, the containment of radical Islam in the southern parts of the country was a major concern, which is why it focused its efforts on this, at times even countering Saudi efforts.[2] The UAE is no longer content to merely follow Riyadh's lead, especially if this does not bring benefits or align fully with national interests and objectives. Understanding the changes experienced by the UAE will allow us to better understand the viability of this trend and its spread among other smaller Gulf Arab states in a lasting manner. This trend has the potential to profoundly affect regional security and the way the Persian Gulf states interact, both among themselves and with the regional hegemons in the longer term.

As established, three regional events fostered the establishment of the UAE's greater assertiveness: the 2011 Arab Spring, the perceived US disengagement from the region and the 2015 nuclear deal with Iran. The wave of protests that swept through parts of the Middle East in 2011 posed several domestic and regional problems for the smaller Gulf Arab states, and provided them with opportunities to fill the power vacuum in the region. This coincided with a nascent impression that the United States sought to limit its involvement in the region, and by extension, would not be as committed to its Gulf Arab partners as it once was,[3] and a perceived rise in the Iranian threat.[4] The combination of threats and opportunities unleashed by the Arab Spring established the UAE's desire to pursue self-sufficiency, while providing it with the opportunity to act more assertively on the regional stage as it pursued its own objectives. The announced US 'Pivot to Asia' called into question the commitment of the United States to its Middle Eastern allies – or, at least, that was how the situation was perceived by the Gulf Arab elites. It served to highlight the Gulf Arab states' reliance on the United States for their security needs, and as a result, vulnerability to the changes in Washington's foreign policy priorities. While the US Pivot had little impact on the ground, the psychological impact on the leadership of the Gulf Arab states was significant. The leadership in the UAE concluded that it was imperative to diversify its sources of security, while committing to increasing its self-sufficiency. The negotiations leading up to the 2015 nuclear deal with Iran and the deal itself worsened the perception of US disengagement from the Middle East, and established a new fear: that the United States would turn to their regional rival, Iran, instead.[5] It also increased fears of what a legitimized and bolstered Tehran would do in the region, thereby infusing the Iranian threat with new significance and further entrenching the trend of assertiveness for the UAE.[6]

The existence of the UAE's assertiveness was established through an examination of several factors. The first was its growing military and non-military capabilities, because no country can be assertive if it does not have the means to do so. While military capabilities are the traditional measures of the means a state possesses, cultural, economic, political and diplomatic capabilities are also considered here because together, they offer a more accurate snapshot of what the country under scrutiny here achieved. The state's intention to use the capabilities outlined above is also key to establishing the existence of a new assertiveness in the UAE's foreign policy. While capabilities provide the means for projecting power and influence and are useful to bolster a state's confidence, they are inadequate if the country in question is not willing to use them. Finally, the resilience of the trend is determined by the state's perception of the use of its capabilities. This is key because in the absence of any mitigating factors, perceived success in deployment of capabilities in pursuit of particular objectives should empower the state in question to continue on its more assertive track.

While the UAE seems to view its policy of assertiveness as one that has brought it a number of benefits, it has also created some potential problems for it.

Overreach?

The UAE embarked on a campaign to improve its image and portray itself as a beacon of stability in an unstable Middle East, as well as an innovative and fast-growing economic powerhouse and a reliable security partner. But 'with increasing exposure comes new risks'.[7] As the UAE became a more prominent political, military and economic actor on the regional and world stage, greater attention was paid to its efforts, leading to greater criticism, both within and outside the region, of its methods and the results of its policy objectives. Criticism was only one side of the coin though. As the UAE's perceived foreign policy successes grew, so did the desire of other countries to emulate what the UAE had done and was doing. This has the potential to chip away at the UAE's lead in this trend. All of these factors will feed into how Abu Dhabi and the rest of the world view the success of the UAE's foreign policy assertiveness and whether it is likely to last or not.

As established, the UAE pursued a multipronged PR campaign to improve its image and influence the outcome of political processes and decision-making in foreign countries, in particular the United States. During the special investigation of President Trump in 2018–19, reports of the UAE's extensive ties to the US political elite increased, including through contact with so-called 'fixers' who were charged with protecting Emirati interests within the Trump administration and advancing their foreign policy goals in Washington.[8] In addition, in the context of its more overt campaigns in Yemen and Libya, the split with Qatar and the investigations into President Trump, the UAE's efforts continued to garner greater scrutiny with a continuous slew of damning media coverage of the UAE's involvement in US politics.[9] But it was not just involvement in US politics that was problematic, Emirati efforts to improve their reputation through funding campaigns to Western academic and research institutions also came under greater scrutiny,[10] particularly following crises such as the detention of British academic Matthew Hedges for alleged espionage,[11] the refusal of work visas for two NYU academics[12] and the poor labour conditions faced by migrants building the NYU campus in Abu Dhabi.[13] Following increasing reports of record spending by the UAE to such institutions,[14] greater attention was paid to their output, leading some to decline additional funding from the UAE.[15] This began to take a toll on the UAE's image in Washington, with greater scrutiny of the country by the US Congress, and efforts to constrain the Trump administration's ability to advance Emirati foreign policy goals, including its involvement in the Yemen war,[16] and the sale of weapons to the UAE[17] – a measure that the Trump administration defied in May 2019 by selling $8 billion worth of weapons to the UAE, Saudi Arabia and Jordan,[18] sparking a renewed effort by the US Senate and Congress to block the sale.[19] In December 2020, new legislation blocking the sale of F-35 fighter jets and the MQ-Reaper drones to the UAE was only narrowly struck down by the US Senate – 49 to 47 against the resolution.[20] But efforts to lobby the vote in favour of blocking the sale were significant, and very public.[21] In January 2021, the Biden administration put a hold on these sales,[22] though they then claimed they were committed to the sale in April and, again, in November of that year.[23] The dilly-dallying of the US government (combined with the pressure it was under from Washington to slow the expansion of ties with China) was immensely frustrating to Abu Dhabi: it chose to suspend talks with the United States over the same weapons sales in December 2021, shortly after it had agreed to an over €17 billion deal with France to buy eighty Rafale jets and twelve helicopters.[24] This was a significant change from the statements made by US officials in 2014 confirming that the US relationship with the UAE is 'the strongest relationship that the United States has in the Arab world today'.[25] US lawmakers in particular did not hesitate to criticize the Emiratis for their contribution to the war effort in Yemen, with Lindsey Graham, a Trump ally and Republican Congressman, referring to the UAE's efforts in Yemen as 'problematic'.[26] US officials were not the only ones that questioned the UAE's tactics in regional conflicts. Greater Emirati assertiveness, as well as its close association with Saudi Arabia and its increasingly brazen crown prince Mohammed bin Salman, became problematic for Europeans and others. Following successive reports of indiscriminate coalition bombing campaigns in Yemen and the brutal Saudi murder of journalist Jamal Khashoggi in October 2018, European countries began to assess their weapons sales to the Gulf Arab states. In fact, all weapons sales to the UAE and the coalition came under international scrutiny as the war waged on.[27] The UAE's stance on various geopolitical events also garnered greater scrutiny of its actions and frustration among the Western world, none more so than its stance on the Ukraine crisis in 2022 when it sought to balance its relationship with the West and its growing ties with Russia, along with the need to display its discontent with its US partner.[28]

While the UAE remained a major regional partner to the United States and Europe, its reputation and carefully built image began to suffer from its greater interventionism in the region and beyond. This included how its allies and friends in the region, including within the GCC, viewed it. The UAE 'is short-sighted, and it is shooting itself in the foot', according to a senior Qatari official,[29] an Omani academic and expert on regional security stated that the UAE was 'overplaying its hand right now'.[30] In an interview conducted in 2017, a former official of the GCC said of the UAE that 'it was playing with fire' with its increasing assertiveness.[31] Emirati assertiveness in the region was, at times, perceived as outright aggressive. The same former GCC official commented on how he believed the Emiratis were involving themselves in Omani affairs: 'Omanis believe the UAE is trying to surround Oman and that Abu Dhabi is planning for the post-Qaboos era. They want to weaken the country.'[32] He questioned Abu Dhabi's goals: 'What are they really trying to achieve here?' he asked.[33] An Omani official believed the UAE was being too assertive: 'The Emiratis are being zealous; you can see this in Yemen.'[34] Another Omani official explained the Saudi position on the UAE in late 2021: 'Saudi Arabia doesn't believe the UAE is genuine in their intervention in Yemen. MBS realised MBZ was a more of a burden than anything else, always holding Saudi Arabia back. Now the UAE is the one chasing Saudi because they want things to go back to normal,' he explained referring to the increasing public differences between Saudi Arabia and the UAE.[35] In Qatar, the view was similar: 'It will be hard for Qatar to get over its differences with the UAE. Abu Dhabi went too far [with the split]. The [Al Ula] resolution is not real. It will take a lot more than that to fix things … The UAE is too belligerent.'[36] In fact, according to some in the region, the UAE's increasing confidence was leading it to miscalculate situations: 'With the Ukraine conflict, the UAE miscalculated. It put itself in opposition to a unified Western front,' explained an expert in Qatar.[37] The UAE's greater assertiveness in the pursuit of its foreign policy objectives and its willingness to pursue them alone in the years following 2011 inevitably garnered greater international scrutiny of its methods and policies. This reversed some of the consequential gains it made in terms of improving its image. It may also make it harder for Abu Dhabi to maintain its assertive stance, as other countries in the region and beyond chip away at its advances in various sectors.

A lasting change?

There is a risk that the greater scrutiny the UAE faces as a result of its more overt interventionism and assertiveness, and the subsequent effect this has on its image and its ability to continue on its current track, would convince it to return to the status quo ante and abandon its more assertive and interventionist policies. This seems unlikely, however, as Abu Dhabi believes the benefits of this more assertive stance outweigh the costs, and that it is achieving the objectives it has laid out for itself in the region and beyond. Simply put, 'they believe they are successful.'[38] In 2019, following a number of years on the current, assertive track, a former advisor to the Emirati government said that the UAE was 'the smartest, most nimble Gulf country',[39] wilfully ignoring some of the negative consequences of the current policy. But if some of these negative consequences endure, then it is possible that the UAE will review its policy of assertiveness.

Several challenges have emerged for the UAE. One is the fruits of the UAE's involvement in Libya: 'There is a visible flexibility in the UAE's approach to foreign policy', but its ability to learn from instances of overreach remains to be seen.[40] Abu Dhabi's ability to change tack in the country and build meaningful relationships with others on the ground will be a testament to the strength of its nimbleness and assertiveness. What is certain is that despite the setbacks, the UAE succeeded in shifting its policy and making itself a key player in Libya, as it shifted its support to Prime Minister Abdul Hamid Dabaiba,[41] and built a network of allies in the country that would ensure lasting influence. Emirati officials view themselves as well-placed mediators in Libya: 'We are engaging and mediating in Libya.'[42] The UAE's perception of the success of its involvement will contribute to its longevity in some way or another. Other problems that may surface for the UAE in the long run are how to ensure it is not overextended in one arena, while facing a need to intervene elsewhere – at one stage the UAE had seven thousand troops in Hodeida in Yemen, 'what would have happened if something had gone wrong elsewhere?'[43] – and how to secure the new assets it has developed internationally. The UAE will face the challenge of 'achieving a sustainable balance on multiple issues', including ensuring 'the hawkish approach to domestic and regional security does not weaken the integrative bonds among the seven emirates, particularly as the conflict in Yemen continues and UAE casualties mount'.[44] And yet, the UAE has become increasingly bold and unafraid of the consequences of its actions as time goes on.

One fundamental reason explaining why the UAE's growing assertiveness remains and has been strengthened is the perceived US disengagement from the region. Many in the UAE now believe that the US desire to disengage from the region was not only restricted to President Obama's administration but also felt by the Trump and Biden administrations and was therefore an indicator of a long-term trend. Though there may be instances where the United States was willing to flex its muscles in defence of its partners' interests – for example, following the deployment of an additional three thousand troops to the Persian Gulf after the events of early 2020,[45] and following the US assassination of leader of the Quds Force Qassem Soleimani and Iranian promises to avenge his death[46] – the belief was that the United States 'does not have a long-term strategy for the Middle East', and that 'America is just as inflicted with short-termism in pursuing its own interests as every other country in the world'.[47] In fact, the view of the United States became increasingly negative as the disappointment with the Trump administration settled in. 'It didn't take much time for MBZ to realise that Trump was fickle. He was further proof of American disengagement from the region,' said an advisor to the Emirati leadership.[48] The sentiment worsened further during the presidency of Democrat Joe Biden. In August 2021, the Biden administration went through with US withdrawal from Afghanistan that had been planned by his predecessor, President Trump, even though the planning, optics and execution were rife with problems. This was a shock to the UAE and some of its smaller neighbours. From their perspective, the United States had made it clear they were leaving the region, but up until then, they had been somewhat careful about how they did that. After Afghanistan, the genie was out of the bottle. The perception was that not only did the United States want to leave but Washington did not care how it left or what mess it left behind.[49] This was the new reality for the region, and it was a reality that stood little chance of changing. It further impressed the necessity of staying on track with their assertive foreign policy and their desire to build their self-sufficiency with whatever means necessary, adding longevity to the trend. According to Abdulkhaleq Abdulla, 'There's a trust deficit with America which is growing by the day. The trend is ... less of America on all fronts, not just economically but politically, militarily and strategically in the years to come. There's nothing America can do about it.'[50] In fact, over time, this 'trust deficit' turned into frustration and anger with the United States. The UAE believed that the United States had not done enough to come to their assistance following the Houthis strikes on the UAE in early 2021, believing they had been abandoned by their main security partner during their '9/11 moment'.[51] In 2022, it was outraged that the United States and its allies were asking them to choose sides in the Ukraine conflict:

> Ukraine is a new Cold War, where the battlelines have been drawn, and we're being asked to choose sides. While we understand policies are dictated by national interests, we don't understand why the US is asking us to send weapons to Ukraine, when they asked us not to in the region! Such double standards are giving us a different impression of the West.[52]

The worsening of the relationship with the United States only further entrenched the need to maintain the UAE's assertive course.

Finally, despite the setbacks it faced in its foreign policy as it involved itself in more arenas, the UAE continued to believe that its policy was the right one, though it made an effort to present it differently at different times. At the end of 2021, there was a push to rebrand the UAE's foreign policy away from assertive and militaristic, and focus more on soft power, outreach and engagement.[53] 'We're aiming for a zero enemy foreign policy,' explained an official in late 2021.[54] This meant the UAE pursued engagement more actively, including with countries it had previously shunned, like Turkey and Syria. 'It's about building relations and tackling issues of common concern,' said another Emirati official.[55] Abdulkhaleq

Abdulla explained that the change was not a result of greater optimism but of greater Emirati confidence in its abilities.[56] 'We need to take the lead in the Arab world and on the economy. We have to be number one, be stable, be accepted by different international partners and be strong economically, politically and militarily. We can't adhere to these ambitions while engaged in conflict,' explained an Emirati foreign ministry official.[57] Focusing on soft power, which included political, social and media tools, was less expensive than resorting to military power.[58] In addition, 'just relying on military power wasn't working', explained an Emirati foreign policy analyst,[59] indicating that the UAE had learned some lessons from its military involvement in the region and beyond, and that it aspired to a greater role internationally, which includes economic and political influence and acting as a mediator. 'The UAE has a long-term vision now. It doesn't want to be blind-sighted, there is fatigue in managing crises. So, we will ensure we have greater foresight through the use of alternative levers of power in our foreign policy.'[60] Aside from the buzzwords, these statements tell us a great deal about how the Emirati decision-makers viewed themselves: this was not a country that felt itself overstretched but rather one that saw itself as nimble, fast-acting and adaptable, with an assertive foreign policy that was fit for purpose.

As a result, it would appear that this trend of growing assertiveness may well endure for the UAE. The trend has already had a significant impact on regional security, including on the GCC's ability to work as a unit, especially following the outbreak of the crisis with Qatar, and the region's ability to manage tensions. It will have an even greater impact if the UAE's influence continues to grow and it is able to increase its involvement in regional conflicts or in the domestic politics of countries of interest such as the United States, unchecked.

***

The UAE exemplifies the broader shift that appears to be shaping the region. It remains to be seen whether the smaller Gulf Arab states will also follow the same path as the UAE and display greater assertiveness in a lasting manner, or periodically display assertiveness in specific arenas of importance to them. Regardless of this, the change in the UAE's foreign policy, and the temporary forays into greater assertiveness displayed by the smaller Gulf Arab states, has already begun to change security relations in the region, as smaller states, no longer content to follow Riyadh's lead, pursue their own interests, even when these do not coincide with those of their allies and partners. For some states, the regional context is likely to favour this type of development: after reversing some of its assertiveness following overstretch after the Arab Spring, Qatar found itself being forced into following a more assertive and individualistic foreign policy after the summer 2017 blockade led by Saudi Arabia and the UAE. For example, Qatar began to pursue its own bilateral relations both in the region and beyond, including with countries such as Iran and the United States, with whom it sought to increase ties actively.[61] Doha believes this has paid off; 'we are more needed today than before 2017, sitting in the middle between different parties in the region and beyond', said a Qatari official in February 2020. The elite's perception of success in Qatar's greater assertiveness would indicate the beginnings of a lasting change for Qatar as well.

The growing assertiveness displayed by the smaller Gulf Arab states, and the UAE in particular, leads to a number of broader questions that require consideration: What will happen when disagreements are no longer manageable? Are we witnessing the end of the GCC? Will the Gulf Arab states be better equipped to deal with threats and changing regional security relations as a result of this shift? How will this affect relations with Iran in the long run: are we likely to see an escalation in tensions or a slow easing of tensions as Iran begins to mend ties with the neighbours that are willing to engage it? What is certain, however, is that the new trend of assertiveness has important implications for security relations in the region.

NOTES

Introduction

1 Shahram Chubin and Charles Tripp, 'Iran-Saudi Arabia Relations and Regional Order', *IISS Adelphi Paper* 304 (1996): 3.

2 Ibid., 8.

3 (Supreme Leader Ayatollah Ruhollah) Imam Khomeini, *Governance of the Jurist: Islamic Government* (Tehran: Institute for Compilation and Publication of Imam Khomeini's Works – International Affairs Department, 1970), 23–4; Supreme Leader Ayatollah Ruhollah Khomeini, 'We Shall Confront the World with Our Ideology', speech on Radio Tehran, 21 March 1980, in 'Iran's Revolution: The First Year', *Middle East Reports*, vol. 10 (May/June 1980).

4 Eugene Rogan, *The Arabs – A History* (New York: Basic Books, 2009), 455.

5 The formation of the UAE will be discussed in greater detail later in the chapter.

6 For more on the formation of the UAE, see Christopher M. Davidson, *After the Sheikhs: The Coming Collapse of the Gulf Monarchies* (London: Hurst, 2012), 11–37; Christopher M. Davidson, 'The United Arab Emirates', in Christopher Davidson (eds), *Power and Politics in the Persian Gulf Monarchies* (London: Hurst, 2011); Kristian Coates Ulrichsen, *The United Arab Emirates – Power, Politics, and Policymaking* (Abingdon: Routledge, 2017), 17–60.

7 For more on the Dhofar rebellion, see chapter 3 in Calvin H. Allen and W. Lynn Rigsbee II, *Oman under Qaboos: From Coup to Constitution, 1970–1996* (London: Routledge, 2013).

8 David Commins, *The Gulf States: A Modern History* (London: I.B. Tauris, 2012), 189.

9 Matteo Legrenzi, *The GCC and the International Relations of the Gulf – Diplomacy, Security, and Economic Coordination in a Changing Middle East* (London: I.B. Tauris, 2015), 77, 78, 81; WikiLeaks, 'A Long Hot Summer for UAE-Saudi Relations', 15 October 2009, https://wikileaks.org/plusd/cab les/09ABUDHABI981_a.html, last accessed: 11 July 2022.

10 WikiLeaks, 'A Long Hot Summer for UAE-Saudi Relations'.

11 For more on the formation of the GCC see Legrenzi, *The GCC and the International Relations of the Gulf*.

12 Ibid., 78.

13 Ibid.

14 Elizabeth Becker, 'US and Bahrain Reach a Free Trade Agreement', *New York Times*, 28 May 2004, http://www.nytimes.com/2004/05/28/busin ess/us-and-bahrain-reach-a-free-trade-agreement.html.

15 For more on Qatar's foreign policy, see Mehran Kamrava, *Qatar – Small State, Big Politics* (Ithaca, NY: Cornell University Press, 2013).

16 See the crisis in 2014 and again in 2017, David D. Kirkpatrick, '3 Gulf Countries Pull Ambassadors from Qatar over Its Support of Islamists', *New York Times*, 5 March 2014, https://www.nytimes.com/2014/03/06/world/middleeast/3-persian-gulf-states-pull-ambassadors-from-qatar.html; Kareem Faheem and Karen Young, 'Four Arab Nations Sever Diplomatic Ties with Qatar, Exposing Rifts', *Washington Post*, 5 June 2017, https://www.washingtonpost.com/world/four-arab-nations-sever-diplomatic-ties-with-qatar-exposing-rift-in-region/2017/06/05/15ad2 284-49b4-11e7-9669-250d0b15f83b_story.html?utm_term=.30140b5ff3ad.

17 Author interviews with GCC lawmakers, officials and experts, Dubai, Abu Dhabi, Muscat, Doha and Kuwait City (2014–17).

18 At the end of the 1990s, the UAE sought to take on a more active international role to test its forces and kit. As a result, it contributed 1,200 troops, along with battle-tanks and armoured vehicles to the NATO peacekeeping mission in Kosovo. It complemented this effort with aid and assistance, followed by commercial investments. In May 2000, the general commander of NATO troops in Europe hailed the UAE's involvement in Kosovo and declared the intervention a success.

19 For more on the formation of the UAE, see Davidson, *After the Sheikhs*, 11–37; Davidson, 'The United Arab Emirates'; Ulrichsen, *United Arab Emirates*, 17–60.

20 Ibid., 17.

21 Ibid.

22 'Emirates Act to End Coup Crisis', *Chicago Tribune*, 19 June 1987, http://articles.chicagotribune.com/1987-06-19/news/8702150353_1_ras-al-khai mah-al-qassimi-uae.

23 F. Gregory Gause III, *The International Relations of the Persian Gulf* (Cambridge: Cambridge University Press, 2010), 25.

24 Christopher M. Davidson, *Dubai: The Vulnerability of Success* (London: Hurst, 2008), 276.

25 Legrenzi, *GCC and the International Relations of the Gulf*, 77, 81; Davidson, *Dubai*, 275.

26 Davidson, 'The United Arab Emirates', 25.

27 Legrenzi, *The GCC and the International Relations of the Gulf*, 15.

28 Karim Sadjadpour, 'The Battle of Dubai: The United Arab Emirates and the U.S.–Iran Cold War', *Carnegie Papers* (2011), 9.

29 See, for example, WikiLeaks, 'MbZ Hosts Gulf Security Dinner with Isa Asd Vershbow and PM A/S Shapiro', 23 July 2009, https://wikileaks.org/plusd/cables/09ABUDHABI746_a.html, last accessed: 11 July 2022.

30 Abdullah Baabood, 'Dynamics and Determinants of the GCC States' Foreign Policy with Special Reference to the EU', in Gerd Nonneman (ed.), *Analyzing Middle East Foreign Policies and the Relationship with Europe* (London: Routledge, 2005), 146; Legrenzi, *The GCC and the International Relations of the Gulf*, 129–30.

31 Christin Marschall, *Iran's Persian Gulf Policy: From Khomeini to Khatami* (Oxon: Routledge, 2003), 134.

32 This will also be examined in Chapter 4.

33 Christopher M. Davidson, 'Government in the United Arab Emirates: Progress and Pathologies', in Abbas Kadhim (ed.), *Governance in the Middle East: A Handbook* (London: Routledge, 2013), 281–3.

34 Ibid., 276.

35 Ulrichsen, *The United Arab Emirates*, 175.

36 Davidson, 'The United Arab Emirates', 27–8; Ulrichsen, *The United Arab Emirates*, 117.

37 See Luay Al-Khatteeb, 'Gulf Oil Economies Must Wake Up or Face Decades of Decline', Middle East Economic Survey, 14 August 2015; Yoel Guzansky and Nizan Feldman, 'Plunging Oil Prices: The Challenge for the Gulf Oil Economies', INSS Insight, No. 675, 22 March 2015, http://www.inss.org.il/publication/plunging-oil-prices-the-challenge-for-the-gulf-oil-economies/, last accessed: 11 July 2022; Gause III, *The International Relations of the Persian Gulf*, 33.

38 Davidson, *After the Sheikhs*, 44.

39 Ibid.

40 Davidson, *Dubai*, 102, 106.

41 Davidson, 'Government in the United Arab Emirates', 275.

42 Jonathan Shainin, 'Zaki Nusseibeh: Before and After', *Bidoun Interviews*, no. 18, 2009, https://www.bidoun.org/articles/zayed-zaki-nusseibeh.

43 Peter Salisbury, 'Risk Perception and Appetite in UAE Foreign and National Security Policy', Chatham House Research Paper, July 2020, https://www.chathamhouse.org/sites/default/files/2020-07-01-risk-in-uae-salisbury.pdf, 3.

44 Davidson, 'The United Arab Emirates', 25; Legrenzi, *The GCC and the International Relations of the Gulf*, 15.

45 Abdulkhaleq Abdulla, 'New Assertiveness in UAE Foreign Policy', *Gulf News*, 9 October 2012, https://gulfnews.com/opinion/op-eds/new-assertiveness-in-uae-foreign-policy-1.1086667.

46 Hussein Lbish, 'The UAE's Evolving National Security Strategy', The Arab Gulf States Institute in Washington Report, 6 April 2017, https://agsiw.org/wp-content/uploads/2017/04/UAE-Security_ONLINE.pdf, 6.

47 Ibid., 4–6; see also several WikiLeaks cables describing the UAE's fears of Iran, including UAE Cable, 'Abu Dhabi Crown Prince Warns DOE DepSec Poneman about Iran', 17 December 2009; US Department of State, 'US-UAE Cooperation against Taliban Finance Continues', 24 January 2010; US Department of State, 'Strong Words in Private from MBZ at IDEX – Bashes Iran, Qatar, Russia', 25 February 2009.

48 David B. Roberts, 'Bucking the Trend: The UAE and the Development of Military Capabilities in the Arab World', *Security Studies*, vol. 29, no. 2 (2020): 323.

49 Author interview with lawmakers and officials, experts and academics, Dubai, Abu Dhabi (2014–17).

50 Emma Soubrier, 'Evolving Foreign and Security Policies: A Comparative Study of Qatar and the UAE', in Khalid Almezaini and Jean-Marc Rickli (eds), *The Small Gulf States: Foreign and Security Policies* (Abingdon: Routledge, 2016), 133.

51 Author interview with UK official, London, 25 June 2019.

52 Kevin Narizny, *The Political Economy of Grand Strategy* (Ithaca, NY: Cornell University Press, 2007), 11.

53 Author interview with Emirati officials, Abu Dhabi, 24 November 2021.

Chapter 1

1 Marc Lynch, *The New Arab Wars – Uprisings and Anarchy in the Middle East* (New York: Public Affairs, 2016), 27.

2 Ibid., 13.

3 Author interviews with GCC lawmakers, officials, experts and academics, Dubai, Abu Dhabi, Muscat, Doha and Kuwait City (2014–17).

4 Author interview with an official from a regional Central Bank, Manama, 9 December 2012.

5 Author interviews with GCC lawmakers, officials, experts and academics, Dubai, Abu Dhabi, Muscat, Doha and Kuwait City (2014–17).

6 Ibid.

7 Ibid.; author interview with a former Emirati national security advisor, New York, 31 October 2019; author interview with Michael Hanna, senior fellow, The Century Foundation, New York, 30 October 2019; Lynch, *The New Arab Wars*, 22–3, 54, 55, 146.

8 Marc Fisher, 'In Tunisia, Act of One Fruit Vendor Sparks Wave of Revolution through Arab World', *Washington Post*, 26 March 2011, https://www.washingtonpost.com/world/in-tunisia-act-of-one-fruit-vendor-spa rks-wave-of-revolution-through-arab-world/2011/03/16/AFjfsueB_story. html?utm_term=.ca7af8075dbd.

9 Ibid.; Bilal Randeree, 'Protests Continue in Tunisia', *Al Jazeera*, 26 December 2010, https://www.aljazeera.com/news/africa/2010/12/2010122682433751 904.html.

10 Steven A. Cook, Lorenzo Moretti and David Rudin, 'Corruption and the Arab Spring', *Brown Journal of World Affairs*, vol. 18, no. 2 (Spring/Summer 2012): 21–8; Matthew Partridge, 'How the Economic Policies of a Corrupt Elite Caused the Arab Spring', *New Statesman*, 7 June 2011.

11 Lynch, *The New Arab Wars*, 7.

12 For more on the origins of the Arab Spring in Tunisia, see Christopher Alexander, *Tunisia: From Stability to Revolution in the Maghreb* (New York: Routledge, 2016).

13 See, for example, the repression of protestors at Redeyef in 2008, Jean-Marie Lemaire and Rim Mathlouti, 'Redeyef, the Precursor of the Tunisian Revolution', *France 24*, 15 February 2011, https://www.france24.com/en/20110215-reporters-tunisia-redeyef-gafsa-mining-phosphate-accusati ons-competition-rigged-ben-ali-supporters-protests-journalists.

14 Gregory F. Gause III, 'Why Middle East Studies Missed the Arab Spring: The Myth of Authoritarian Stability', *Foreign Affairs*, vol. 90, no. 4 (July/August 2011): 88.

15 See Elena Ianchovichina, Lili Mottaghi and Shantayanan Devarajan, 'Inequality, Uprisings, and Conflict in the Arab World', The World Bank, 21 October 2015, http://documents.worldbank.org/curated/en/3034414 67992017147/Inequality-uprisings-and-conflict-in-the-Arab-World; see also 'Socio-Economic Context and Impact of the 2011 Events in the Middle East and North Africa Region', MENA-OECD Investment Programme Reports, December 2011, http://www.oecd.org/mena/competitiven ess/49171115.pdf.

16 Grause, 'Why Middle East Studies Missed the Arab Spring', 86.

17 Lina Khatib and Ellen Lust (eds), *Taking to the Streets: The Transformation of Arab Activism* (Baltimore, MD: John Hopkins University Press, 2014), viii.

18 International Monetary Fund, 'Libya: 2013 Article IV Consultation', IMF Country Report No. 12/150, May 2013, https://www.imf.org/external/ pubs/ft/scr/2013/cr13150.pdf, 12.

19 Lili Mottaghi, 'The Problem of Unemployment in the Middle East and North Africa Explained in Three Charts', The World Bank – Voices and Views: Middle East and North Africa, 25 August 2014, http://blogs.worldb ank.org/arabvoices/problem-unemployment-middle-east-and-north-afr ica-explained-three-charts.

20 Lynch, *The New Arab Wars*, 2, 65, 66.

21 Frederic M. Wehrey, *Sectarian Politics in the Gulf: From the Iraq War to the Arab Uprisings* (New York: Columbia University Press, 2014), 70–83.

22 Ibid., xiv; Vali Nasr, *The Shia Revival: How Conflicts within Islam Will Shape the Future* (New York: W. W. Norton, 2006), 108.

23 Toby Matthiesen, *The Other Saudis: Shiism, Dissent and Sectarianism* (Cambridge: Cambridge University Press, 2015), 8, 10, 16, 217–18; Wehrey, *Sectarian Politics in the Gulf*, 16, 105, 121.

24 Grause, 'Why Middle East Studies Missed the Arab Spring', 88.

25 Author interview with Michael Hanna, senior fellow, The Century Foundation, New York, 30 October 2019.

26 For more on the role of technology and social media in the Arab Spring, see Philip N. Howard, *The Digital Origins of Dictatorship and*

Democracy – Information, Technology and Democracy (Oxford: Oxford University Press, 2011); Mahmood Monshipouri, Democratic Uprisings in the New Middle East: Youth, Technology, Human Rights and US Foreign Policy (London: Routledge, 2014); Zeynep Tufekci, Twitter and Tear Gas: The Power and Fragility of Networked Protest (New Haven, CT: Yale University Press, 2017); Wael Ghonim, Revolution 2.0: The Power of the People Is Greater Than the People in Power – A Memoir (Boston, MA: Houghton Mifflin Harcourt, 2012); Philip N. Howard and Muzammil M. Hussain, Democracy's Fourth Wave? Digital Media and the Arab Spring (Oxford: Oxford University Press, 2013); Victoria Carty, 'Arab Spring in Tunisia and Egypt: The Impact of New Media on Contemporary Social Movements and Challenges for Social Movement Theory', International Journal of Contemporary Sociology, vol. 51, no. 1 (2014): 51–80; Gadi Wolfsfeld, Elad Segev and Tamir Sheafer, 'Social Media and the Arab Spring: Politics Comes First', International Journal of Press/Politics, vol. 18, no. 2 (2013): 115–37.

27 Lynch, The New Arab Wars, 49.

28 Anas El Gomati, 'The Libyan Revolution Undone – The Conversation Will Not Be Televised', in Andreas Krieg (ed.), Divided Gulf: The Anatomy of a Crisis (London: Palgrave Macmillan, 2019), 182–3.

29 May Seikaly and Khawla Mattar, 'Introduction – The Arab Spring: How Immune Are the Gulf Arab States?' in May Seikaly and Khawla Mattar (eds), The Silent Revolution: The Arab Spring and the Gulf Arab States (Berlin: Gerlach Press, 2014), 4.

30 This also applies to Qatar.

31 Christopher M. Davidson, After the Sheikhs: The Coming Collapse of the Gulf Monarchies (London: Hurst, 2012), 144.

32 Russel E. Lucas, 'The Persian Gulf Monarchies and the Arab Spring', in Mehran Kamrava (ed.), Beyond the Arab Spring: The Evolving Ruling Bargain in the Middle East (London: Hurst, 2014), 315–16, 327; Abdulkhaleq Abdulla, 'Repercussions of the Arab Spring on GCC States', Arab Center for Research and Policy Studies Research Paper, May 2012, https://www.dohainstitute.org/en/lists/ACRPS-PDFDocumentLibrary/Repercussions_of_the_Arab_Spring.pdf, 18; Angela Shah, 'Why the Arab Spring Never Came to the UAE', Time Magazine, 18 July 2011, http://content.time.com/time/world/article/0,8599,2083768,00.html.

33 Christopher M. Davidson, 'Government in the United Arab Emirates: Progress and Pathologies', in Abbas Kadhim (ed.), Governance in the Middle East: A Handbook (London: Routledge, 2013), 276, 278.

34 Davidson, 'Government in the United Arab Emirates', 276.

35 Davidson, After the Sheikhs, 34–7.

36 Thomas Atkins, 'Boom Turns to Gloom as Crisis Hits Dubai', Reuters, 21 November 2008, https://www.reuters.com/article/us-dubai-crisis/boom-turns-to-gloom-as-crisis-hits-dubai-idUSTRE4AJ65C20081121.

37 Author interview with Michael Hanna, senior fellow, The Century Foundation, New York, 20 October 2019.

38 See, for example, 'Workers Gather in Protest against Unpaid Salaries', *The National*, 19 June 2011, https://www.thenational.ae/uae/workers-gather-in-protest-against-unpaid-salaries-1.377290.

39 Christopher M. Davidson, 'Fear and Loathing in the Emirates', Sada Blog – Carnegie Endowment for International Peace, 18 September 2012, http://carnegieendowment.org/sada/49409.

40 'Local Views on Prospects for UAE', US embassy cable, 04ABUDHABI3210, 16 September 2004, http://wikileaks.wikimee.org/cable/2004/09/04ABUDHABI3210.html.

41 Lucas, 'The Persian Gulf Monarchies and the Arab Spring', 316.

42 Ingo Forstenlechner, Emilie Rutledge and Rashed Salem Alnuaimi, 'The UAE, the "Arab Spring" and Different Types of Dissent', *Middle East Policy Council*, vol. 19, no. 4 (Winter 2012), https://www.mepc.org/uae-arab-spring-and-different-types-dissent; Abdulla, 'Repercussions of the Arab Spring on GCC States', 18.

43 Abdulla, 'Repercussions of the Arab Spring on GCC States', 18.

44 Davidson, 'Fear and Loathing in the Emirates'. The government's crackdown will be examined further in the chapter.

45 Lynch, *The New Arab Wars*, 18.

46 Author roundtable with a team of government officials, Abu Dhabi, 14 April 2016.

47 See Chapter 3.

48 For more on the rise of Arab nationalism in the region, see, for example, Rashid Khalidi, Lisa Anderson, Muhammad Muslih and Reeva S. Simon (eds), *The Origins of Arab Nationalism* (New York: Columbia University Press, 1991); Adeed Dawisha, *Arab Nationalism in the Twentieth Century – From Triumph to Despair* (Princeton, NJ: Princeton University Press, 2003); Fawaz A. Gerges, *Making the Arab World: Nasser, Qutb, and the Clash that Shaped the Middle East* (Princeton, NJ: Princeton University Press, 2018).

49 For more on the rise of Syria and Libya, see, for example, Allison Pargeter, *Libya: The Rise and Fall of Qaddafi* (New Haven, CT: Yale University Press, 2012); Bente Scheller, *The Wisdom of Syria's Waiting Game* (London: Hurst, 2013); Leon T. Goldsmith, *Cycle of Fear: Syria's Alawites in War and Peace* (London: Hurst, 2015).

50 Author interview with Riad Kahwaji, founder and chief executive officer, INEGMA, Dubai, 13 November 2016.

51 Author interview with Omani analyst, Doha, 15 May 2016.

52 Author interview with Riad Kahwaji, founder and chief executive officer, INEGMA, Dubai, 13 November 2016; author interviews with GCC lawmakers and officials, Dubai, Abu Dhabi, Muscat, Doha and Kuwait City (2014–17).

53 Victor Gervais, 'The Changing Security Dynamic in the Middle East and Its Impact on Smaller Gulf Cooperation Council States' Alliance Choices and Policies', in Khalid S. Almezaini and Jean-Marc Rickli (eds), *The Small Gulf States: Foreign and Security Policies Before and After the Arab Spring* (London: Routledge, 2017), 31–46.

54 This is examined in greater detail in Chapter 3. Lynch, *The New Arab Wars*, 246; author interview with Saif Al Maskery, former assistant secretary of the GCC, Muscat, 5 March 2017; author interview with senior Ministry of Foreign Affairs official, Muscat, 5 March 2017.

55 Mehran Kamrava, *Qatar – Small State, Big Politics* (Ithaca, NY: Cornell University Press, 2013), xvii.

56 Ibid.; author roundtable with Qatari delegation of academics and experts, New York, 26 September 2018.

57 See F. Gregory Gause III, 'Threats and Threat Perceptions in the Persian Gulf Region', MESA Roundtable: Mutual Threat Perceptions in the Gulf, *Middle East Policy*, vol. 14, no. 2 (Summer 2007): 119–24.

58 Emma Soubrier, 'Evolving Foreign and Security Policies: A Comparative Study of Qatar and the UAE', in Khalid S. Almezaini and Jean-Marc Rickli (eds), *The Small Gulf States: Foreign and Security Policies Before and After the Arab Spring* (London: Routledge, 2017), 127.

59 Author roundtable with the Al Jazeera Research Center, Doha, 16 May 2016; author interview with former Emirati government advisor, New York, 30 October 2019.

60 Statement by high-level UAE government official, Seventh Sir Bani Yas Forum, Abu Dhabi, 18–20 November 2016.

61 Author roundtable with officials and academics, Qatar University, 14 May 2016.

62 Abdulla, 'Repercussions of the Arab Spring on GCC States', 23.

63 Ibid.

64 'Khamenei hails "Islamic" Uprisings', *Al Jazeera*, 4 February 2011, https://www.aljazeera.com/news/middleeast/2011/02/201124101233510493.html.

65 Shahram Chubin, 'Iran and the Arab Spring: Ascendancy Frustrated', GRC Gulf Papers, September 2012, https://carnegieendowment.org/files/Iran_and_Arab_Spring_2873.pdf, 8.

66 Rusi Jaspal, 'Representing the Arab Spring in the Iranian Press: Islamic Awakening or Foreign-Sponsored Terror?' *Politics, Groups and Identities*, vol. 2, no. 3 (2014): 424; Payam Mohseni, 'The Islamic Awakening: Iran's Grand Narrative of the Arab Uprisings', Middle East Brief, Crown Center for Middle East Studies Brandeis University, No. 71, April 2013, https://www.brandeis.edu/crown/publications/meb/MEB71.pdf.

67 Author roundtable with B'huth, Dubai, 29 February 2017.

68 Supreme Leader Ayatollah Khamenei, Speech to officials and ambassadors of Islamic countries on Mab'ath, 16 May 2015, http://english.khamenei.ir/news/2069/Leader-s-Speech-to-Officials-and-Ambassadors-of-Islamic-Countries.

69 Jaspal, 'Representing the Arab Spring in the Iranian Press', 423.

70 Author roundtable with the Al Jazeera Research Center, Doha, 16 May 2016.

71 Author interview with Michael Hanna, senior fellow, The Century Foundation, New York, 30 October 2019.

72   Ibid.
73   Author interviews with GCC lawmakers, officials, experts and academics, Dubai, Abu Dhabi, Muscat, Doha and Kuwait City (2014–17).
74   Author roundtable with officials and academics, Qatar University, Doha, 14 May 2016.
75   For more on Iranian involvement in Syria, see Ben Hubbard, Isabel Kershner and Anne Barnard, 'Iran, Deeply Embedded in Syria, Expands "Axis of Resistance"', *New York Times*, 19 February 2018; 'Bitter Rivals: Iran and Saudi Arabia, Part II: Syrian War', PBS Frontline Series, 27 February 2018, https://www.pbs.org/wgbh/frontline/article/watch-why-iran-bac ked-assad-in-syria/; Dina Esfandiary and Ariane Tabatabai, 'Iran's ISIS Policy', *International Affairs*, vol. 91, no. 1 (2015): 1–15; Farnaz Fassihi, Jay Solomon and Sam Dagher, 'Iranians Dial Up Presence in Syria', *Wall Street Journal*, 16 September 2013.
76   Hussein Ibish, 'What's at Stake for the Gulf Arab States in Syria?' The Arab Gulf States Institute in Washington, 30 June 2016, 1.
77   Author interview with Professor Abdullah Baabood, Qatar University, Doha, 15 March 2016.
78   Author interview with former official of Emirati military intelligence, Abu Dhabi, 28 February 2017.
79   Ibid.
80   Ibid.
81   'Bahrain Hints at Evidence of Iran Protest Links', *The Telegraph*, 24 November 2011, https://www.telegraph.co.uk/news/worldnews/middlee ast/bahrain/8912240/Bahrain-hints-at-evidence-of-Iran-protest-links.html.
82   Author interview with Bahraini officials, Manama, September 2021 and March 2022, London, January 2022; Simon Mabon, *Saudi Arabia and Iran: Power and Rivalry in the Middle East* (London: I.B. Tauris, 2013), 70.
83   Ethan Bronner and Michael Slackman, 'Saudi Troops Enter Bahrain to Put Down Unrest', *New York Times*, 14 March 2011, https://www.nytimes.com/2011/03/15/world/middleeast/15bahrain.html.
84   Simon Henderson, 'Saudi Arabia's Fears for Bahrain', The Washington Institute, Policy Watch 1759, 17 February 2011, https://www.washingtonin stitute.org/policy-analysis/view/saudi-arabias-fears-for-bahrain.
85   Author interview with Bahraini official, Manama, 13 March 2022.
86   Remarks by President Barack Obama, Cairo University, Cairo, 4 June 2009, https://obamawhitehouse.archives.gov/the-press-office/remarks-presid ent-cairo-university-6-04-09.
87   Fawaz Gerges quoted in David Lepeska, 'Obama and the Middle East: Why the US Is Disengaging', *The National*, 27 January 2012, https://www.then ational.ae/arts-culture/books/obama-and-the-middle-east-why-the-us-is-disengaging-1.404554.
88   Remarks by President Barack Obama, Cairo University.
89   Author interviews with GCC lawmakers and officials, Dubai, Abu Dhabi, Muscat, Doha and Kuwait City (2014–17).

90 Lynch, *The New Arab Wars*, 18–19.
91 Author interviews with GCC lawmakers and officials, Dubai, Abu Dhabi, Muscat, Doha and Kuwait City (2014–17).
92 Author interview with former Emirati government advisor, New York, 30 October 2019.
93 For more analysis on the Egyptian revolution in 2011, including its causes, the revolution itself and the aftermath, see Ashraf Khalil, *Liberation Square: Inside the Egyptian Revolution and the Rebirth of a Nation* (New York: St Martin's Press, 2011); David D. Kirkpatrick, *Into the Hands of the Soldiers* (London: Bloomsbury, 2018); Ghonim, *Revolution 2.0*; M. Cherif Bassiouni, *Chronicles of the Egyptian Revolution and Its Aftermath: 2012–2016* (Cambridge: Cambridge University Press, 2017); Thanassis Cambanis, *Once Upon a Revolution: An Egyptian Story* (New York: Simon & Schuster, 2015); Steven A. Cook, *The Struggle for Egypt: From Nasser to Tahrir Square* (Oxford: Oxford University Press, 2012).
94 Marc Lynch, *The Arab Uprising – The Unfinished Revolutions of the New Middle East* (New York: Public Affairs, 2012), 92.
95 Remarks by the president on the situation in Egypt, The White House – Office of the Press Secretary, 1 February 2011, https://obamawhiteho use.archives.gov/the-press-office/2011/02/01/remarks-president-situat ion-egypt.
96 Aaron David Miller, 'For America, An Arab Winter', *Wilson Quarterly* (Summer 2011), https://wilsonquarterly.com/quarterly/summer-2011-a-changing-middle-east/for-america-an-arab-winter/
97 Lynch, *The Arab Uprising*.
98 Ibid., 94; Lynch, *The New Arab Wars*, 54.
99 Lynch, *The New Arab Wars*, 22–3.
100 Author roundtable with Emirati officials, Abu Dhabi, 14 April 2016.
101 Lynch, *The Arab Uprising*, 94.
102 David Goldfischer, 'The United States and Its Key Gulf Allies: A New Foundation for a Troubled Partnership?' in Khalid S Almezaini and Jean-Marc Rickli (eds), *The Small Gulf States: Foreign and Security Policies Before and After the Arab Spring* (London: Routledge, 2017), 74.
103 Author interview with former Emirati government advisor, New York, 30 October 2019.
104 For more on President Obama's red line, see Jeffrey Lewis and Bruno Tertrais, 'The Thick Red Line: Implications of the 2013 Chemical-Weapons Crisis for Deterrence and Transatlantic Relations', *Survival*, vol. 59, no. 6 (2017): 77–108; 'Obama's Failure to Enforce His "Red-Line" Emboldened and Strengthened Al Assad', *The National*, 20 August 2017; Derek Chollet, 'Obama's Red Line, Revisited', *Politico*, 19 July 2016, https://www.politico.com/magazine/story/2016/07/obama-syria-foreign-policy-red-line-revisi ted-214059.
105 Author interview with Riad Kahwahji, founder and CEO, INEGMA, Dubai, 13 November 2016.

106 Author roundtable with Emirati officials, Abu Dhabi, 14 April 2016.

107 Lynch, *The New Arab Wars*, 58.

108 Author interview with Riad Kahwaji, founder and CEO, INEGMA, Dubai, 13 November 2016.

109 Author roundtable with Al Jazeera Research Center, Doha, 16 May 2016.

110 Ibid.

111 Author roundtable with Emirati officials, Abu Dhabi, 14 April 2016.

112 'GCC to set up $20bn bailout fund for Bahrain and Oman', *The National*, 11 March 2011, https://www.thenational.ae/world/mena/gcc-to-set-up-20bn-bailout-fund-for-bahrain-and-oman-1.413176.

113 Thomas Erdbrink and Toby Warrick, 'Bahrain Crackdown Fuelling Tension between Iran, Saudi Arabia', *Washington Post*, 22 April 2011, https://www.washingtonpost.com/world/bahrain-crackdown-fueling-tensions-betw een-iran-saudi-arabia/2011/04/21/AFVe6WPE_story.html.

114 Kamrava, *Qatar*, xviii.

115 Author interview with a staff member at the Ministry of Foreign Affairs, Abu Dhabi, 14 April 2016.

116 Lynch, *The New Arab Wars*, 15.

117 Ibid., 63.

118 Author email exchange with Marc Lynch, 7 October 2019.

119 Lynch, *The New Arab Wars*, 26.

Chapter 2

1 'Remarks by President Barack Obama at Suntory Hall', The White House – Office of the Press Secretary, 14 November 2009, https://obamawhiteho use.archives.gov/the-press-office/remarks-president-barack-obama-sunt ory-hall.

2 Kenneth G. Lieberthal, 'The American "Pivot to Asia"', *Foreign Policy*, 21 December 2011, https://www.brookings.edu/articles/the-ameri can-pivot-to-asia/.

3 Ambassador Susan Rice, 'Explaining President Obama's Rebalance Strategy', *Medium*, 5 September 2016, https://medium.com/@ObamaWhi teHouse/explaining-president-obamas-rebalance-strategy-eb5f0e81f870.

4 'A New Beginning', Remarks by President Barack Obama, Cairo University, Cairo, 4 June 2009, https://obamawhitehouse.archives.gov/the-press-office/ remarks-president-cairo-university-6-04-09.

5 Ibid.

6 Author interviews with GCC lawmakers, officials, experts and academics, Dubai, Abu Dhabi, Muscat, Doha and Kuwait City (2014–17); Fawaz Gerges, *Obama and the Middle East: The End of America's Moment?* (New York: Palgrave Macmillan, 2012), 102.

7 Ibid., 10; Ben Rhodes, quoted in Ryan Lizza, 'The Consequentialist: How the Arab Spring Remade Obama's Foreign Policy', *New Yorker*, 2 May 2011, https://www.newyorker.com/magazine/2011/05/02/the-consequentialist.

8 Hillary Clinton, 'America's Pacific Century', *Foreign Policy*, 11 October 2011, https://foreignpolicy.com/2011/10/11/americas-pacific-century/.

9 For more on US foreign policy in the Middle East during the Cold War, see, for example, Ray Takeyh and Steven Simon, *The Pragmatic Superpower: Winning the Cold War in the Middle East* (New York: W. W. Norton, 2016); Douglas Little, *American Orientalism: The United States and the Middle East since 1945* (London: I.B. Tauris, 2003); Rashid Khalidi, *Sowing Crisis: The Cold War and American Dominance in the Middle East* (Boston, MA: Beacon Press, 2009); Bryan R. Gibson, *Sold Out? US Foreign Policy, Iraq, the Kurds and the Cold War* (New York: Palgrave Macmillan, 2015); Geoffrey Wawro, *Quicksand: America's Pursuit of Power in the Middle East* (New York: Penguin Press, 2010); Roham Alvandi, *Nixon, Kissinger, and the Shah: The United States and Iran in the Cold War* (Oxford: Oxford University Press, 2014).

10 Eugene Rogan, *The Arabs – a History* (New York: Basic Books, 2009), 583; F. Gregory Gause III, *The International Relations of the Persian Gulf* (Cambridge: Cambridge University Press, 2010), 88, 127, 128.

11 President Richard Nixon, 'Address to the Nation on the War in Vietnam', 3 November 1969, https://www.nixonfoundation.org/2017/09/address-nat ion-war-vietnam-november-3-1969/.

12 Gause, *The International Relations of the Persian Gulf*, 21–2.

13 For more on the hostage crisis, see Mark Bowden, *Guests of the Ayatollah: The Iran Hostage Crisis – The First Battle in America's War with Militant Islam* (New York: Grove Press, 2006); David Farber, *Taken Hostage: The Iran Hostage Crisis and America's First Encounter with Radical Islam* (Princeton, NJ: Princeton University Press, 2006); Gary Sick, *All Fall Down: America's Fateful Encounter with Iran* (London: I.B. Tauris, 1985).

14 President Jimmy Carter, State of the Union Address, 23 January 1980.

15 Gause, *The International Relations of the Persian Gulf*, 105.

16 Ibid., 104.

17 Ibid., 128.

18 Matteo Legrenzi, *The GCC and the International Relations of the Gulf – Diplomacy, Security, and Economic Coordination in a Changing Middle East* (London: I.B. Tauris, 2015), 75.

19 Ibid., 75; Christopher M. Davidson, *After the Sheikhs: The Coming Collapse of the Gulf Monarchies* (London: Hurst, 2012), 179.

20 F. Gregory Gause III, 'The Illogic of Dual Containment', *Foreign Affairs* (March/April 1994); Gause, *The International Relations of the Persian Gulf*, 127.

21 Statement by a regional analyst, Regional focus group involving officials and established regional academics, Dubai, 19 April 2016.

22 Christopher M. Davidson, 'The United Arab Emirates', in Christopher M. Davidson (ed.), *Power and Politics in the Persian Gulf Monarchies*

(London: Hurst, 2011), 10; Christin Marschall, *Iran's Persian Gulf Policy: From Khomeini to Khatami* (Oxon: Routledge, 2003), 94, 116; Frederic M. Wehrey, *Sectarian Politics in the Gulf: From the Iraq War to the Arab Uprisings* (New York: Columbia University Press, 2014), xvi.

23 For more on President Bush's strategy towards the Middle East, see, for example, Timothy Andres Sayle, Jeffrey A. Engel, Hal Brands and William Inboden (eds), *The Last Card: Inside George W Bush's Decision to Surge in Iraq* (Ithaca, NY: Cornell University Press, 2019); Craig Unger, *House of Bush, House of Saud: The Secret Relationship between the World's Two Most Powerful Dynasties* (New York: Scribner, 2004); William J. Burns, *The Back Channel: A Memoir of American Diplomacy and the Case for Its Renewal* (New York: Random House, 2019); Bob Woodward, *State of Denial: Bush at War, Part III* (New York: Simon and Schuster, 2006); Stanley A. Renson and Peter Suedfeld (eds), *Understanding the Bush Doctrine: Psychology and Strategy in an Age of Terrorism* (New York: Routledge, 2007); Kenneth Stein, 'The Bush Doctrine Is Selective Engagement: Continuity in American Foreign Policy toward the Middle East', *Politique Etrangere*, vol. 67, no. 1 (January 2002): 149–71; Dennis Ross, 'The Middle East Predicament', *Foreign Affairs*, vol. 84, no. 1 (January–February 2005): 61; Pierre Noel, 'The Bush Doctrine and Oil Security', *Politique Etrangere*, Summer, no. 2 (July 2006): 246–53; Robert Jervis, 'Understanding the Bush Doctrine', *Political Science Quarterly*, vol. 118, no. 3 (Fall 2003): 365–90.

24 Gerges, *Obama and the Middle East*, 70.

25 The National Security Strategy of the United States of America, Office of the White House, September 2002, https://georgewbush-whitehouse.archi ves.gov/nsc/nss/2002/index.html.

26 David Goldfischer, 'The United States and Its Key Gulf Allies: A New Foundation for a Troubled Partnership?' in Khalid S. Almezaini and Jean-Marc Rickli (eds), *The Small Gulf States: Foreign and Security Policies Before and After the Arab Spring* (London: Routledge, 2017), 71.

27 Ibid.

28 Marc Lynch, *The Arab Uprising – The Unfinished Revolutions of the New Middle East* (New York: Public Affairs, 2012), 224.

29 See 'Global Public Opinion in the Bush Years (2001–2008)', Pew Research Center, 18 December 2008, https://www.pewresearch.org/glo bal/2008/12/18/global-public-opinion-in-the-bush-years-2001-2008/.

30 Barack Obama, 'Renewing American Leadership', *Foreign Affairs*, vol. 86, no. 4 (July–August 2007): 2–16.

31 Ibid., 4.

32 Gerges, *Obama and the Middle East*, 8.

33 Rhodes, quoted in Lizza, 'The Consequentialist'.

34 Author interviews with GCC lawmakers, officials, experts and academics, Dubai, Abu Dhabi, Muscat, Doha and Kuwait City (2014–17).

35 'Full Transcript of Obama's Al-Arabiya Interview', Transcript, *NBC News*, 27 January, 2009, http://www.nbcnews.com/id/28870724/ns/politics-whit e_house/t/full-transcript-obamas-al-arabiya-interview/.

36 Ibid.

37 'President Obama's Remarks in Turkey', Transcript, *New York Times*, 6 April 2009, https://www.nytimes.com/2009/04/06/us/politics/06ob ama-text.html.

38 'A New Beginning', Remarks by President Barack Obama.

39 Ibid.

40 Gerges, *Obama and the Middle East*, 66–7.

41 Author interviews with GCC lawmakers, officials, experts and academics, Dubai, Abu Dhabi, Muscat, Doha and Kuwait City (2014–17); Lynch, *The Arab Uprising*, 222.

42 Gerges, *Obama and the Middle East*, 66–7.

43 Lizza, 'The Consequentialist'.

44 Jeffrey Goldberg, 'The Obama Doctrine', *The Atlantic*, April 2016, https:// www.theatlantic.com/magazine/archive/2016/04/the-obama-doctr ine/471525/.

45 Obama, 'Renewing American Leadership', 12.

46 Nicholas D. Anderson and Victor D. Cha, 'The Case of the "Pivot to Asia": System Effects and the Origins of Strategy', *Political Science Quarterly*, vol. 132, no. 4 (2017): 602.

47 Remarks by President Barack Obama at Suntory Hall.

48 Chi Wang, *Obama's Challenge to China: The Pivot to Asia* (Abingdon: Routledge, 2017), 6.

49 Ibid., 59.

50 Dennis Wilder, 'The US-China Strategic and Economic Dialogue: Continuity and Change in Obama's China Policy', The Brooking Institution, 15 May 2009, https://www.brookings.edu/artic les/the-u-s-china-strategic-and-economic-dialogue-continuity-and-cha nge-in-obamas-china-policy/.

51 Helene Cooper, 'China Holds Firm on Major Issues in Obama's Visit', *New York Times*, 17 November 2009, https://www.nytimes. com/2009/11/18/world/asia/18prexy.html.

52 Goldberg, 'The Obama Doctrine'.

53 Mark Landler, 'Obama Urges China to Check North Korea', *New York Times*, 6 December 2010, https://www.nytimes.com/2010/12/07/world/ asia/07diplo.html.

54 Wang, *Obama's Challenge to China*, 73–4.

55 Mark Landler, 'Offering to Aid Talks, US Challenges China on Disputed Islands', *New York Times*, 23 July 2010, https://www.nytimes. com/2010/07/24/world/asia/24diplo.html.

56 Wang, *Obama's Challenge to China*, 83–7.

57 Mark Landler, 'Obama's Journey to Tougher Tack on a Rising China', *New York Times*, 20 September 2012, https://www.nytimes.com

/2012/09/21/us/politics/obamas-evolution-to-a-toug
her-line-on-china.html.

58 For a timeline of America's war in Afghanistan, see 'The U.S. War in Afghanistan – Timeline', The Council on Foreign Relations, https://www. cfr.org/timeline/us-war-afghanistan.

59 Transcript of Obama speech on Afghanistan, *CNN*, 2 December 2009, http://www.cnn.com/2009/POLITICS/12/01/obama.afghanistan.speech.tra nscript/index.html.

60 For a timeline of America's war in Iraq, see 'The Iraq War – Timeline', The Council on Foreign Relations, https://www.cfr.org/timeline/iraq-war.

61 Mark Landler, 'U.S. Troops to Leave Afghanistan by End of 2016', *New York Times*, 27 May 2014, https://www.nytimes.com/2014/05/28/world/asia/ us-to-complete-afghan-pullout-by-end-of-2016-obama-to-say.html.

62 Lizza, 'The Consequentialist'.

63 Lieberthal, 'The American "Pivot to Asia"'.

64 Remarks by President Obama at APEC CEO Business Summit Q&A, The White House, 12 November 2011, https://obamawhitehouse.archives.gov/ the-press-office/2011/11/12/remarks-president-obama-apec-ceo-business-summit-qa.

65 Remarks by President Obama to the Australian Parliament, Canberra, 17 November 2011, https://obamawhitehouse.archives.gov/the-press-off ice/2011/11/17/remarks-president-obama-australian-parliament.

66 Anderson and Cha, 'The Case of the "Pivot to Asia"', 598; see also Remarks by President Obama to the Australian Parliament.

67 Jackie Calmes, 'A U.S. Marine Base for Australia Irritates China', *New York Times*, 16 November 2011, https://www.nytimes.com/2011/11/17/world/ asia/obama-and-gillard-expand-us-australia-military-ties.html.

68 US Trade Representative, 'The United States in the Trans-Pacific Partnership', November 2011, cited in David W. Barno, Nora Bensahel and Travis Sharp, 'Pivot but Hedge: A Strategy for Pivoting to Asia While Hedging in the Middle East', *Orbis*, vol. 56, no. 2 (December 2012): 158–76.

69 Lieberthal, 'The American "Pivot to Asia"'.

70 Clinton, 'America's Pacific Century'.

71 Ibid.

72 'Remarks by National Security Advisor Tom Donilon – As prepared for Delivery', The White House, 15 November 2012, https://obamawhitehouse. archives.gov/the-press-office/2012/11/15/remarks-national-security-advi sor-tom-donilon-prepared-delivery.

73 Secretary of Defense Ash Carter, 'Remarks on the Next Phase of the U.S. Rebalance to the Asia-Pacific' (McCain Institute, Arizona State University), Tempe, 6 April 2015, https://dod.defense.gov/News/Speeches/Spe ech-View/Article/606660/.

74 Rice, 'Explaining President Obama's Rebalance Strategy'.

75 Ibid.

76 'Advance Policy Questions for Admiral Harry B. Harries Jr., U.S. Navy, Nominee to be Commander, U.S. Pacific Command', Senate Hearing, https://www.armed-services.senate.gov/imo/media/doc/Harris_12-02-14.pdf; see also Mark E. Manyin, Stephen Daggett, Ben Dolven, Susan V. Lawrence, Michael F. Martin, Ronald O'Rourke and Bruce Vaughn, 'Pivot to the Pacific? The Obama Administration's "Rebalancing" toward Asia', Congressional Research Service Reports, 28 March 2012, 15.

77 David W. Barno, Nora Bensahel and Travis Sharp, 'Pivot but Hedge: A Strategy for Pivoting to Asia while Hedging in the Middle East', *Orbis*, vol. 56, no. 2 (Spring 2012): 159.

78 Amitai Etzioni, 'The United States' Premature Pivot to "Asia"', *Society*, vol. 49, no. 5 (September 2012): 395–9.

79 See factsheet on 'UAE-US Economic Relationship', Embassy of the UAE in Washington DC, https://www.uae-embassy.org/uae-us-relations/key-areas-bilateral-cooperation/uae-us-economic-relationship.

80 Statement by former Emirati official, Regional focus group involving officials and established regional academics, Dubai, 19 April 2016.

81 Author interviews with GCC lawmakers, officials, experts and academics, Dubai, Abu Dhabi, Muscat, Doha and Kuwait City (2014–17).

82 Ibid.

83 Goldberg, 'The Obama Doctrine'.

84 Ibid.

85 Statement by former Emirati military intelligence official, Dubai, 10 April 2016.

86 Remarks by President Obama in Address to the United Nations General Assembly, United Nations, New York, 24 September 2013, https://obamawhitehouse.archives.gov/the-press-office/2013/09/24/remarks-presid ent-obama-address-united-nations-general-assembly.

87 Mark Landler, 'Rice Offers a More Modest Strategy for the Mideast', *New York Times*, 26 October 2013, https://www.nytimes.com/2013/10/27/world/middleeast/rice-offers-a-more-modest-strategy-for-mideast.html.

88 Author interviews with GCC lawmakers, officials, experts and academics, Dubai, Abu Dhabi, Muscat, Doha and Kuwait City (2014–17).

89 Statement by a Middle East analyst, Bani Yas conference, Abu Dhabi, 18–19 November 2016.

90 Author interview with Youssef Al Otaiba, UAE ambassador to the USA, Washington, 2 March 2016.

91 Author interviews with GCC lawmakers, officials, experts and academics, Dubai, Abu Dhabi, Muscat, Doha and Kuwait City (2014–17).

92 Author interview with UAE think tank director, Dubai, 1 March 2017.

93 Author round table with experts and analysts, Al Jazeera Research Center, Doha, 16 May 2016.

94 Round table with professors and researchers, Qatar University, Doha, 15 May 2016.

95 Author interview with former Omani member of the *Majles Shura*, Muscat, 21 May 2016.

96 Author interview with Omani central bank board member, Muscat, 5 March 2017.

97 See, for example, Louis Jacobson, 'Donald Trump Says Kuwait Never Paid U.S. Back for Ousting Saddam Hussein', *Politifact*, 27 April 2011, https://www.politifact.com/truth-o-meter/statements/2011/apr/27/donald-trump/donal-trump-says-kuwait-never-paid-us-back-ousting/.

98 Author interview with Abdullah Baabood, former professor, Qatar University, Doha, 15 May 2016.

99 Philip Rucker and Karen DeYoung, 'Trump Signs "Tremendous" Deals with Saudi Arabia on His First Day Overseas', *Washington Post*, 20 May 2017, https://www.washingtonpost.com/politics/trump-gets-elaborate-welcome-in-saudi-arabia-embarking-on-first-foreign-trip/2017/05/20/679f2766-3d1d-11e7-a058-ddbb23c75d82_story.html.

100 See, for example, the immediate aftermath of the strikes on Saudi oil installations in September 2019 and the lack of US response to the attacks, Rory Jones and Sune Engel Rasmussen, 'What We Know about the Saudi Oil Attacks', *Wall Street Journal*, 20 September 2019, https://www.wsj.com/articles/what-we-know-about-the-saudi-oil-attacks-11568991017.

101 See Chapter 3. See Rajiv Chandrasekran, 'In the UAE, the United States Has a Quiet, Potent Ally Nicknamed "Little Sparta"', *Washington Post*, 9 November 2014, https://www.washingtonpost.com/world/national-security/in-the-uae-the-united-states-has-a-quiet-potent-ally-nicknamed-little-sparta/2014/11/08/3fc6a50c-643a-11e4-836c-83bc4f26eb67_story.html?utm_term=.a92d2e0ed1d6; David Hearst, 'Revealed: How Trump Confidant Was Ready to Share Inside Information with UAE', *Middle East Eye*, 28 June 2018, https://www.middleeasteye.net/news/revealed-how-trump-confidant-was-ready-share-inside-information-uae.

102 Author interview with UAE official, Washington, DC, 2 March 2016.

103 Ibid.

104 Author interview with a former Emirati national security advisor, New York, 31 October 2019; author interviews with Emirati lawmakers, officials, experts and academics, Dubai, Abu Dhabi (2014–17).

105 Ibid.

106 Author round table with experts and analysts, Al Jazeera Research Center, 16 May 2016.

107 Author interview with Omani analyst, Doha, 15 May 2016.

108 Ibid.

109 Kenneth Katzman, 'The United Arab Emirates (U.A.E): Issues for U.S. Policy', Congressional Research Service reports, 28 November 2016, https://www.refworld.org/pdfid/58453f2a4.pdf, 19.

110 Ibid., 20.

111 Author interviews with GCC lawmakers, officials, experts and academics, Dubai, Abu Dhabi, Muscat, Doha and Kuwait City (2014–17).

112 'Middle East 2016: Current Conditions and the Road Ahead', Zogby Research Services, Prepared for the Sir Bani Yas Forum, November 2016, 5.

113 Ibid., 7.

114 Ibid., 8.

115 Author interviews with GCC lawmakers, officials, experts and academics, Dubai, Abu Dhabi, Muscat, Doha and Kuwait City (2014–17).

116 'Remarks by President Barack Obama at Suntory Hall'.

117 'A New Beginning', Remarks by President Barack Obama.

118 Clinton, 'America's Pacific Century'.

Chapter 3

1 The time it would take for Iran to develop all the raw materials needed for one nuclear device. See Ernest Moniz, 'A Nuclear Deal That Offers a Safer World', *Washington Post*, 12 April 2015, https://www.washingtonpost.com/opinions/a-safer-iran/2015/04/12/ae3a7f78-dfae-11e4-a1b8-2ed88bc190d2_story.html?utm_term=.9eae4bab7b12.

2 Ibid.

3 Author interviews with GCC lawmakers, officials, experts and academics, Dubai, Abu Dhabi, Muscat, Doha, and Kuwait City (2014–17).

4 Author interview with Sami Al Faraj, president, Kuwait Centre for Strategic Studies, Kuwait, 24 May 2016; author interview with Abdullah Baabood, former professor, Qatar University, Doha, 15 May 2016.

5 For more on the environmental concerns sparked by Iran's nuclear programme for the UAE, see Dina Esfandiary, 'Two Tremors in Two Weeks, and Many Questions for Iran', *The National*, 22 April 2013, https://www.thenational.ae/two-tremors-in-two-weeks-and-many-questions-for-iran-1.324812.

6 Author interviews with GCC lawmakers, officials, experts and academics, Dubai, Abu Dhabi, Muscat, Doha, and Kuwait City (2014–17).

7 Ibid; author interview with Emirati official, New York, 11 March 2016; Youssef Al Otaiba, 'One Year after the Iran Nuclear Deal', *Wall Street Journal*, 3 April 2016, https://www.wsj.com/articles/one-year-after-the-iran-nuclear-deal-1459721502; Suleiman Al-Khalidi, 'Saudi FM says Riyadh Determined to Confront Iranian Expansion in Region', *Reuter*s, 9 July 2015, https://www.reuters.com/article/uk-saudi-iran/saudi-fm-says-riyadh-determined-to-confront-iranian-expansion-in-region-idUKKCN0PJ2GJ20150709; Gregory F. Gause III, 'Why the Iranian Deal Scares Saudi Arabia', *New Yorker*, 26 November 2013, https://www.newyorker.com/news/news-desk/why-the-iran-deal-scares-saudi-arabia; Angus McDowall, 'Region Will Lose Sleep over Iran Deal: Saudi Advisor', Reuters, 24 November 2013, https://www.reuters.com/article/us-iran-nuclear-saudi-fears/region-will-lose-sleep-over-iran-deal-saudi-adviser-idUSBRE9AN07C20131124.

8 Author round table with government officials, Abu Dhabi, 14 April 2016.

9 Author interviews with Emirati lawmakers, officials, experts and academics, Dubai, Abu Dhabi (2014–17).

10 Ibid.

11 Author interview with Emirati official, Washington, 2 March 2016, Author interview with Emirati official, New York, 11 March 2016.

12 McDowall, 'Region Will Lose Sleep over Iran Deal'.

13 The Pahlavis came to power in December 1925 under Reza Shah until 1979, when his son, Mohammed Reza Shah, was deposed following the Iranian Revolution.

14 For more on the shah's vision for Iran, see Mohammed Reza Pahlavi, *Answer to History* (New York: Stein & Day, 1980); Abbas Milani, *The Shah* (New York: St Martin's Press, 2012).

15 For example, the shah's claims to Bahrain and influence prevented the Sheikhdom from joining the federation that was being negotiated following the British withdrawal from the region. See Matteo Legrenzi, *The GCC and the International Relations of the Gulf – Diplomacy, Security, and Economic Coordination in a Changing Middle East* (London: I.B. Tauris, 2015), 17. While he finally relinquished his claim, allowing Bahrain to declare independence on 16 December 1971, he maintained his claims to three islands off the coast of the UAE: Abu Musa, which it disputed with the emirate of Sharjah, and Greater and Lesser Tunbs, which it disputed with Ras Al Khaimeh.

16 (Supreme Leader Ayatollah Ruhollah) Imam Khomeini, *Governance of the Jurist: Islamic Government* (Tehran: The Institute for Compilation and Publication of Imam Khomeini's Works – International Affairs Department, 1970), 23–4, Supreme Leader Ayatollah Ruhollah Khomeini, 'We Shall Confront the World with Our Ideology', speech on Radio Tehran, 21 March 1980, in 'Iran's Revolution: The First Year', *Middle East Reports, Vol 10* (May/June 1980).

17 Simon Mabon, *Saudi Arabia and Iran: Power and Rivalry in the Middle East* (London: I.B. Tauris, 2013), 5.

18 Alidad Mafinezam and Aria Mehrabi, *Iran and Its Place among Nations* (Greenwood: Praeger, 2008), 37; Ali Ansari, *The Politics of Nationalism in Modern Iran* (New York: Cambridge University Press, 2012), 221; Shireen T. Hunter, *Iran after Khomeini* (Santa Barbara: Praeger, 1992), 93.

19 Author interviews with Iranian officials, Berlin, Vienna, New York, Lausanne, Doha (2015–22); Ansari, *The Politics of Nationalism in Modern Iran*, 226, Hunter, *Iran after Khomeini*, 93; Ali Ansari, *Modern Iran: Reform and Revolution* (Abingdon: Routledge, 2003), 283; Daniel Byman, Shahram Chubin, Anoushiravan Ehteshami and Jerrold D. Green, *Iran's Security Policy in a Post-Revolutionary Era* (Santa Monica: RAND Corporation, 2001), 9; Christin Marschall, *Iran's Persian Gulf Policy: From Khomeini to Khatami* (Oxon: Routledge, 2003), 11. For more on the means Iran uses to involve itself in the region, see Gregory F. Rose, 'The Post-Revolutionary Purge of Iran's Armed Forces: A Revisionist Assessment', *Iranian Studies,* vol. 17, nos. 2/3 (Spring–Summer 1984): 153–94; Nikola B. Schahgaldian, 'The Iranian Military under the Islamic Republic', *RAND Report*, March 1987; Frederic Wehrey, Jerrold D. Green, Brian Nichiporuk, Alireza Nader, Lydia Hansell, Rasool Nafisi and S. R. Bohandy, *The Rise of the Pasdaran: Assessing the Domestic Roles of Iran's Islamic Revolutionary Guards Corps* (Santa Monica: RAND Corporation, 2009); Daniel Byman, *Deadly Connections: States That Sponsor Terrorism* (Cambridge: Cambridge University Press, 2005), 53–78, Bruce Hoffman, *Inside Terrorism* (New York: Columbia University Press, 1998), 258–67; Kenneth Katzman, 'Iran's Foreign and Defence Policies', Congressional Research Service Report, 7 November 2017, https://fas.org/sgp/crs/mideast/R44017.pdf

20 Author interviews with Iranian officials, Berlin, New York, Lausanne, Doha (2015–19).

21 Author interviews with GCC lawmakers and officials, Dubai, Abu Dhabi, Muscat, Doha and Kuwait City (2014–22).

22 Author round table with Emirati think tank, Dubai, 29 February 2017.

23 Author interview with Salim bin Mohamed Al Riyami, former Omani ambassador to Vienna, Muscat, 19 May 2016; author interview with Saif bin Hashil Al Maskery, former assistant secretary of the GCC, former ambassador to Switzerland and former member of the Majles Ashura, Muscat, 5 March 2017. For more on Oman's relations with Iran, see Gertjan Hoetjes, 'Iran-GCC Relations: The Case of Oman', in Maiike Warnaar, Luciano Zaccara and Paul Aarts (eds), *Iran's Relations with the Arab States of the Gulf* (London: Gerlach Press, 2016).

24 Author interview with Ministry of Foreign Affairs officials, Abu Dhabi, 28 February 2017; author interview with Central Bank Board member, Muscat, 5 March 2017; author interview with *Majles Ashura* member, Muscat, 5 March 2017.

25 Author interview with UAE Ministry of Foreign Affairs officials, Abu Dhabi, 28 February 2017; author interview with Ambassador Youssef Al Otaiba, UAE ambassador to the USA, Washington DC, 2 March 2016; author interview with Ambassador Lana Nusseibeh, UAE ambassador to the United Nations, New York, 11 March 2016; Abdullah bin Zayed Al Nahyan, 'Iran Is Threatening the Stability in the Middle East', *Financial Times*, 30 January 2018, https://www.ft.com/content/5254f 36a-05a2-11e8-9e12-af73e8db3c71; Adel bin Ahmed Al-Jubeir, 'Can Iran Change?' *New York Times*, 19 January 2016, https://www.nytimes. com/2016/01/19/opinion/saudi-arabia-can-iran-change.html.

26 Author interviews with Kuwaiti officials, officials in the navy and academics, Kuwait City, 25–26 May 2016; author interviews with Qatari officials, experts and academics, Doha, 14–17 May 2016.

27 F. Gregory Gause III, *The International Relations of the Persian Gulf* (Cambridge: Cambridge University Press, 2010), 131; Marschall, *Iran's Persian Gulf Policy*, 97, 102.

28 WikiLeaks, 'Former GCC Secretary General: "No Common GCC Strategy on Iran"', 24 September 2006.

29   For more on the origins of Iran's nuclear programme, see, for example, Steven Hurst, *The United States and the Iranian Nuclear Programme: A Critical History* (Edinburgh: Edinburgh University Press, 2018); Jeremy Bernstein, *Nuclear Iran* (Cambridge, MA: Harvard University Press, 2014); David Patrikarakos, *Nuclear Iran: The Birth of an Atomic State* (London: I.B. Tauris, 2012); Seyed Hossein Mousavian, *The Iranian Nuclear Crisis: A Memoir* (Washington, DC: Carnegie Endowment for International Peace, 2012).

30   See Greg Bruno, 'Iran's Nuclear Program', Council on Foreign Relations Backgrounder, 10 March 2010, https://www.cfr.org/backgrounder/irans-nuclear-program; Andrew Koch and Jeanette Wolf, 'Iran's Nuclear Procurement Program: How Close to the Bomb?', *Nonproliferation Review* (Fall 1997), https://www.nonproliferation.org/wp-content/uploads/npr/koch51.pdf, 131; Seyed Hossein Mousavian and Mohammad Mehdi Mousavian, 'Building on the Iran Nuclear Deal for International Peace and Security', *Journal for Peace and Nuclear Disarmament*, vol. 1, no. 1 (2018): 171.

31   For more information, see Wyn Bowen, Matthew Moran and Dina Esfandiary, *Living on the Edge: Iran and the Practice of Nuclear Hedging* (London: Palgrave Macmillan, 2016).

32   For more on sanctions on Iran, see Ali Vaez, 'Spider Web: The Making and Unmaking of Iran Sanctions', *International Crisis Group Report*, no. 138, 25 February 2013, https://www.crisisgroup.org/middle-east-north-africa/gulf-and-arabian-peninsula/iran/138-spider-web-making-and-unmaking-iran-sanctions.

33   Remarks by Alireza Jafarzadeh on New Information on Top Secret Projects of the Iranian Regime's Nuclear Program, *IranWatch*, 14 August 2002, https://www.iranwatch.org/library/ncri-new-information-top-secret-nuclear-projects-8-14-02.

34   For more on the negotiations between Iran and the P5+1 and the importance of the nuclear programme to Iran, see Bowen, Moran and Esfandiary, *Living on the Edge*.

35   'Secret US-Iran Talks Cleared the Way for Historic Nuclear Deal', *Associated Press*, 24 November 2013, https://www.telegraph.co.uk/news/worldnews/middleeast/iran/10471030/Secret-US-Iran-talks-cleared-way-for-historic-nuclear-deal.html.

36   Jeff Mason and Louis Charbonneau, 'Obama, Iran's Rouhani Hold Historic Phone Call', *Reuters*, 27 September 2013, https://www.reuters.com/article/us-un-assembly-iran/obama-irans-rouhani-hold-historic-phone-call-idUSBRE98Q16S20130928.

37   Joint Plan of Action (JPOA), Geneva, 24 November 2011, http://www.isisnucleariran.org/assets/pdf/Joint_plan_24Nov2013.pdf.

38   Julian Borger and Paul Lewis, 'Iran Nuclear Deal: Negotiators Announce "Framework" Agreement', *The Guardian*, 2 April 2015, https://www.theguardian.com/world/2015/apr/02/iran-nuclear-deal-negotiators-announce-framework-agreement.

39   The Joint Comprehensive Plan of Action (JCPOA), Vienna, 14 July 2015,
      https://www.state.gov/documents/organization/245317.pdf.

40   Iran's old IR-1 centrifuges were cut from 19,500 to 6,104; of those,
      5,060 would enrich uranium to less than 5 per cent (only at the Natanz
      enrichment plant). The remainder would be dismantled and stored under
      IAEA seal. See The Joint Comprehensive Plan of Action (JCPOA), Vienna,
      14 July 2015, https://www.state.gov/documents/organization/245317.pdf,
      section A.

41   Ibid.

42   Ali Ahmad, Frank von Hippel, Alexander Glaser and Zia Mian, 'A
      Win-Win Solution for Iran's Arak Reactor', *Arms Control Today*, 1 April
      2014, https://www.armscontrol.org/act/2014_04/A-Win-Win-Solut
      ion-for-Irans-Arak-Reactor.

43   The Joint Comprehensive Plan of Action, section B.

44   Ibid., section C.

45   Vaez, 'Spider Web'.

46   See, for example, James Phillips, 'The Most Glaring Flaws in Obama's Iran
      Deal', The Heritage Foundation, 14 July 2015, https://www.heritage.org/glo
      bal-politics/commentary/the-most-glaring-flaws-obamas-iran-deal; Alan
      J. Kuperman, 'The Iran Deal's Fatal Flaw', *New York Times*, 23 June 2015,
      https://www.nytimes.com/2015/06/23/opinion/the-iran-deals-fatal-flaw.
      html; Charles Krauthammer, 'The Fatal Flaw in the Iran Deal', *Washington
      Post*, 26 February 2015, https://www.washingtonpost.com/opinions/
      the-fatal-flaw-in-the-iran-deal/2015/02/26/9186c70e-bde1-11e4-8668-4e7
      ba8439ca6_story.html. Strictly speaking, the permitted enrichment
      programme is beyond what Iran needs for a peaceful nuclear programme,
      see Michael Singh, 'The Case for Zero Enrichment in Iran', *Arms Control
      Today*, March 2014, https://www.armscontrol.org/act/2014-03/case-zero-
      enrichment-iran.

47   Dina Esfandiary and Ariane Tabatabai, 'Meeting Iran's Nuclear Fuel
      Supply Needs', *Bulletin of Atomic Scientists*, 5 June 2014, https://thebulletin.
      org/2014/06/meeting-irans-nuclear-fuel-supply-needs/.

48   Author interviews with the Iranian negotiating team, Geneva, Lausanne,
      Vienna (2013-2015); author interview with US official, Vienna, 13
      May 2015.

49   Senator Bob Menendez, speech on Iran Nuclear Deal, Seton Hall
      University, 18 August 2015, https://www.menendez.senate.gov/
      news-and-events/press/menendez-delivers-remarks-on-iran-nucl
      ear-deal-at-seton-hall-universitys-school-of-diplomacy-and-internatio
      nal-relations; Ambassador Eric Edelman, 'The Iran Nuclear Deal after
      One Year: Assessment and Options for the Next President', Report, JINSA's
      Gemunder Center Iran Task Force, July 2016, https://jinsa.org/wp-content/
      uploads/2016/07/The-Iran-Nuclear-Deal-After-One-Year-Assessment-and-
      Options_web-1.pdf.

50   Emile Hokayem and Matteo Legrenzi, 'The Arab Gulf States in the Shadow
      of the Iranian Nuclear Challenge', The Stimson Center Working Paper,

26 May 2006, 4; Legrenzi, *The GCC and the International Relations of the Gulf*, 117.

51 Sammy Salama and Heidi Weber, 'The Emerging Arab Response to Iran's Unabated Nuclear Program', NTI Report, 22 December 2006, https://www. nti.org/analysis/articles/arab-response-irans-nuclear-program/; Frederic Wehrey, David E. Thaler, Nora Bensahel, Kim Cragin, Jerrold D. Green, Dalia Dassa Kaye, Nadia Oweidat and Jennifer Li, *Dangerous but Not Omnipotent: Exploring the Reach and Limitations of Iranian Power in the Middle East* (Santa Monica: RAND Corporation, 2009), 134.

52 Wehrey, Thaler, Bensahel, Cragin, Green, Kaye, Oweidat and Li, *Dangerous but Not Omnipotent*, 134.

53 Ibid., 115.

54 Ibid., 117–18.

55 Hokayem and Legrenzi, 'The Arab Gulf States in the Shadow of the Iranian Nuclear Challenge', 2.

56 Dalia Dassa Kaye and Frederic M. Wehrey, 'A Nuclear Iran: The Reactions of Neighbours', *Survival*, vol. 49, no. 2 (2007): 117.

57 Dina Esfandiary, 'Two Tremors in Two Weeks, and Many Questions for Iran', *The National*, 22 April 2013, https://www.thenational.ae/two-trem ors-in-two-weeks-and-many-questions-for-iran-1.324812; Tariq Khaitous, 'Why Arab Leaders Worry about Iran's Nuclear Program', *Bulletin of Atomic Scientists*, 23 May 2008, https://thebulletin.org/2008/05/why-arab-lead ers-worry-about-irans-nuclear-program/.

58 Author interview with two officials from the Emirates Nuclear Energy Corporation (ENEC), Abu Dhabi, November 2017.

59 Esfandiary, 'Two Tremors in Two Weeks, and Many Questions for Iran'.

60 Gause III, *The International Relations of the Persian Gulf*, 147.

61 Hokayem and Legrenzi, 'The Arab Gulf States in the Shadow of the Iranian Nuclear Challenge', 3–6.

62 Ibid., 4.

63 Videotaped Remarks by the President in Celebration of Nowruz, The White House, 20 March 2009, https://obamawhitehouse.archives.gov/ the-press-office/videotaped-remarks-president-celebration-nowruz.

64 'Iran Confirms Exchange of Letters with Obama', *Reuters*, 17 September 2013, https://www.reuters.com/article/us-iran-usa/iran-confirms-excha nge-of-letters-with-obama-idUSBRE98G0MT20130917.

65 Author interview with Emirati lawmakers, officials, experts and academics, Dubai, Abu Dhabi (2014–17); author interview with Sami Al Faraj, president, Kuwait Centre for Strategic Studies, Kuwait, 24 May 2016; author interview with Abdullah Baabood, former professor, Qatar University, Doha, 15 May 2016; author interview with Bahraini official, Manama, 13 March 2022.

66 Author interviews with GCC lawmakers, officials, experts and academics, Dubai, Abu Dhabi, Muscat, Doha and Kuwait City (2014–17).

67 Legrenzi, *The GCC and the International Relations of the Gulf*, 89; Christopher M. Davidson, *After the Sheikhs: The Coming Collapse of the*

Gulf Monarchies (London: Hurst, 2012), 35; Christopher M. Davidson, *Dubai: The Vulnerability of Success* (London: Hurst, 2008), 227.

68 Marschall, *Iran's Persian Gulf Policy*, 135.

69 Hokayem and Legrenzi, 'The Arab Gulf States in the Shadow of the Iranian Nuclear Challenge', 21.

70 Tariq Khaitous, 'Arab Reactions to a Nuclear-Armed Iran', *Policy Focus #94*, The Washington Institute for Near East Policy, June 2009, 21.

71 Hokayem and Legrenzi, 'The Arab Gulf States in the Shadow of the Iranian Nuclear Challenge', 14.

72 Author interviews with GCC lawmakers, officials, experts and academics, Dubai, Abu Dhabi, Muscat, Doha and Kuwait City (2014–17).

73 Ibid; Youssef Al Otaiba, 'One Year after the Iran Nuclear Deal', *Wall Street Journal*, 3 April 2016, https://www.wsj.com/articles/one-year-after-the-iran-nuclear-deal-1459721502; Suleiman Al-Khalidi, 'Saudi FM Says Riyadh Determined to Confront Iranian Expansion in Region', *Reuters*, 9 July 2015, https://www.reuters.com/article/uk-saudi-iran/saudi-fm-says-riyadh-determined-to-confront-iranian-expansion-in-region-idUKKCN0PJ2GJ20150709; Gregory F. Gause III, 'Why the Iranian Deal Scares Saudi Arabia', *New Yorker*, 26 November 2013, https://www.newyorker.com/news/news-desk/why-the-iran-deal-scares-saudi-arabia; McDowall, 'Region Will Lose Sleep over Iran Deal'.

74 Author interview with Youssef Al Otaiba, UAE ambassador to the United States, Washington, DC, 2 March 2016.

75 Statement by UAE official, author round table with regional experts, officials and academics, Dubai, 19 April 2016.

76 Author interview with government officials, Abu Dhabi, 14 April 2016.

77 Author round table with think tank experts, Doha, 16 May 2016.

78 Statement by a US negotiator of the Iran deal, Sir Bani Yas Conference, Abu Dhabi, 18–19 November 2016.

79 Author interviews with GCC lawmakers, officials, experts and academics, Dubai, Abu Dhabi, Muscat, Doha and Kuwait City (2014–17).

80 A senior Gulf official quoted in Julian Borger, 'Gulf States to Push for a US Plan for Containing Iran', *The Guardian Global Security Blog*, 1 May 2015, https://www.theguardian.com/world/julian-borger-global-security-blog/2015/may/01/gulf-states-to-push-for-a-us-plan-for-containing-iran.

81 Ibid.

82 'US, Gulf Allies Seek Agreement on New Security Measures: Kerry', *Reuters*, 8 May 2015, https://www.reuters.com/article/us-usa-gulf-kerry/u-s-gulf-allies-seek-agreement-on-new-security-measures-kerry-idUSKBN0NT1CY20150508.

83 Dan Roberts, 'Obama Summit with Arab Allies Begins despite Saudi King's Absence', *The Guardian*, 14 May 2015, https://www.theguardian.com/us-news/2015/may/14/barack-obama-arab-gulf-leaders-camp-david-summit.

84 Author interview with former Emirati national security advisor, New York, 31 October 2019.

85 The UAE's Sheikh Khalifa bin Zayed al Nahyan sent a congratulatory note to President Hassan Rouhani for reaching the nuclear deal on 14 July 2015, see 'UAE Congratulations Iran on Atomic Deal, First Official Gulf Comment', *Reuters*, 14 July 2015, https://www.reuters.com/article/us-iran-nuclear-emirates/uae-congratulates-iran-on-atomic-deal-first-official-gulf-comment-idUSKCN0PO1QV20150714.

86 Author round table with experts and analysts, B'huth, Dubai, 29 February 2017.

87 Author interview with Emirati official, Washington, DC, 2 March 2016.

88 Hussein Ibish, 'For Gulf Countries, Iran's Regional Behavior Overshadows Nuclear Deal', The Arab Gulf States Institute in Washington, 17 July 2015, https://agsiw.org/for-gulf-countries-irans-regional-behavior-overshadows-nuclear-deal/; 'In Gulf Press, Fear and Criticism of Iran Nuclear Agreement: Obama Is Leaving the Middle East a Legacy of Disaster', The Middle East Media Research Institute, Special Dispatch No. 6107, 15 July 2015, https://www.memri.org/reports/gulf-press-fear-and-criticism-iran-nuclear-agreement-obama-leaving-middle-east-legacy.

89 'UAE Congratulates Iran on Atomic Deal, First Official Gulf Comment'; 'UAE Leaders Congratulate Rouhani on Nuclear Deal', *Khaleej Times*, 14 July 2015, https://www.khaleejtimes.com/nation/government/uae-leaders-congratulate-rohani-on-nuclear-agreement.

90 Author interview with Emirati official, New York, 11 March 2016.

91 Author interview with Emirati officials, Dubai and Abu Dhabi (2014–17); author interview with Youssef Al Otaiba, UAE ambassador to the United States, Washington, DC, 2 March 2016; author interview with a former Emirati national security advisor, New York, 31 October 2019.

92 'Iran Nuclear Deal: An Overview of Global Reactions', *Euronews*, 15 July 2015, https://www.euronews.com/2015/07/15/iran-nuclear-deal-reactions-from-around-the-world-overview.

93 Author round table with Emirati officials, Abu Dhabi, 28 February 2017.

94 Author interview with Emirati official, Washington, DC, 2 March 2016.

95 Author round table with Emirati foreign ministry officials, Abu Dhabi, 14 April 2016.

96 Ibid.

97 Statement by head of an Emirati think tank, author round table with regional experts, officials and academics, Dubai, 19 April 2016.

98 Author round table with experts and analysts, Al Jazeera Research Center, Doha, 16 May 2016.

99 See, for example, David Rothkopf, 'Iran's $300 Billion Shakedown', *Foreign Policy*, 16 April 2015, https://foreignpolicy.com/2015/04/16/irans-300-billion-shakedown-sanctions-nuclear-deal/.

100 Author interviews with GCC lawmakers, officials, experts and academics, Dubai, Abu Dhabi, Muscat, Doha and Kuwait City (2014–17). JCPOA

supporters countered this argument, see, for example, Richard Nephew, 'Sanctions Relief Won't Be a $100 Billion Windfall for Iran's Terrorist Friends', *Foreign Policy*, 2 July 2015, https://foreignpolicy.com/2015/07/02/iran-rouhani-khamenei-syria-assad-nuclear-sanctions-hezbollah/.

101 Statement by head of an Emirati think tank, author round table with regional experts, officials and academics, Dubai, 19 April 2016.

102 Author interviews with GCC lawmakers, officials, experts and academics, Dubai, Abu Dhabi, Muscat, Doha and Kuwait City (2014–17).

103 Author interview with two senior Emirati foreign ministry officials, Abu Dhabi, 14 April 2016.

104 Ibid; author interview with two officials from the Emirates Nuclear Energy Corporation (ENEC), Abu Dhabi, November 2017.

105 Author interviews with GCC lawmakers, officials, experts and academics, Dubai, Abu Dhabi, Muscat, Doha and Kuwait City (2014–17).

106 Richard Nephew, 'Sanctions Relief Won't Be a $100 Billion Windfall for Iran's Terrorist Friends', *Foreign Policy*, 2 July 2015, https://foreignpolicy.com/2015/07/02/iran-rouhani-khamenei-syria-assad-nuclear-sanctions-hezbollah/.

107 Jonathan Saul, Parisa Hafezi, Michael Georgy, 'Exclusive: Iran Steps Up Support for Houthis in Yemen's War – Sources', *Reuters*, 21 March 2017, https://www.reuters.com/article/us-yemen-iran-houthis/exclusive-iran-steps-up-support-for-houthis-in-yemens-war-sources-idUSKBN16S22R.

108 Hossein Bastani, 'Iran Quietly Deepens Involvement in Syria's War', *BBC News*, 20 October 2015, https://www.bbc.com/news/world-middle-east-34572756; Dugald McConnell and Brian Todd, 'Iran Steps Up Its Forces in Syria', *CNN*, 28 October 2015, https://www.cnn.com/2015/10/27/middleeast/iran-syria-troop-buildup/index.html. Iranian presence in Syria had been limited to military advisory roles, political support and equipment, see Dina Esfandiary and Ariane Tabatabai, 'Iran's ISIS Policy', *International Affairs*, vol. 91, no. 1 (2015): 8, 13.

109 Esfandiary and Tabatabai, 'Iran's ISIS Policy', 2–5; Garrett Nada, 'Part 1: Iran's Role in Iraq', The Wilson Center, 26 April 2018, https://www.wilsoncenter.org/article/part-1-irans-role-iraq.

110 'Iran Has over 1,000 Troops in Iraq, Less Than 2,000 in Syria: US General', *Reuters*, 27 October 2015, https://www.reuters.com/article/us-mideast-crisis-dunford-iranians/iran-has-over-1000-troops-in-iraq-less-than-2000-in-syria-u-s-general-idUSKCN0SL23E20151027.

111 Jonathan Saul, Parisa Hafezi, Michael Georgy, 'Exclusive: Iran Steps Up Support for Houthis in Yemen's War – Sources', *Reuters*, 21 March 2017, https://www.reuters.com/article/us-yemen-iran-houthis/exclusive-iran-steps-up-support-for-houthis-in-yemens-war-sources-idUSKBN16S22R.

112 Author interview with two senior Emirati foreign ministry officials, Abu Dhabi, 14 April 2016.

113 Ibid.

114 Statement by Emirati military official, author round table with regional experts, officials and academics, Dubai, 19 April 2016.

115 Ben Hubbard, 'Arab World Split over Iran Nuclear Deal', *New York Times*, 14 July 2015, https://www.nytimes.com/2015/07/15/world/middleeast/ iran-nuclear-deal-provokes-sharp-reactions-across-the-arab-world.html.

116 According to a Zogby Poll conducted in 2014, significant majorities in both Saudi Arabia (88 per cent) and the UAE (89 per cent) view the United States as having a negative impact on the region, see 'Today's Middle East: Pressures and Challenges', Zogby Research Services LLC, Report prepared for the Sir Bani Yas Forum, November 2014, Section VII, https:// assets.nationbuilder.com/aai/pages/7880/attachments/original/1431629 755/Sir%252520Bani%252520Yas%2525202014%25252011-01.pdf?143 1629755, 29; the 2016 poll showed majorities in those countries were still unfavourable to the United States, but by smaller margins, see 'Middle East 2016: Current Conditions and the Road Ahead', Zogby Research Services, prepared for the Sir Bani Yas Forum, November 2016, Section I, https:// d3n8a8pro7vhmx.cloudfront.net/aai/pages/12021/attachments/origi nal/1481751962/SBY2016_FINAL.pdf?1481751962, 5, 7.

117 Author interview with Emirati officials, Dubai and Abu Dhabi (2014–17); author interview with Youssef Al Otaiba, UAE ambassador to the United States, Washington, DC, 2 March 2016.

118 Jeffrey Goldberg, 'The Obama Doctrine', *The Atlantic*, April 2016, https:// www.theatlantic.com/magazine/archive/2016/04/the-obama-doctr ine/471525/.

119 Author round table with Emirati foreign ministry officials, Abu Dhabi, 14 April 2016.

120 Ibid.

121 Press call by Ben Rhodes, deputy national security advisor for strategic communications, and Jeff Prescott, senior direction for the Middle East, NSC, on the upcoming visit of King Salman of Saudi Arabia, The White House, Office of the Press Secretary, 2 September 2015, https://obamawhi tehouse.archives.gov/the-press-office/2015/09/03/press-call-ben-rhodes- deputy-national-security-advisor-strategic.

122 Author round table with Emirati foreign ministry officials, Abu Dhabi, 14 April 2016.

123 Author interview with Emirati official, Washington, DC, 2 March 2016.

124 Author interview with Emirati think tank expert, Dubai, 13 November 2016.

125 Author interview with two senior Emirati foreign ministry officials, Abu Dhabi, 14 April 2016.

126 Author round table with Emirati foreign ministry officials, Abu Dhabi, 14 April 2016.

127 Author interview with Gary Sick, senior research scholar, Middle East Institute, and adjunct professor, School of International and Public Affairs, Columbia University, New York City, 10 March 2016.

128 Statement by Gulf-based analyst, author round table with regional experts, officials and academics, Dubai, 19 April 2016.

129 Author interviews with GCC lawmakers, officials, experts and academics, Dubai, Abu Dhabi, Muscat, Doha and Kuwait City (2014–17).

130 Ibid.

131 Legrenzi, *The GCC and the International Relations of the Gulf*, 77.

132 Ibid., 78.

133 Kaye and Wehrey, 'A Nuclear Iran, 112.

134 Author interviews with Emirati experts and academics, Dubai, Abu Dhabi (2014–17); author interview with UK Foreign and Commonwealth official, London, 13 March 2019.

135 Author interview with think tank director, Dubai, 16 November 2016.

136 Ibid.

137 Ibid.

138 Author interview with Emirati think tanker, Dubai, 13 November 2016.

139 Neil Partrick, 'The UAE's War Aims in Yemen', *Sada Blog – Carnegie Endowment for International Peace*, 24 October 2017, http://carnegieen dowment.org/sada/73524; Michael Knights and Alexandre Mello, 'The Saudi-UAE War Efforts in Yemen (Part 1): Operation Golden Arrow in Aden', The Washington Institute PolicyWatch 2462, 10 August 2015, https://www.washingtoninstitute.org/policy-analysis/view/the-saudi-uae-war-eff ort-in-yemen-part-1-operation-golden-arrow-in-aden.

140 See Chapter 3.

141 Author interview with UK Foreign and Commonwealth official, London, 13 March 2019; author interview with former Emirati national security advisor, New York, 31 October 2019.

142 Ibid.

143 Author interview with former and current Emirati officials, Dubai and Abu Dhabi (2014–17); author interview with former Emirati national security advisor, New York, 31 October 2019; author interview with UK foreign and Commonwealth official, London, 13 March 2019; author interview with former Emirati national security advisor, New York, 31 October 2019.

Chapter 4

1 Kenneth Katzman, 'The United Arab Emirates (UAE): Issues for US Policy', Congressional Research Service Reports (2014), 12–13.

2 See, for example, the DP World fiasco in 2006, 'Bush Says He Will Veto Any Bill to Stop UAE Port Deal', *Fox News*, 22 February 2006, http://www.foxnews.com/story/2006/02/22/bush-says-will-veto-any-bill-t o-stop-uae-port-deal.html; Stephen E. Flynn, 'The DP World Controversy and the Ongoing Vulnerability of U.S. Seaports', Testimony – Prepared

Remarks, 2 March 2006, https://www.cfr.org/report/dp-world-controve rsy-and-ongoing-vulnerability-us-seaports-prepared-remarks; David E. Sanger, 'Under Pressure, Dubai Company Drops Port Deal', *New York Times*, 10 March 2006, https://www.nytimes.com/2006/03/10/politics/ under-pressure-dubai-company-drops-port-deal.html.

3   Christopher M. Davidson, *After the Sheikhs: The Coming Collapse of the Gulf Monarchies* (London: Hurst, 2012), 81, 83.

4   Emma Soubrier, 'Evolving Foreign and Security Policies: A Comparative Study of Qatar and the UAE', in Khalid S Almezaini and Jean-Marc Rickli (eds), *The Small Gulf States: Foreign and Security Policies Before and After the Arab Spring* (London: Routledge, 2017), 134.

5   Sami G. Hajjar, 'US Military Presence in the Gulf: Challenges and Prospects', US Army War College Strategic Studies Institute, March 2002, 41, https://apps.dtic.mil/sti/pdfs/ADA400834.pdf.

6   Kenneth Katzman, 'The United Arab Emirates (UAE): Issues for US Policy', Congressional Research Service Reports (2017), 19.

7   See, for example, 'UAE Gets Cruise Missiles', *BBC News*, 26 November 1998, http://news.bbc.co.uk/1/hi/world/middle_east/222553.stm; Julian Moxon, 'UAE Orders Mirage 2000-9s and Goes Ahead with Upgrade Work', *Flight Global*, 24 December 1997, https://www.flightglobal.com/ news/articles/uae-orders-mirage-2000-9s-and-goes-ahead-with-upgr ade-30950/.

8   'United Arab Emirates Signs Agreement for the Purchase of 80 Lockheed Martin F-16s', *Defense-aerospace.com*, 5 March 2000, http://www.defe nse-aerospace.com/articles-view/release/3/1775/uae-sign-contract-for-80-lockheed-f_16s-(mar.-6).html.

9   Anthony H. Cordesman and Khalid R. Al Rodhan, *Gulf Military Forces in an Era of Asymmetric Wars* (Westport, CT: Praeger Security International, 2007), 299.

10 Bilal Saab, 'The Gulf Rising: Defense Industrialization in Saudi Arabia and the UAE', The Atlantic Council – Brent Snowcroft Center on International Security Report, May 2014, 4.

11 Fleurant, Tian, D. Wezeman, T. Wezeman, 'Trends in International Arms Transfers, 2016', 11.

12 Author interview with Riad Kahwaji, CEO, INEGMA, Dubai, 13 November 2016.

13 Author interview with Andreas Krieg, lecturer, School of Security Studies, King's College London, London, 8 October 2019; Andreas Krieg, 'The Weaponization of Narratives Amid the Gulf Crisis', in Andreas Krieg (eds), *Divided Gulf: The Anatomy of a Crisis* (London: Palgrave Macmillan, 2019), 96–7; Karen Young, *The Political Economy of Energy, Finance and Security in the United Arab Emirates* (London: Palgrave, 2014), 102–30.

14 Author interview with Andreas Krieg, lecturer, School of Security Studies, King's College London, London, 8 October 2019.

15 Peter D. Wezeman, Aude Fleurant, Alexndra Kuimova, Nan Tian and Siemon T. Wezeman, 'Trends in International Arms Transfers, 2017', *SIPRI Fact Sheet*, March 2018, https://www.sipri.org/sites/default/files/2018-03/fssipri_at2017_0.pdf, 2.

16 Author interview with Riad Kahwaji, CEO, INEGMA, Dubai, 13 November 2016.

17 Scott R. Gourley, 'U.A.E. Becomes First International Customer for THAAD', *Defense Media Network*, 4 January 2012, https://www.defensemedianetwork.com/stories/u-a-e-becomes-first-international-customer-for-thaad/.

18 'Rockets and Reach: UAE Doubles Down on HIMARS, ATACMS', *Defense Industry Daily*, 2 October 2014, https://www.defenseindustrydaily.com/uae-orders-752m-worth-of-himars-launchers-rockets-02659/.

19 'UAE Agrees $1.6 Billion Deal with Lockheed Martin to Upgrade F-16 Fighters', *Reuters*, 12 November 2017, https://www.reuters.com/article/us-emirates-lockheed-airshow/uae-agrees-1-6-billion-deal-with-lockheed-martin-to-upgrade-f-16-fighters-idUSKBN1DC0JH.

20 Jen Judson, 'Thanks to Missile Sales to UAE, US Army Can Buy 100 More Advanced Patriot Missiles', *Defense News*, 6 August 2018, https://www.defensenews.com/land/2018/07/27/thanks-to-missile-sales-to-uae-us-army-can-buy-100-more-advanced-patriot-missiles/.

21 Tony Osborne, 'UAE Taking Delivery of Archangel COIN Aircraft', *Aviation Week Network*, 8 November 2015, https://aviationweek.com/dubai-air-show-2015/uae-taking-delivery-archangel-coin-aircraft.

22 'United Arab Emirates – Foreign Military Sales Order (FMSO) II Case', Press Release, US Defense Security Cooperation Agency, 3 February 2022, https://www.dsca.mil/press-media/major-arms-sales/united-arab-emirates-foreign-military-sales-order-fmso-ii-case#:~:text=WASHINGTON%2C%20February%203%2C%202022%20%2D,estimated%20cost%20of%20%2465%20million.

23 Author interview with Emirati lawmakers and officials, experts and academics, Dubai, Abu Dhabi (2014–17).

24 Kenneth Katzman, 'The United Arab Emirates (U.A.E): Issues for U.S. Policy', Congressional Research Service reports (2014), 12; 'U.S and UAE Hold 4th Joint Military Dialogue', News Release US Department of Defense, 10 April 2019, https://dod.defense.gov/News/News-Releases/News-Release-View/Article/1811503/us-and-uae-hold-4th-joint-military-dialogue/.

25 Katzman, 'The United Arab Emirates (U.A.E)', 12–13.

26 Kenneth Katzman, 'The United Arab Emirates (U.A.E): Issues for U.S. Policy', Congressional Research Service reports (2016), 18.

27 Author interview with Emirati experts, officials, academics, Abu Dhabi and Dubai (2014–17).

28 Author interview with Emirati Ministry of Foreign Affairs official, Abu Dhabi, 14 April 2016.

29 Interviews in the region highlighted the link between the effects of the catalysts identified in this dissertation (including perceived growth of the Iranian threat as well as US perceived disengagement from the region) and a new urgency for weapons procurements. Author interview with GCC lawmakers and officials, experts and academics, Dubai, Abu Dhabi, Muscat, Doha and Kuwait City (2014–17); Kenneth Katzman, 'The United Arab Emirates (U.A.E): Issues for U.S. Policy', Congressional Research Service reports (2012), 15.

30 Emmanuel Jarry, 'France, UAE Sign Military and Nuclear Agreements', *Reuters*, 15 January 2008, https://www.reuters.com/article/us-france-sark ozy-gulf/france-uae-sign-military-and-nuclear-agreements-idUSL15174 72620080115.

31 'France and Security in the Asia-Pacific', French Ministry of Defence, April 2013, 2, 10.

32 Author interview with Andreas Krieg, lecturer, School of Security Studies, King's College London, London, 8 October 2019.

33 'France Sees More Joint Defence Ventures with UAE', *Emirates 247*, 17 February 2013, https://www.emirates247.com/business/fra nce-sees-more-joint-defence-ventures-with-uae-2013-02-17-1.495279.

34 Theodore Karasik, 'UAE People and Politics: UAE and France's Robust Cooperation in Fighting Extremists', *The National*, 7 May 2015.

35 'Mohammed Lauds Military Exercise', *Khaleej Times*, 3 May 2012, https://www.khaleejtimes.com/article/mohammed-lauds-military-exercise.

36 'UAE and French Armed Forces Conclude "Gulf 2016" Joint Military Exercise', *The National*, 24 November 2016, https://www.thenational.ae/uae/uae-and-french-armed-forces-conclude-gulf-2016-joint-military-exerc ise-1.192384.

37 Theodore Karasik, 'UAE People and Politics: UAE and France's Robust Cooperation in Fighting Extremists', *The National*, 7 May 2015.

38 Author interview with Emirati experts, officials, academics, Abu Dhabi and Dubai (2014–17).

39 'Joint Defence Partnership between UK and the UAE Announced', *BBC News*, 6 November 2012, https://www.bbc.co.uk/news/uk-politics-20216028.

40 Simeon Kerr, 'UAE Stops Using Former British Officers as Military Trainers', *Financial Times*, 22 May 2014, https://www.ft.com/content/53cc2 584-e1ab-11e3-9999-00144feabdc0.

41 Craig Hoyle, 'Picture: Saab Unveils First GlobalEye for UAE', *Flight Global*, 23 February 2018, https://www.flightglobal.com/news/articles/pict ure-saab-unveils-first-globaleye-for-uae-446155/.

42 'First UAE Spyplane Breaks Its Cover', *Arabian Aerospace*, 27 December 2017, https://www.arabianaerospace.aero/first-uae-spyplane-bre aks-its-cover.html.

43 'Chinese Military Drone Sales Hover over Middle East', *Associated Press*, 26 February 2018, https://www.scmp.com/news/china/diplomacy-defe

nce/article/2134680/chinese-military-drone-display-united-arab-emira tes; Aniseh Bassiri Tabrizi and Justin Bronk, 'Armed Drones in the Middle East: Proliferation and Norms in the Region', RUSI Occasional Paper, December 2018, 27.

44 Natasha Turak, 'Pentagon Is Scrambling as China "Sells the Hell Out of" Armed Drones to US Allies', *CNBC*, 21 February 2019, https://www. cnbc.com/2019/02/21/pentagon-is-scrambling-as-china-sells-the-hell-ou t-of-armed-drones-to-americas-allies.html.

45 Ibid.

46 Tabrizi and Bronk, 'Armed Drones in the Middle East', 22, 30.

47 Peter Apps, 'Chinese, Local Drones Reflecting Changing Middle East', *Reuters*, 7 March 2019, https://in.reuters.com/article/apps-drones/column- chinese-local-drones-reflect-changing-middle-east-idINKCN1QO0FT.

48 Tabrizi and Bronk, 'Armed Drones in the Middle East', 30; Agnes Al Helou and Chirine Mouchantaf, 'Source: UAE Wants to Buy 24 F-35s', *DefenseNews*, 12 November 2017, https://www.defensenews.com/digi tal-show-dailies/dubai-air-show/2017/11/12/uae-undertakes-air-force- restructuring-plan/.

49 Quoted in Tabrizi and Bronk, 'Armed Drones in the Middle East', 30.

50 David Axe, 'One Nation Is Selling Off Its Chinese Combat Drones', *National Interest*, 5 June 2019, https://nationalinterest.org/blog/buzz/one- nation-selling-its-chinese-combat-drones-61092.

51 Camille Lons, Jonathan Fulton, Degang Sun and Naser Al-Tamimi, 'China's Great Game in the Middle East', ECFR Policy Brief, October 2019, https:// www.ecfr.eu/page/-/china_great_game_middle_east.pdf; Dina Esfandiary and Ariane Tabatabai, *Triple Axis: Iran's Relations with Russia and China* (London: Bloomsbury, 2018). There is a debate emerging about China's role in the Middle East and whether it should go beyond its current transactional approach to the region, see Wang Huiyao, 'From the Syrian civil war to Yemen to energy, China has a larger role to play in the Middle East', *South China Morning Post*, 13 November 2019, https://www.scmp. com/comment/opinion/article/3037353/syrian-civil-war-yemen-ene rgy-china-has-larger-role-play-middle.

52 Author interview with Andreas Krieg, lecturer, School of Security Studies, King's College London, London, 8 October 2019.

53 Oksana Antonenko, 'Russia's Military Involvement with the Middle East', in Thomas Keaney, Barry Rubin (eds), *Armed Forces in the Middle East: Politics and Strategy* (London: Frank Cass, 2002).

54 Clayton Thomas, 'Arms Sales in the Middle East: Trends and Analytical Perspectives for U.S. Policy', Congressional Research Service Reports, 11 October 2017, https://fas.org/sgp/crs/mideast/R44984.pdf, 7.

55 'UAE buys Russia's Kornet, Pantsir Missile Systems – General', *TASS*, 17 February 2019, http://tass.com/world/1045135.

56 Kirikk Semenov, 'Russia seeks closer military-technical cooperation with the UAE', *Al Monitor*, November 2017, https://www.al-monitor.com/pulse/fa/originals/2017/11/russia-eyes-closer-military-cooperation-uae.html.

57 This policy was also the result of internal efforts towards economic diversification and Emiratization.

58 Sandra I. Erwin, 'Defense Industry Eyes Growth in the Middle East', *National Defense*, 2 May 2014, http://www.nationaldefensemagazine.org/articles/2014/5/2/defense-industry-eyes-growth-in-the-middle-east.

59 Bilal Y. Saab, 'Arms and Influence in the Gulf – Riyadh and Abu Dhabi Get to Work', *Foreign Affairs*, 5 May 2014, https://www.foreignaffairs.com/artic les/middle-east/2014-05-05/arms-and-influence-gulf.

60 Florence Gaub and Zoe Stanley-Lockman, 'Defence Industries in Arab States: Players and Strategies', *European Union Institute for Security Studies Chaillot Paper*, no. 141 (March 2017), 47.

61 Sandra I. Erwin, 'Defense Industry Eyes Growth in the Middle East', *National Defense*, 2 May 2014, http://www.nationaldefensemagazine.org/articles/2014/5/2/defense-industry-eyes-growth-in-the-middle-east.

62 Gaub and Stanley-Lockman, 'Defence Industries in Arab States', 47–52.

63 DB Des Roches, 'IDEX 2019 Highlights Gulf States' Move to Develop Domestic Defense Industries', The Arab Gulf States Institute in Washington, 11 March 2019, https://agsiw.org/idex-2019-highlights-gulf-states-move-to-develop-domestic-defense-industries/.

64 'UAE Merger Creates Defense Services, Manufacturing Company', *Reuters*, 2 December 2014, https://www.reuters.com/article/us-emirates-defe nce-m-a/uae-merger-creates-defense-services-manufacturing-company-idUSKCN0JG1IE20141202.

65 Florence Gaub and Zoe Stanley-Lockman, 'Defence Industries in Arab States: Players and Strategies', *European Union Institute for Security Studies Chaillot Paper*, no. 141 (March 2017), 53.

66 Agnes Helou, 'UAE Launches "Edge" Conglomerate to Address "Antiquated Military Industry"', *DefenseNews*, 6 November 2019, https://www.defensenews.com/digital-show-dailies/dubai-air-show/2019/11/06/uae-launches-edge-conglomerate-to-address-its-antiquated-military-industry/.

67 'Russia and UAE to Work on Fifth Generation Fighter Jet', *TASS*, 20 February 2017, http://tass.com/defense/931828.

68 Gaub and Stanley-Lockman, 'Defence Industries in Arab States', 53.

69 See table in Florence Gaub and Zoe Stanley-Lockman, 'Defence Industries in Arab States: Players and Strategies', *European Union Institute for Security Studies Chaillot Paper*, no. 141 (March 2017), 54, 61.

70 Author interview with academics and experts, Washington, DC and New York, February 2016.

71 'Bush says he will veto any bill to stop UAE port deal', *Fox News*, 22 February 2006, http://www.foxnews.com/story/2006/02/22/bush-say s-will-veto-any-bill-to-stop-uae-port-deal.html; Stephen E. Flynn, 'The

DP World Controversy and the Ongoing Vulnerability of U.S. Seaports', Testimony – Prepared Remarks, 2 March 2006, https://www.cfr.org/report/dp-world-controversy-and-ongoing-vulnerability-us-seaports-prepared-remarks.

72 Edward Simpkins and Sylvia Pfeiger, 'Dubai "Will Not Drop" £3.9 Billion bid for P&O', *The Telegraph*, 26 February 2006, https://www.telegraph.co.uk/finance/2933078/Dubai-will-not-drop-3.9bn-bid-for-PandO.html.

73 David E. Sanger, 'Under Pressure, Dubai Company Drops Port Deal', *New York Times*, 10 March 2006, https://www.nytimes.com/2006/03/10/politics/under-pressure-dubai-company-drops-port-deal.html.

74 Larry Luxner, 'Oil-Rich UAE, Reaching for the Stars, Gets Pulled Back Down to Earth', *Washington Diplomat*, 18 November 2010, http://www.washdiplomat.com/index.php?option=com_cont ent&view=article&id=6048:oil-rich-uae-reaching-for-stars-gets-pul led-back-down-to-earth-&catid=204:march-2010&Itemid=240.

75 Author interview with Youssef Al Otaiba, UAE ambassador to the United States, Washington, DC, 2 March 2016.

76 Lindsay Young, 'What Countries Spent the Most to Influence in the USA in 2013', *Sunlight Foundation*, 8 May 2014, https://sunlightfou ndation.com/2014/05/08/what-countries-spent-the-most-to-influe nce-the-usa-in-2013/; Colby Itkowitz, 'Which Foreign Countries Spent the Most to Influence U.S. Politics?', *Washington Post*, 14 May 2014, https://www.washingtonpost.com/blogs/in-the-loop/wp/2014/05/14/which-foreign-countries-spent-the-most-to-influence-u-s-politics/?noredir ect=on&utm_term=.d164a2624fd9.

77 Jennifer LaFleur, 'Adding It Up: The Top Players in Foreign Agent Lobbying', *ProRepublica*, 18 August 2009, https://www.propublica.org/arti cle/adding-it-up-the-top-players-in-foreign-agent-lobbying-718.

78 Author interview with officials in Europe's External Action Service, Brussels, 24 June 2019; David Rose, 'Cameron and the Arab Sheiks' Web of Influence That Infiltrated Britain: The Shadowy Nexus of PM's Cronies That Secretively Lobbied for Middle East Paymasters', *The Mail on Sunday*, 18 October 2015, http://www.dailymail.co.uk/news/article-3277345/Came ron-Arab-Sheiks-web-influence-infiltrated-Britain-shadowy-nexus-PM-s-cronies-secretively-lobbied-Middle-East-paymasters.html.

79 Zaid Jilani, 'The UAE Secretly Picked Up the Tab for the Egyptian Dictatorship's D.C. Lobbying', *The Intercept*, 4 October 2017, https://thein tercept.com/2017/10/04/egypt-lobbying-uae-otaiba-trump-sisi/.

80 Ryan Grim, 'Diplomatic Underground – The Sordid Double Life of Washington's Most Powerful Ambassador', *The Intercept*, 30 August 2017, https://theintercept.com/2017/08/30/uae-ambassador-yousef-al-otaiba-double-life-prostitutes-sex-work/.

81 David Hearst, 'Revealed: How Trump Confidant Was Ready to Share Inside Information with UAE', *Middle East Eye*, 28 June 2018, https://www.middle easteye.net/news/revealed-how-trump-confidant-was-ready-share-inside-information-uae.

82 Bradley Hope and Tom Wright, 'Stolen Emails Show Ties between UAE Envoy and 1MDB Fund's Central Figure', *Wall Street Journal*, 1 August 2017, https://www.wsj.com/articles/stolen-emails-show-ties-betw een-u-a-e-envoy-and-1mdb-funds-central-figure-1501579801.

83 Bethany Allen-Ebrahimian, 'New UAE Documentary Claims Qatar Complicit in 9/11 Attacks', *Foreign Policy – The Cable*, 24 July 2017, http:// foreignpolicy.com/2017/07/24/new-uae-documentary-claims-qatar-compli cit-in-911-attacks-gulf-crisis-saudi-arabia-doha/.

84 Suzanne Kianpour, 'Emails Show UAE-Linked Effort against Tillerson', *BBC News*, 5 March 2018, http://www.bbc.co.uk/news/world-us-canada-43281519.

85 Kenneth P. Vogel and David D. Kirkpatrick, 'Fund-Raiser Held Out Access to Trump as a Prize for Prospective Clients', *New York Times*, 25 March 2018, https://www.nytimes.com/2018/03/25/us/politics/elliott-bro idy-trump-access-circinus-lobbying.html.

86 Author interview with Emirati official, Washington, DC, 2 March 2016.

87 Author interview with former Emirati official, New York, 30 October 2019.

88 Author interview with Emirati official, Washington, DC, 2 March 2016.

89 Author interview with Emirati experts, officials, academics, Abu Dhabi and Dubai (2014–17).

90 Youssef Al Otaiba, 'A Vision for a Moderate, Modern Muslim World', *Foreign Policy*, 2 December 2015, http://foreignpolicy.com/2015/12/02/a-vision-for-a-moderate-modern-muslim-world-uae-abu-dhabi-isis/.

91 Youssef Al Otaiba, 'ISIL Can't Be Beat on the Battlefield Alone', *Politico*, 16 February 2015, https://www.politico.com/magazine/story/2015/02/ isil-cant-be-beat-on-the-battlefield-alone-115233.

92 'On Woman's Day, the UAE Ambassador to the US Writes an Open Letter to His Daughter', *Harpers Bazaar Arabia*, 8 March 2017, https://www.harp ersbazaararabia.com/for-womens-day-the-uae-ambassador-to-the-us-wri tes-an-open-letter-to-his-daughter.

93 Karen Zraick, 'Arab Woman Led Airstrikes over Syria', *New York Times*, 25 September 2014, https://www.nytimes.com/2014/09/26/world/middlee ast/emirates-first-female-fighter-pilot-isis-airstrikes.html; 'Woman Who Reached for the Skies', *The National*, 10 June 2014, https://www.thenational. ae/uae/government/woman-who-reached-for-the-skies-1.586232.

94 See, for example, HH Sheikh Mohammed bin Rashid, ruler of Dubai's tweets on 7 March 2017.

95 For example, in 2010, Sheikh Mohammed bin Rashid Al Maktoum, vice president and prime minister of the UAE and the ruler of Dubai, launched Vision 2021, which 'enshrined as its objective the transformation of the UAE into a knowledge-based economy in which growth is driven by research, development, and innovation and the creation of internationally competitive high value-added economic sectors'. See Ulrichsen, *The United Arab Emirates*, 125.

96 Davidson, *After the Sheikhs*, 8, 44.

97 Ibid., 43.

98 Toby Matthiesen, 'Renting the Casbah', in Kristian Coates Ulrichsen (ed.), *The Changing Security Dynamics of the Persian Gulf* (London: Hurst, 2017)

99 Stanley Carvalho, 'East meets West as Louvre Abu Dhabi opens in the Gulf', *Reuters*, 7 November 2017, https://www.reuters.com/article/us-emira tes-louvre/east-meets-west-as-louvre-abu-dhabi-opens-in-the-gulf-idUSKBN1D719F.

100 Amna Ehtesham Khaishgi, 'UAE Has Become the Leading Donor to Charitable Causes around the World', *The National*, 21 August 2014, https://www.thenational.ae/uae/government/uae-has-become-the-lead ing-donor-to-charitable-causes-around-the-world-1.263786.

101 Stephanie Strom, 'Abu Dhabi Gives US Hospital 4150 Million', *New York Times*, September 15, 2009, https://www.nytimes.com/2009/09/16/us/16d onation.html?mtrref=www.google.co.uk.

102 Karen E. Young, 'A New Politics of GCC Economic Statecraft: The Case of UAE Aid and Financial Intervention in Egypt', *Journal of Arabian Studies: Arabia, the Gulf and the Red Sea*, vol. 7, no. 1: Special Section: New Perspectives on UAE Foreign Policy (2017): 124

103 Ibid., 125.

104 Ibid., 116.

105 Soubrier, 'Evolving Foreign and Security Policies', 134.

106 Young, 'A New Politics of GCC Economic Statecraft: The Case of UAE Aid and Financial Intervention in Egypt', 113–36.

107 Ibid., 116.

108 David D. Kirkpatrick, 'Recordings Suggest Emirates and Egyptian Military Pushed Ousting of Morsi', *New York Times*, 1 March 2015, https://www.nyti mes.com/2015/03/02/world/middleeast/recordings-suggest-emirates-and-egyptian-military-pushed-ousting-of-morsi.html.

109 Along with $5 billion from Saudi Arabia and $4 billion from Kuwait, a significant increase on the contributions from the United States and Europe of $1.5 billion and $1.3 billion, respectively. See Rod Nordland, 'Saudi Arabia Promises to Aid Egypt's Regime', *New York Times*, 19 August 2013, https://www.nytimes.com/2013/08/20/world/middleeast/saudi-ara bia-vows-to-back-egypts-rulers.html.

110 Lisa Watanabe, 'Gulf States' Engagement in North Africa', in Khalid S. Almezaini and Jean-Marc Rickli (eds), *The Small Gulf States: Foreign and Security Policies Before and After the Arab Spring* (London: Routledge, 2017), 175.

111 For more on how much the UAE allocated to assisting Egypt, see Sebastian Sons, Inken Wiese, 'The Engagement of Arab Gulf States in Egypt and Tunisia since 2011 – Rationale and Impact', DGAP Analysis, vol. 9 (October 2015): 31–8. This reportedly did not include another $4 billion that Sheikh Mohammed bin Rashid Al Maktoum announced during the Egypt Economic Development Conference in March 2015, see ibid., 34.

112 Karen E. Young, 'A New Politics of GCC Economic Statecraft: The Case of UAE Aid and Financial Intervention in Egypt', *Journal of Arabian*

Studies: Arabia, the Gulf and the Red Sea, vol. 7, no. 1: Special Section: New Perspectives on UAE Foreign Policy (2017): 116.

113 Sons, Wiese, 'The Engagement of Arab Gulf States in Egypt and Tunisia since 2011 – Rationale and Impact', 34.

114 Sebastian Sons, Inken Wiese, 'The Engagement of Arab Gulf States in Egypt and Tunisia since 2011 – Rationale and Impact', DGAP Analysis, vol. 9 (October 2015): 35.

115 Karen E. Young, 'A New Politics of GCC Economic Statecraft: The Case of UAE Aid and Financial Intervention in Egypt', *Journal of Arabian Studies: Arabia, the Gulf and the Red Sea*, vol. 7, no. 1: Special Section: New Perspectives on UAE Foreign Policy (2017): 116.

116 Ibid.

117 See Chapters 1 and 4.

118 For more on China's relations with Iran, see Esfandiary and Tabatabai, *Triple Axis*.

119 Theodore Karasik, 'The GCC's New Affair with China', Middle East Institute (24 February 2016), https://www.mei.edu/publications/gccs-new-affair-china.

120 Esfandiary and Tabatabai, *Triple Axis*.

121 Dania Thafer, 'After the Financial Crisis: Dubai-China Economic Relations', Middle East Institute (15 September 2013), https://www.mei.edu/publications/after-financial-crisis-dubai-china-economic-relations.

122 'China, UAE to build strategic partnership: Wen', *The China Daily*, 16 January 2012, http://www.chinadaily.com.cn/china/2012-01/16/content_14456913.htm. For more on China's economic and political ties with the UAE; see Jonathan Fulton, 'China's Changing Role in the Middle East', Atlantic Council Rafik Hariri Center for the Middle East Report (June 2019), https://www.atlanticcouncil.org/images/publications/Chinas_Changing_Role_in_the_Middle_East.pdf.

123 Nick Webster, 'UAE and China Declare Deep Strategic Partnership as State Visit Ends', *The National*, 21 July 2018, https://www.thenational.ae/uae/uae-and-china-declare-deep-strategic-partnership-as-state-visit-ends-1.752515.

124 Kristian Coates Ulrichsen, *The United Arab Emirates – Power, Politics, and Policymaking* (Abingdon: Routledge, 2017), 156.

125 Kanika Saigal, 'Middle East: Emirates NBD Prints Gulf's First Dim Sum Bond', *Euromoney*, 2 April 2012, https://www.euromoney.com/article/b12kjmj0qjjwj8/middle-east-emirates-nbd-prints-gulfs-first-dim-sum-bond; Dania Saadi, 'UAE Financial Ties with China Were Years in the Making', *The National*, 11 January 2015, https://www.thenational.ae/business/uae-financial-ties-with-china-were-years-in-the-making-1.115095.

126 'UAE, China Launch $10b Joint Strategic Fund', *Gulf News*, 17 December 2015, https://gulfnews.com/uae/government/uae-china-launch-10b-joint-strategic-fund-1.1636147.

127 Muhammad Zufika Rakhmat, 'Institutionalising China's Relations with the Gulf', *International Policy Digest*, 15 April 2019, https://intpolicydigest. org/2019/04/15/institutionalising-china-s-relations-with-the-gulf/.

128 Statement by Mohammed Baharoon, director general, B'huth Center for Strategic Studies, at Middle East Institute Webinar on 'Covid-19, Oil Prices, and Prospects for Iran-GCC Relations', 6 May 2020.

129 Theodore Karasik, Giorgio Cafiero, 'Geopolitics Drive Russia and the UAE Closer', Middle East Institute, 4 April 2017, https://www.mei.edu/publicati ons/geopolitics-drive-russia-and-uae-closer.

130 'UAE's "Look East" Policy Is Developing', *The National*, 16 February 2017, https://www.thenational.ae/opinion/uae-s-look-east-policy-is-develop ing-1.49919.

131 Florence Gaub and Zoe Stanley-Lockman, 'Defence Industries in Arab States: Players and Strategies', *European Union Institute for Security Studies Chaillot Paper*, no. 141 (March 2017): 62.

132 Marc Lynch, 'The New Arab Order: Power and Violence in Today's Middle East', *Foreign Affairs* (September/October 2018 Issue), https://www.for eignaffairs.com/articles/middle-east/2018-08-13/new-arab-order; Victor Gervais, 'The Changing Security Dynamic in the Middle East and Its Impact on Smaller Gulf Cooperation Council States' Alliance Choices and Policies', in Khalid S. Almezaini and Jean-Marc Rickli (eds), *The Small Gulf States: Foreign and Security Policies Before and After the Arab Spring* (London: Routledge, 2017), 32.

133 Lynch, 'The New Arab Order'.

134 Saudi Arabia aimed to curb the perceived Iranian presence on its border. Author interview with Mohammed Al-Ghandi, political officer, Saudi embassy in Qatar, Doha, 18 May 2016; author interviews with former and current Gulf Arab officials and academics, Abu Dhabi, Doha, Muscat and Kuwait City, April and May 2016; Mubarak Ali AlSabah, Flotilla Commander, Kuwait Coast Guard, Kuwait City, 24 May 2016; Marc Lynch, *The New Arab Wars: Uprising and Anarchy in the Middle East* (New York: PublicAffairs, 2016), 64; author interview with Majdi Al-Dhafiri, Kuwaiti ambassador to Iran, Kuwait City, 24 May 2016.

135 Author round table with high-level Emirati officials, Abu Dhabi, 14 April 2016.

136 Sam Wilkin, 'UAE Troops Dig in for a Long War in Yemen', *Reuters*, 2 December 2015, https://www.reuters.com/article/us-yemen-security-emirates/uae-troops-dig-in-for-a-long-war-in-yemen-idUSKBN0TL14T2 0151202.

137 Leah Sherwood, 'Risk Diversification and the United Arab Emirates' Foreign Policy', in Khalid S. Almezaini and Jean-Marc Rickli (eds), *The Small Gulf States: Foreign and Security Policies Before and After the Arab Spring* (London: Routledge, 2017), 151.

138 Mina Aldroubi, 'UAE Humanitarian Aid to Yemen almost $4bn', *The National*, 26 June 2018, https://www.thenational.ae/world/mena/uae-humanitarian-aid-to-yemen-almost-4bn-1.744471.

139 Author email interview with Peter Salisbury, Crisis Group Senior Analyst for Yemen, 3 November 2021.

140 Ola Salem, 'UAE Military Intervention in Yemen Was "Inevitable"', *The National*, 26 March 2015, https://www.thenational.ae/uae/uae-military-intervention-in-yemen-was-inevitable-1.82859.

141 Author interviews with Emirati officials, Abu Dhabi, 14 April 2016.

142 Eleonora Ardemadni, 'UAE's Military Priorities in Yemen: Counterterrorism and the South', ISPI Commentary, 28 July 2016, https://www.ispionline.it/sites/default/files/pubblicazioni/commentary_ardemagni_28_07.2016.pdf, 1.

143 Noah Browning and Alexander Cornwell, 'UAE Extends Military Reach in Yemen and Somalia', *Reuters*, 11 May 2018, https://www.reuters.com/article/us-uae-security-yemen-somalia/uae-extends-military-reach-in-yemen-and-somalia-idUSKBN1IC12A; Abdulwahab Al Qassab, 'Strategic Considerations of the UAE's Role in Yemen', Arab Center Washington DC Policy Analysis, 9 March 2018, http://arabcenterdc.org/policy_analyses/strategic-considerations-of-the-uaes-role-in-yemen/.

144 'The Ambitious United Arab Emirates – the Gulf's "Little Sparta"', *The Economist*, 6 April 2017, https://www.economist.com/middle-east-and-africa/2017/04/06/the-ambitious-united-arab-emirates.

145 Also called the Yemeni Congregation for Reform, founded in 1990.

146 For more on the growth of AQAP in Yemen, see 'Yemen's Al Qaeda: Expanding the Base', International Crisis Group Report, no. 174, 2 February 2017, https://www.crisisgroup.org/middle-east-north-africa/gulf-and-arabian-peninsula/yemen/174-yemen-s-al-qaeda-expanding-base.

147 Ibid.

148 Elana DeLozier, 'UAE Drawdown May Isolate Saudi Arabia in Yemen', The Washington Institute Policywatch 3148, 2 July 2019, https://www.washingtoninstitute.org/policy-analysis/view/uae-drawdown-in-yemen-may-isolate-saudi-arabia.

149 Author phone interview with Elizabeth Dickinson, senior analyst, Arabian Peninsula, International Crisis Group, 28 August 2019.

150 Neil Partrick, 'The UAE's War Aims in Yemen', Sada Blog – Carnegie Endowment for International Peace, 24 October 2017, http://carnegieendowment.org/sada/73524.

151 Ibid.

152 '3 Killed in Inter-militia Fighting at Yemen's Aden Airport', *Associated Press*, 12 February 2017, http://www.foxnews.com/world/2017/02/12/3-killed-in-inter-militia-fighting-at-yemen-aden-airport.html.

153 'Yemen Conflict: Southern Separatists Seize Control of Aden', *BBC News*, 11 August 2019, https://www.bbc.co.uk/news/world-middle-east-49308199

154 Jo Adetunji, Peter Beaumont and Martin Chulov, 'Libya Protests: More Than 100 Killed as Army Fires on Unarmed Demonstrators', *The Guardian*, 20 February 2011, https://www.theguardian.com/world/2011/

feb/20/libya-protests-benghazi-muammar-gaddafi; Laila Fadel and Liz Sly, 'Gaddafi Forces Fire on Protestors in Tripoli; Defiant Leader Urges Thousands of Supporters to Take Up Arms', *Washington Post*, 26 February 2011, http://www.washingtonpost.com/wp-dyn/content/arti cle/2011/02/25/AR2011022502731.html?noredirect=on; 'World Report 2012: Libya – Events of 2011', Human Rights Watch, https://www.hrw.org/ world-report/2012/country-chapters/libya.

155 Soubrier, 'Evolving Foreign and Security Policies, 135.

156 Author email interview with Claudia Gazzini, Crisis Group Senior Libya analyst, 31 October 2021.

157 Sherwood, 'Risk Diversification and the United Arab Emirates' Foreign Policy', 150.

158 Kareem Shaheen, 'UAE Warplanes Will Patrol Libyan No-Fly Zone', *The National*, 25 March 2011, https://www.thenational.ae/uae/uae-warpla nes-will-patrol-libyan-no-fly-zone-1.417396; Haneed Dajani, 'UAE Warplanes in Sardinia Ahead of Dispatch to Libya', *The National*, 29 March 2011, https://www.thenational.ae/uae/uae-warplanes-in-sardinia-ahead-of-dispatch-to-libya-1.409823; for more on other Emirati efforts in Libya, see Jean-Marc Rickli, 'The Political Rational and Implications of the United Arab Emirates' Military Involvement in Libya', in Dag Henriksen and Ann Karin Larssen (eds), *Political Rational and International Consequences of the War in Libya* (Oxford: Oxford University Press, 2016), 144–6.

159 Ibid., 148.

160 For more on the contribution of the GCC states to the NATO-led intervention in Libya, see Bruce R. Nardulli, 'The Arab States Experience', in Karl P. Mueller (ed.), *Precision and Purpose: Airpower in the Libyan Civil War* (Santa Monica: RAND Corporation, 2015), 339–72.

161 Ibid., 359.

162 Hussein Lbish, 'The UAE's Evolving National Security Strategy', The Arab Gulf States Institute in Washington Report, 6 April 2017, https://agsiw.org/ wp-content/uploads/2017/04/UAE-Security_ONLINE.pdf, 23; Rickli, 'The Political Rational and Implications of the United Arab Emirates' Military Involvement in Libya'.

163 Author interview with Riad Kahwaji, CEO, INEGMA, Dubai, 13 November 2016.

164 For more on Qatar's involvement in Libya, see David Roberts, 'Behind Qatar's Intervention in Libya', *Foreign Affairs*, 28 September 2011, https:// www.foreignaffairs.com/articles/libya/2011-09-28/behind-qatars-intervent ion-libya.

165 Nardulli, 'The Arab States Experience', 362.

166 According to Gomati,

The Muslim Brotherhood's Justice and Construction Party (J&C) lost the political party votes, only winning 15% of their allocated 80 party seats. The UAE backed secular party – the National Forces Alliance (NFA) led by Mahmoud Jibril – won around 40% of the political party votes. However, the 120 independent seats, of which 25 had affiliation to the NFA was not enough for the NFA and Jibril to control the parliament.

See Anas El Gomati, 'The Libyan Revolution Undone – the Conversation Will Not Be Televised', in Andreas Krieg (eds), *Divided Gulf: The Anatomy of a Crisis* (London: Palgrave Macmillan, 2019), 188.

167 David B. Roberts, 'Qatar and the UAE: Exploring Divergent Responses to the Arab Spring', *Middle East Journal*, vol. 71, no. 4 (Autumn 2017): 547.

168 Qatar reportedly assisted the Libya Dawn coalition, see ibid., 24.

169 David D. Kirkpatrick, 'Libyan Militias Seize Control of Capital as Chaos Rises', *New York Times*, 1 September 2014, https://www.nytimes.com/2014/09/02/world/africa/militias-seize-control-of-libyan-capital.html.

170 Anne Gearan, 'Egypt and the UAE Strike Islamist Militias in Libya', *Washington Post*, 25 August 2014, https://www.washingtonpost.com/world/national-security/egypt-and-uae-strike-islamist-militias-in-libya/2014/08/25/8685ef04-2c98-11e4-be9e-60cc44c01e7f_story.html?utm_term=.f09f7c6f3c04.

171 Fahmy Howeidi, 'The Emirati Airstrikes on Libya', *Al-Shorouk*, 27 August 2014.

172 UN Security Council Resolution 2292, 14 June 2016, http://unscr.com/en/resolutions/doc/2292

173 SPIRI Arms Transfer Database, https://sipri.org/databases/armstransfers (accessed 17 June 2019).

174 Final report of the Panel of Experts on Libya established pursuant to resolution 1973 (2011), UN Security Council, 1 June 2017, 24, 33–4, 43–4, https://reliefweb.int/sites/reliefweb.int/files/resources/N1711623.pdf.

175 'Libya embargo violations: UN panel to report findings to UNSC', *Al Jazeera*, 1 March 2018, https://www.aljazeera.com/news/2018/03/libya-embargo-violations-panel-report-findings-unsc-180301080019627.html. Reporting in 2019 stated that missile strikes attributed to General Haftar were conducted using Wing Loong variants. See 'Libya Missile Strikes Point to Possible UAE Role: UN Report', *France 24*, 6 May 2019, https://www.france24.com/en/20190506-libya-missile-strikes-point-possible-uae-role-un-report.

176 Zachary Cohen and Joshua Berlinger, 'Libyan General Praise by Trump Accused of Possible War Crimes', *CNN*, 15 May 2019, https://www.cnn.com/2019/05/15/politics/libya-war-crimes-allegations-intl/index.html.

177 Hussein Ibish, 'The UAE's Evolving National Security Strategy', The Arab Gulf States Institute in Washington Report, 6 April 2017, https://agsiw.org/wp-content/uploads/2017/04/UAE-Security_ONLINE.pdf, 28.

178 'Libya's Shifting Sands: Derna and Sirte', *Al Jazeera Reports*, 22 June 2017, https://www.aljazeera.com/program/al-jazeera-world/2017/6/22/libyas-shifting-sands-derna-and-sirte; Sasha Toperich, 'Khafa Haftar Is No Longer Part of Libya's Solution', *The Hill*, 1 May 2019, https://thehill.com/opinion/international/441552-khalifa-haftar-is-no-longer-part-of-libyas-solution.

179 Ami Rojkes Dombe, 'Report: The UAE Is Expanding the al-Khadim Air Base in Libya', *Israel Defense*, 17 December 2017, https://www.israeldefense. co.il/en/node/32228.

180 Eleonora Ardemagni, Frederica Saini Fasanotti, 'The UAE in Libya and Yemen: Different Tactics, One Goal', ISPI, 31 July 2020, https://www. ispionline.it/en/pubblicazione/uae-libya-and-yemen-different-tact ics-one-goal-27138.

181 Benoit Faucon, Jared Malsin, Summer Said, 'U.A.E. Backed Militia Leader's Bid to Take Control of Libyan Oil Exports', *Wall Street Journal*, 13 July 2018, https://www.wsj.com/articles/u-a-e-backed-militia-lead ers-bid-to-take-control-of-libyan-oil-exports-1531474200.

182 'Stopping the War for Tripoli', Crisis Group Briefing 69, 23 May 2019, https://www.crisisgroup.org/middle-east-north-africa/north-africa/libya/ b069-stopping-war-tripoli.

183 Tom Kington, 'UAE Allegedly Using Chinese Drones for Deadly Airstrikes in Libya', *Defense News*, 2 May 2019, https://www.defensenews.com/unman ned/2019/05/02/uae-allegedly-using-chinese-drones-for-deadly-airstri kes-in-libya/.

184 Eleonora Ardemagni, Frederica Saini Fasanotti, 'The UAE in Libya and Yemen: Different Tactics, One Goal', ISPI, 31 July 2020, https://www. ispionline.it/en/pubblicazione/uae-libya-and-yemen-different-tact ics-one-goal-27138.

Chapter 5

1 This has been examined extensively in the literature, see, for example, David A. Baldwin, 'Success and Failure in Foreign Policy', *Annual Review of Political Science*, vol. 3 (June 2000): 167–82; George A. Boyne, 'What Is Public Service Improvement?', *Public Administration*, vol. 81, no. 2 (June 2003); David Marsh and Allan McConnell, 'Towards a Framework for Establishing Policy Success', *Public Administration*, vol. 88, no. 2 (2010): 564–83.

2 Declan Walsh and David D. Kirkpatrick, 'U.A.E Pulls Most Forces from Yemen in Blow to Saudi War Effort', *New York Times*, 11 July 2019, https://www.nytimes.com/2019/07/11/world/middleeast/yemen-emira tes-saudi-war.html.

3 Author interview with AlBadr Al Shateri, professor, UAE National Defense College, Abu Dhabi, 28 February 2017.

4 Author interviews with Emirati experts, officials, academics, Abu Dhabi and Dubai (2014–17).

5 Author interview AlBadr Al Shateri, professor, UAE National Defense College, Abu Dhabi, 28 February 2017.

6   Andrew England and Simeon Kerr, 'UAE: The Middle East's Power Broker Flexes Its Muscles', *Financial Times*, 24 October 2017, https://www.ft.com/content/1b2b7f54-b411-11e7-a398-73d59db9e399.

7   Quoted by Abdullah Baabood who was on the same panel as Abdulkhaleq Abdullah when he made that statement. Author interview with Abdullah Baabood, former professor, Qatar University, 28 February 2020.

8   Author interview with Abdulkhaleq Abdulla, Dubai, 23 November 2021.

9   Statement by Barbara A. Leaf, ambassador-designate to the UAE, to the Senate Foreign Relations Committee, 10 September 2014, https://www.fore ign.senate.gov/imo/media/doc/Leaf_Testimony.pdf.

10 For more on this and the UAE's reliance on surrogates, see Andreas Krieg and Jean-Marc Rickli, *Surrogate Warfare: The Transformation of War in the Twenty-First Century* (Washington, DC: Georgetown University Press, 2019).

11 Author interview with UAE think tank analyst, Dubai, 13 November 2016.

12 Ibid.

13 Author interview with Riad Kahwaji, CEO, INEGMA, Dubai, 13 November 2016.

14 Author interview with Emirati official, Abu Dhabi, 24 November 2021.

15 Ibid.

16 Ibid.

17 Author interview with Emirati foreign ministry official, Abu Dhabi, 24 November 2021.

18 Author interview with Emirati official, Abu Dhabi, 24 November 2021.

19 Author round table with officials and academics, Qatar University, Doha, 14 May 2016.

20 Author round table with regional experts, officials and academics, Dubai, 19 April 2016.

21 Author interview with Emirati official, Abu Dhabi, 9 March 2022.

22 Author interview with AlBadr Al Shateri, professor, UAE National Defense College, Abu Dhabi, 10 March 2022.

23 Author interview with military official, Abu Dhabi, 24 November 2021.

24 Xi Jinping, 'UAE, Chinese People Never Give Up Their Dreams: President Xi', *Gulf News*, 17 July 2018, https://gulfnews.com/opinion/thinkers/uae-chinese-people-never-give-up-their-dreams-president-xi-1.2253147.

25 'UAE and China Sign Strategic Agreements as Sheikh Mohamed bin Zayed Visits Beijing', *The National*, 22 July 2019, https://www.thenational.ae/uae/government/uae-and-china-sign-strategic-agreements-as-sheikh-moha med-bin-zayed-visits-beijing-1.889051.

26 See Chapter 4.

27 Simeon Kerr, 'UAE to Produce China's Sinopharm Covid Vaccine', *Financial Times*, 28 March 2021, https://www.ft.com/content/040e8 67b-a0d1-4e6a-9a58-888da31a220c.

28 'Abdullah bin Zayed, Chinese Foreign Minister Review Global Fight against Covid-19', *Gulf News*, 10 April 2020, https://gulfnews.com/uae/

abdullah-bin-zayed-chinese-foreign-minister-review-global-fight-agai
nst-covid-19-1.1586538805682.

29 Paul Schemm, 'Third Dose of Sinopharm Coronavirus Vaccine Needed for some in the UAE after Low Immune Response', *Washington Post*, 22 March 2021, https://www.washingtonpost.com/world/middle_east/uae-sinoph arm-third-dose/2021/03/21/588fcf0a-8a26-11eb-a33e-da28941cb9ac_st ory.html.

30 Ni Jian, 'Why China's Relationship with the UAE Is Brotherly', *The National*, https://www.thenationalnews.com/opinion/comment/why-china-s-relat ionship-with-the-uae-is-brotherly-1.868032.

31 Andrew England and Simeon Kerr, ' "More of China, Less of America": How Superpower Fight Is Squeezing the Gulf', *Financial Times*, 20 September 2021, https://www.ft.com/content/4f82b560-4744-4c53-bf4b-7a37d3afeb13.

32 Gordon Lubold and Warren P. Strobel, 'Secret Chinese Port Project in Persian Gulf Rattles U.S. Relations with U.A.E.', *Wall Street Journal*, 19 November 2021.

33 Author interview with current US official, Washington, September 2021.

34 Author interview with Emirati experts, officials and academics, Dubai and Abu Dhabi (2014–22).

35 'UAE, Russia Forge Strategic Partnership', *Gulf News*, 1 June 2018, https://gulfnews.com/uae/government/uae-russia-forge-strategic-partners hip-1.2230246; 'Declaration on the Strategic Partnership between the Russian Federation and the United Arab Emirates', 1 June 2018, http://en.kremlin.ru/supplement/5309.

36 Li-Chen Sim, 'Russia and the UAE Are Now Strategic Partners: What's Next?', *LobeLog*, 7 June 2018, https://lobelog.com/rus sia-and-the-uae-are-now-strategic-partners-whats-next/.

37 Ibid.

38 For more on this, see Julian Barnes Dacey and Cinzia Bianco, 'Order of Engagement: Assad's Visit to Abu Dhabi', European Council on Foreign Relations, 24 March 2022, https://ecfr.eu/article/order-of-engagement-ass ads-visit-to-abu-dhabi/.

39 Declan Walsh, 'Waves of Russian and Emirati Flights Fuel Libyan War, U.N. Finds', *New York Times*, 3 September 2020, https://www.nytimes. com/2020/09/03/world/middleeast/libya-russia-emirates-mercenar ies.html.

40 'Delegation from Yemen Separatists Flies to Russia', Anadolu Agency, 31 January 2021, https://www.aa.com.tr/en/middle-east/delegat ion-from-yemen-separatists-flies-to-russia/2129007.

41 Author interview with Emirati official, Abu Dhabi, 9 March 2022.

42 Michelle Nichols, 'U.N. arms embargo imposed on Yemen's Houthis amid vote questions', *Reuters*, 28 February 2022, https://www.reuters.com/world/ middle-east/un-security-council-imposes-arms-embargo-yemens-hou thi-group-2022-02-28/.

43 'The Impact of Russia's Invasion of Ukraine in the Middle East and North Africa', Crisis Group Commentary, 14 April 2022, https://www.crisisgr oup.org/middle-east-north-africa/impact-russias-invasion-ukraine-mid dle-east-and-north-africa#gulf.

44 Author interview with Emirati official, Abu Dhabi, 24 November 2021.

45 Author interview with head of a research institute, Kuwait City, 24 May 2016; author interview with officials, Abu Dhabi, 14 April 2016.

46 'UAE Arrests Opponents of Israel Peace Deal', *Middle East Monitor*, 17 August 2020, https://www.middleeastmonitor.com/20200817-uae-arrests-opponents-of-israel-peace-deal/.

47 Aya Batrawy, 'UAE and Israel Press Ahead with Ties after Gaza Cease-Fire', *AP News*, 27 May 2021, https://apnews.com/article/israel-middle-east-business-israel-palestinian-conflict-lifestyle-cf5054de2ee04e43d0749a91c 2e3b6ab.

48 Jacob Magid, 'UAE Summons Israel Envoy over "Attacks on Civilians, Incursions into Holy Places"', *Times of Israel*, 19 April 2022, https://www. timesofisrael.com/uae-summons-israeli-envoy-over-attacks-on-civilians-incursions-into-holy-places/.

49 Author interview with military official, Abu Dhabi, 24 November 2021.

50 'UAE Reopens Damascus Embassy after Seven Years', *Al Jazeera*, 28 December 2018, https://www.aljazeera.com/news/2018/12/28/uae-reop ens-damascus-embassy-after-seven-years.

51 Author interview with the former head of a think tank based in the UAE, Dubai, 23 November 2021.

52 'UAE Most Important Trading Partner of Syrian Regime', The Syrian Observer, 7 October 2021, https://syrianobserver.com/news/70294/ uae-most-important-trading-partner-of-the-syrian-regime.html.

53 Aziz el Massassi, 'US "Profoundly Disappointed" by UAE hosting Syria', *Times of Israel*, 19 March 2022, https://www.timesofisrael.com/us-profoun dly-disappointed-by-uae-hosting-syrias-assad/.

54 Yunus Paksoy, 'UAE Allegedly Funnelled $3bn to Topple Erdogan, Turkish Government', *Daily Sabah*, 13 June 2017, https://www.dailysabah.com/polit ics/2017/06/13/uae-allegedly-funneled-3b-to-topple-erdogan-turkish-gov ernment.

55 Author interview with the former head of a think tank based in the UAE, Dubai, 23 November 2021.

56 Suzan Fraser and Aya Batrawy, 'Top UAE Security Chief Visits Turkey after Years of Tension', *Associated Press*, 19 August 2021, https://apnews.com/ article/europe-middle-east-business-turkey-059bc288038fd6c46b1c44431 9f9f683.

57 Orhan Coskun, 'Abu Dhabi Crown Prince to Visit Turkey after Years of Tension – Officials', *Reuters*, 15 November 2021, https://www.reuters.com/ world/middle-east/abu-dhabi-crown-prince-visit-turkey-soon-nov-24-turkish-officials-2021-11-15/; 'Turkey's Erdogan Visits the United Arab Emirates in bid to Improve Long-Strained Ties', *France 24*, 15 February

2022, https://www.france24.com/en/middle-east/20220215-turkey-s-erdo
gan-visits-the-united-arab-emirates-to-improve-long-strained-ties.

58 Onur Ant, 'Turkey, UAE Sign FX Swap Deal Worth $5 Billion', *Bloomberg*, 19 January 2022, https://www.bloomberg.com/news/articles/2022-01-19/turkey-uae-sign-fx-swap-deal-worth-around-5-billion.

59 'UAE Announces $10 Billion Turkey Investment Fund', *AFP*, 24 November 2021, https://www.khaleejtimes.com/uae/uae-announces-10-bill ion-fund-for-investments-in-turkey.

60 Mumin Altas, 'Turkiye, UAE Sign 13 Agreements in Various Areas', *Anadolu Agency*, https://www.aa.com.tr/en/politics/turkiye-uae-sign-13-agreements-in-various-areas/2502456.

61 Author interview with Emirati experts, officials, academics, Abu Dhabi and Dubai (2014–22).

62 Frank Kane, 'Interview: UAE Ambassador to Washington on Building Economic Relations with US', *The National*, 2 August 2016, https://www.thenational.ae/business/interview-uae-ambassador-to-washington-on-building-economic-relations-with-us-1.145104.

63 'Dubai Aerospace to Buy Carlyle Aircraft Service Units for $1.8 Billion', *Associated Press*, 2 April 2017, https://www.cnbc.com/id/17902964.

64 Anshuman Daga, 'Dubai Aerospace to Buy Aircraft Lessor AWAS, Catapults to Top Tier', *Reuters*, 24 April 2017, https://www.reuters.com/arti cle/us-awas-m-a-dubaiaerospace-idUSKBN17Q0QI.

65 Kristian Coates Ulrichsen, *The United Arab Emirates – Power, Politics, and Policymaking* (Abingdon: Routledge, 2017), 87.

66 Ibid., 99–103.

67 Ulrichsen, *The United Arab Emirates – Power, Politics, and Policymaking*, 90, 91.

68 Author interview with Emirati experts, officials, academics, Abu Dhabi and Dubai (2014–22).

69 'Defining UAE as World's Leading Business Hub', *Gulf News*, 2 February 2015, https://gulfnews.com/opinion/editorials/defining-uae-as-worlds-lead ing-business-hub-1.1450459.

70 See Chapter 6.

71 Toby Matthiesen, 'Renting the Casbah', in Kristian Coates Ulrichsen (ed.), *The Changing Security Dynamics of the Persian Gulf* (London: Hurst, 2017), 51–2.

72 Ibid., 51.

73 Sebastian Sons and Inken Wiese, 'The Engagement of Arab Gulf States in Egypt and Tunisia since 2011 – Rationale and Impact', DGAP Analysis, vol. 9 (October 2015): 37.

74 Robert F. Worth, 'Mohammed Bin Zayed's Dark Vision of the Middle East's Future', *New York Times Magazine*, 9 January 2020, https://www.nytimes.com/2020/01/09/magazine/united-arab-emirates-moham med-bin-zayed.html.

75 For more on the UAE's involvement in the Horn of Africa, see 'The United Arab Emirates in the Horn of Africa', *International Crisis Group Middle East Briefing*, no. 65, 6 November 2018; Alex Mello and Michael Knights, 'West of Suez for the United Arab Emirates', *War on the Rocks*, 2 September 2016, https://warontherocks.com/2016/09/west-of-suez-for-the-uni ted-arab-emirates/.

76 Peter Salisbury, 'Yemen's Southern Transitional Council: A Delicate Balancing Act', Istituto Per Gli Studi Di Politica Internazionale (ISPI), 30 March 2021, https://www.crisisgroup.org/middle-east-north-africa/ gulf-and-arabian-peninsula/yemen/yemens-southern-transitional-coun cil-delicate-balancing-act.

77 Mello and Knights, 'West of Suez for the United Arab Emirates'.

78 See Iona Craig, 'Bombed into Famine: How the Saudi Air Campaign Targets Yemen's Food Supplies', *The Guardian*, 12 December 2017, https://www.theguardian.com/world/2017/dec/12/bombed-into- famine-how-saudi-air-campaign-targets-yemens-food-supplies; 'Indiscriminate Bombings and Unreliable Reassurances from Saudi-led Coalition Force MSF to Evacuate Staff from Six Hospitals in the North', Medecins sans Frontieres Press Release, 16 August 2016, https://www. msf.org/yemen-indiscriminate-bombings-and-unreliable-reassuran ces-saudi-led-coalition-force-msf-evacuate; 'Yemen: Coalition Airstrikes Deadly for Children', Human Rights Watch, 12 September 2017, https:// www.hrw.org/news/2017/09/12/yemen-coalition-airstrikes-deadly- children; Nour Youssef, 'Airstrikes in Yemen Kill 68 Civilians in a Single Day', *New York Times*, 28 December 2017, https://www.nytimes. com/2017/12/28/world/middleeast/un-yemen-war.html.

79 Author email interview with Peter Salisbury, Crisis Group senior analyst for Yemen, 3 November 2021.

80 Author interview with Emirati experts, officials, academics and the military, Abu Dhabi and Dubai (2014–22).

81 Author interview with former Emirati national security advisor, New York, 31 October 2019.

82 Author interview with Emirati official, Abu Dhabi, 9 March 2022.

83 Abdulkhaleq Abdulla, 'The UAE Drawdown in Yemen Is a Welcome Step, but It Needs to Be Reciprocated', Middle East Institute, 11 July 2019, https://www.mei.edu/publications/uae-drawdown-yemen-welc ome-step-it-needs-be-reciprocated.

84 Author email interview with Peter Salisbury, Crisis Group senior analyst for Yemen, 3 November 2021.

85 Author interview with high-level military official, Abu Dhabi, 24 November 2021.

86 Peter Salisbury, 'Risk Perception and Appetite in UAE Foreign and National Security Policy', Chatham House Research Paper, 1 July 2020, https://www.chathamhouse.org/2020/07/risk-perception-and-appetite-uae- foreign-and-national-security-policy-0/8-case-study-uae.

87   Peter Salisbury, 'Risk Perception and Appetite in UAE Foreign and National Security Policy', Chatham House Research Paper, 1 July 2020, https://www.chathamhouse.org/2020/07/risk-perception-and-appetite-uae-foreign-and-national-security-policy-0/8-case-study-uae.

88   Author interview with head of an Emirati think tank, Dubai, 13 November 2016.

89   Aya Batrawy, 'UAE Draws Down Troops in Yemen in "Strategic Redeployment"', *AP News*, 8 July 2019, https://apnews.com/article/eed97 5cc4db84d41b690f046a00e3072.

90   Author interview with Emirati experts, officials and academics, Abu Dhabi and Dubai (2019–22).

91   Author interview with high-level military official, Abu Dhabi, 24 November 2021.

92   Ibid; author interview with Emirati officials, Abu Dhabi, November 2021; author interview with Emirati officials, Abu Dhabi, March 2022.

93   'Yemeni Pro-Government Forces Say They Have Retaken Shabwa from Houthis', *Reuters*, 10 January 2022, https://www.reuters.com/world/mid dle-east/yemeni-forces-say-they-have-retaken-energy-producing-provi nce-houthis-2022-01-10/.

94   Emile Roy, 'Who Are the UAE-Backed Forces Fighting on the Western Front in Yemen?' ACLED, 20 July 2018, https://acleddata.com/2018/07/20/who-are-the-uae-backed-forces-fighting-on-the-western-front-in-yemen/; Jonathan Fenton-Harvey, 'Divisions Restrict Southern Transitional Council, UAE Ambitions in Yemen', Al-Monitor, 10 October 2019, https://www.al-monitor.com/originals/2019/10/yemen-southern-movements-divisions-uae-influence.html; Raiman al-Hamdani and Helen Lackner, 'War and Pieces: Political Divides in Southern Yemen', ECFR Policy Brief, 22 January 2020, https://ecfr.eu/publication/war_and_pieces_political_di vides_in_southern_yemen/.

95   Simeon Kerr and Samer Al-Atrush, 'Yemen's Houthi Rebels Strike UAE', *Financial Times*, 17 January 2022, https://www.ft.com/content/e7c87 c71-8e43-48a1-bfea-bfc2b6e9c6b2.

96   U.S. Central Command Statement on Use of Patriots to Defend U.S. Forces, US Centcom Press Release, 24 January 2022, https://www.centcom.mil/MEDIA/PRESS-RELEASES/Press-Release-View/Article/2909334/us-cent ral-command-statement-on-use-of-patriots-to-defend-us-forces/.

97   Natasha Turak, 'UAE Forces Say They Intercepted Houthi Missile Strike, the Third Attack This Month', CNBC, 31 January 2022, https://www.cnbc.com/2022/01/31/uae-forces-say-they-intercepted-houthi-missile-str ike.html.

98   'United Arab Emirates Intercepts Two Ballistic Missiles Targeting Abu Dhabi', *Associated Press*, 24 January 2022, https://www.theguardian.com/world/2022/jan/24/united-arab-emirates-intercepts-two-ballistic-missiles-targeting-abu-dhabi.

99   Author interview with Emirati official, Abu Dhabi, 9 March 2022.

100 Phil Stewart, 'After Houthi Attacks, Senior U.S. General in UAE to Bolster Defenses', *Reuters*, 6 February 2022, https://www.reuters.com/world/middle-east/after-houthi-attacks-senior-us-general-uae-bolster-defenses-2022-02-06/.

101 Author interview with Emirati military analyst, Abu Dhabi, 10 March 2022.

102 Author interview with Emirati official, Abu Dhabi, 9 March 2022.

103 Ibid.

104 Author interview with Emirati officials and experts, Abu Dhabi and Dubai, March 2022; Natasha Turak, 'Drone and Missile Attacks on the UAE Shows Its Strengths More Than Vulnerabilities, Security Analysts Say', CNBC, 11 February 2022, https://www.cnbc.com/2022/02/11/attacks-on-uae-shows-its-strengths-more-than-vulnerabilities-analysts.html.

105 Tom Allinson, 'Libya: Khalifa Haftar's Repressive Proto-State and the "Myth" of Stability', *DeutscheWelle*, 26 February 2020.

106 Jean-Marc Rickli, 'The Political Rational and Implications of the United Arab Emirates' Military Involvement in Libya', in Dag Henriksen and Ann Karin Larssen (eds), *Political Rational and International Consequences of the War in Libya* (Oxford: Oxford University Press, 2016), 148.

107 Ibid., 146–7.

108 Kristian Coates Ulrichsen, *The United Arab Emirates – Power, Politics, and Policymaking* (Abingdon: Routledge, 2017), 195.

109 Ibid., 196.

110 Ibid; Helene Cooper and Robert Worth, 'In Arab Spring, Obama Finds a Sharp Test', *New York Times*, 24 September 2012, https://www.nytimes.com/2012/09/25/us/politics/arab-spring-proves-a-harsh-test-for-obamas-diplomatic-skill.html.

111 The Berlin Conference on Libya, Conference Conclusions, Press Release, Berlin, 19 January 2010, https://www.bundesregierung.de/breg-en/news/the-berlin-conference-on-libya-1713882.

112 Author interview with head of an Emirati think tank, Dubai, 13 November 2016.

113 'Stopping the War for Tripoli', Crisis Group Briefing 69, Middle East and North Africa, 23 May 2019, https://www.crisisgroup.org/middle-east-north-africa/north-africa/libya/b069-stopping-war-tripoli.

114 'Stopping the War for Tripoli', Crisis Group Briefing 69, Middle East and North Africa, 23 May 2019, https://www.crisisgroup.org/middle-east-north-africa/north-africa/libya/b069-stopping-war-tripoli.

115 'Stopping the War for Tripoli', Crisis Group Briefing 69, Middle East and North Africa, 23 May 2019, https://www.crisisgroup.org/middle-east-north-africa/north-africa/libya/b069-stopping-war-tripoli.

116 'Turkey Wades into Libya's Troubled Waters', Crisis Group Report 257, Europe and Central Asia, 30 April 2020, https://www.crisisgroup.org/europe-central-asia/western-europemediterranean/turkey/257-turkey-wades-libyas-troubled-waters.

117 Jared Malsin, 'U.A.E. Boosted Arms Transfers to Libya to Salvage Warlord's Campaign, U.N. Panel Finds', *Wall Street Journal*, 29 September 2020, https://www.wsj.com/articles/u-a-e-boosted-arms-transfers-tolibyato-salv age-warlords-campaign-u-n-panel-finds-11601412059.

118 Amy Mackinnon and Jack Detsch, 'Pentagon Says UAE Possibly Funding Russia's Shadowy Mercenaries in Libya', *Foreign Policy*, 30 November 2020, https://foreignpolicy.com/2020/11/30/pentagon-trump-russia-libya-uae/.

119 Author interview with former Emirati national security advisor, New York, 31 October 2019.

120 Author phone and message conversations with Emirati experts and officials (2020).

121 Zainab Fattah, 'UAE Hints at Frustration with Beleaguered Libyan Ally Haftar', Bloomberg, 17 June 2020, https://www.bloomberg.com/news/artic les/2020-06-17/uae-hints-at-frustrations-with-beleaguered-libyan-ally-haftar.

122 'Libya Update 4', International Crisis Group Briefing Note, 15 February 2021, https://www.crisisgroup.org/middle-east-north-africa/north-africa/libya/libya-update-4.

123 Ibid.

124 Author interview with Emirati official, Abu Dhabi, 24 November 2021.

125 For example, the National Oil Company of Libya accused the Emiratis of being behind the Libyan National Army's (LNA) oil blockade in July 2020. See 'Libya's NOC Accuses UAE of Being behind the Oil Blockade', *Reuters*, 12 July 2020, https://www.reuters.com/article/us-libya-oil-idUSKC N24D0NH.

126 Author email interview with Claudia Gazzini, Crisis Group's senior analyst on Libya, 31 October 2021.

127 Author interview with Emirati experts, officials and academics, Abu Dhabi and Dubai (2014–17).

Chapter 6

1 Mehran Kamrava, *Qatar – Small State, Big Politics* (Ithaca, NY: Cornell University Press, 2013), xvii.

2 Author interview with senior Qatar official, Ministry of Foreign Affairs, Doha, Qatar, 15 December 2019.

3 Author interview with former member of the Omani *Majles Shura*, Muscat, 21 May 2017.

4 Victor Gervais, 'The Changing Security Dynamic in the Middle East and its Impact on Smaller Gulf Cooperation Council States' Alliance Choices and Policies', in Khalid S. Almezaini Jean-Marc Rickli (eds), *The Small Gulf States: Foreign and Security Policies Before and After the Arab Spring* (London: Routledge, 2017), 40.

5 'GCC Leaders Conclude 32nd Session of Supreme Council', Embassy of the Kingdom of Saudi Arabia in Washington, DC, 21 December 2011, https://

www.saudiembassy.net/news/gcc-leaders-conclude-32nd-session-supreme-council.

6 'Oman Will Withdraw from GCC If a Union Is Formed: Foreign Minister', *The National*, 7 December 2013, https://www.thenational.ae/world/oman-will-withdraw-from-gcc-if-a-union-is-formed-foreign-minis ter-1.314873.

7 Carine Malek, 'UAE Recalls Envoy from Qatar over "Interference"', *The National*, 5 March 2014, https://www.thenationalnews.com/uae/governm ent/uae-recalls-envoy-from-qatar-over-interference-1.452598.

8 Ian Black, 'Arab States Withdraw Ambassadors from Qatar in Protest at "Interference"', *The Guardian*, 5 March 2014, https://www.theguardian. com/world/2014/mar/05/arab-states-qatar-withdraw-ambassadors-protest.

9 David D. Kirkpatrick, 'Gulf States and Qatar Gloss over Differences, but Split Still Hampers Them', *New York Times*, 20 December 2014, https:// www.nytimes.com/2014/12/21/world/gulf-states-and-qatar-gloss-over-diff erences-but-split-still-hampers-them.html.

10 Erika Solomon, 'The $1bn Hostage Deal That Enraged Qatar's Gulf Rivals', *Financial Times*, 5 June 2017, https://www.ft.com/content/dd033 082-49e9-11e7-a3f4-c742b9791d43.

11 Evan Perez and Shimon Prokupecz, 'Exclusive: US Suspects Russian Hackers Planted News behind Qatar Crisis', *CNN*, 7 June 2017, https://edition.cnn.com/2017/06/06/politics/russian-hackers-plan ted-fake-news-qatar-crisis/index.html.

12 Jane Kinninmont, 'The Gulf Divided: The Impact of the Qatar Crisis', Chatham House Research Paper, 30 May 2019, 15.

13 Neil Partrick, 'The UAE's War Aims in Yemen', Sada Blog – Carnegie Endowment for International Peace, 24 October 2017, http://carnegieen dowment.org/sada/73524.

14 Round table with Qatari officials hosted by RUSI, London, 20 February 2020; author interview with an advisor to Al Jazeera, Doha, 24 March 2022.

15 Ibid; author interview with Abdullah Baabood, former professor, Qatar University, London, 28 February 2020.

16 Round table with Qatari officials hosted by RUSI, London, 20 February 2020.

17 Full text of the al Ula GCC Summit Declaration, 6 January 2021, https://english.alarabiya.net/News/gulf/2021/01/06/Full-transcr ipt-of-AlUla-GCC-Summit-Declaration-Bolstering-Gulf-unity.

18 'UAE Official Said Rebuilding Trust Required to End Gulf Dispute', *Reuters*, 5 January 2021, https://www.reuters.com/article/us-gulf-summit-emira tes-idUSKBN29A279.

19 Andrew England, 'Qatar Says Deal to End Gulf Crisis Will Not Changes Its Ties with Iran', *Financial Times*, 7 January 2021, https://www.ft.com/cont ent/ea1e7058-960d-416c-93dc-f4f8c7945c12.

20 'Manama Responds To Doha's Provocation with New Documentary', *Arab Weekly*, 22 March 2021, https://thearabweekly.com/manama-respo nds-dohas-provocation-new-documentary.

21 Author interview with an advisor to Al Jazeera, Doha, 24 March 2022.

22 Nader Kabbani, 'The High Cost of High Stakes: Economic Implications of the 2017 Gulf Crisis', *Markaz – Brookings Institute*, 15 June 2017, https://www.brookings.edu/blog/markaz/2017/06/15/the-high-cost-of-high-sta kes-economic-implications-of-the-2017-gulf-crisis/.

23 Ibid.

24 Paul Danahar, *The New Middle East: The World After the Arab Spring* (London: Bloomsbury, 2013), 237.

25 Author interview with Qatari experts, officials and academics, Doha, May 2016.

26 Author interview with Abdullah Baabood, former professor, Qatar University, Doha, 15 May 2016.

27 Kamrava, *Qatar – Small State, Big Politics*.

28 Ibid.

29 Hela Miniaoui, Patrick Irungu, Simeon Kaitibie, 'Contemporary Issues in Qatar's Food Security', *Middle East Insights No. 185*, Middle East Institute Singapore, 31 May 2018, 3.

30 Ibid., 5.

31 Ibid.

32 'Iran Sends Five Planes of Vegetables to Help Qatar after Five Arab Nations Cut Ties over "Extremism" Links', *The Telegraph*, 11 June 2017, https://www.telegraph.co.uk/news/2017/06/11/iran-sends-five-planes-vegetab les-qatar/.

33 'How Turkey Stood by Qatar Amid the Gulf Crisis', *Al Jazeera*, 14 November 2017, https://www.aljazeera.com/news/2017/11/14/how-tur key-stood-by-qatar-amid-the-gulf-crisis.

34 Ibid.

35 Thierry Colville, 'Update on Trade Relations between UAE/Iran and Qatar/ Iran', Fondation pour la Recherche Strategique, April 2019, https://www.frst rategie.org/web/documents/programmes/observatoire-du-monde-arabo-musulman-et-du-sahel/publications/en/201915.pdf.

36 'Qatar's Hamad Port Breaks Blockade with Five New Shipping Lines', *Albawaba*, 20 July 2017, https://www.albawaba.com/business/qat ars-hamad-port-breaks-blockade-five-new-shipping-lines-999642

37 'Qatar Opens New $7.4 Billion Port in Bid to Circumvent Blockade', *Reuters*, 5 September 2017, https://www.dailysabah.com/mide ast/2017/09/05/qatar-opens-new-74-billion-port-in-bid-to-circumvent-blockade.

38 'Food Production in Qatar Grows by 400% since 2017', *The Peninsula*, 13 March 2017, https://thepeninsulaqatar.com/article/13/03/2019/Food-pro duction-in-Qatar-grows-by-400-since-2017.

39 Laura Wellesly, 'How Qatar's Food System Has Adapted to the Blockade', Chatham House, 14 November 2019, https://www.chathamhouse. org/2019/11/how-qatars-food-system-has-adapted-blockade.

40 Eric Knecht, 'With Cows, Chickens and Greenhouses, Qatar Takes on Regional Boycott', *Reuters*, 5 June 2019, https://www.reuters.com/article/ us-gulf-qatar/with-cows-chickens-and-greenhouses-qatar-takes-on-regio nal-boycott-idUSKCN1T6165.

41 Round table with Qatari officials hosted by RUSI, London, 20 February 2020; author interview with Qatari official, London, 3 March 2020.

42 Round table with Qatari officials hosted by RUSI, London, 20 February 2020.

43 Andrew England, 'Qatar Says Deal to End Gulf Crisis Will Not Change Its Ties to Iran'.

44 Ibid.

45 Author interview with academic, Qatar University, Doha, 24 March 2022.

46 Taimoor Shah and Rod Nordland, 'U.S. Diplomats Held Face-to-Face Talks with Taliban, Insurgents Say', *New York Times*, 28 July 2018, https://www. nytimes.com/2018/07/28/world/asia/us-taliban-afghanistan-talks.html.

47 Agreement for Bringing Peace to Afghanistan, US State Department, 29 February 2020, https://www.state.gov/wp-content/uploads/2020/02/ Agreement-For-Bringing-Peace-to-Afghanistan-02.29.20.pdf.

48 Remarks by Secretary Blinken at a joint press conference, US State Department, Doha, Qatar, 7 September 2021, https://www.state.gov/secret ary-antony-j-blinken-and-secretary-of-defense-lloyd-j-austin-qatari-dep uty-prime-minister-and-foreign-minister-mohammed-bin-abdulrah man-al-thani-and-qatari-deputy-prime-minister-and-defense/.

49 'Qatar Calls Taliban Moves on Girls Education "Very Disappointing"', *Al Jazeera*, 30 September 2021, https://www.aljazeera.com/news/2021/9/30/ qatar-taliban-afghanistan-eu-borrell.

50 Author interview with Qatari advisor to government, Doha, 25 March 2022.

51 Author interview with academic, Qatar University, Doha, 24 March 2022; author interview with an advisor to Al Jazeera, Doha, 24 March 2022.

52 Marwa Rashad, Davide Barbuschia, Hadeel Al Sayegh, 'Analysis: Saudi Arabia Eyes Dubai's Crown with HQ Ultimatum', *Reuters*, 16 February 2021, https://www.reuters.com/article/us-saudi-economy-emirates-analy sis-idUSKBN2AG1I5.

53 Aziz El Yaakoubi, Marwa Rashad and Davide Barbuschia, 'Saudi Arabia Amends Import Rules from Gulf in Challenge to the UAE', *Reuters*, 5 July 2021, https://www.reuters.com/world/middle-east/saudi-arabia-amends- import-rules-gulf-challenge-uae-2021-07-05/.

54 Author interview with Emirati experts, officials and academics, Abu Dhabi and Dubai (2021–2).

55 Author round table with regional experts and analysts, Emirati think tank, Dubai, 29 February 2017.

56   Statement by a regional analyst, Regional focus group involving officials and established regional academics, Dubai, 19 April 2016.

57   Christin Marschall, *Iran's Persian Gulf Policy: From Khomeini to Khatami* (Oxon: Routledge, 2003), 76, 97.

58   Ibid., 169.

59   Author interview with Mahjoob Zweiri, professor, Qatar University, Dubai, 19 April 2016.

60   Author interview with Iranian Ministry of Foreign Affairs official, phone interview, 19 May 2016.

61   Author interview with senior Iranian official, Berlin, 26 June 2017.

62   Author round table with two Iranian officials and a former Iranian ambassador, Oslo, 8 March 2019.

63   Author interview with Iranian Ministry of Foreign Affairs official, phone interview, 19 May 2016; Statement by Alex Vatanka, senior fellow, Middle East Institute, at Middle East Institute webinar on 'Covid-19, Oil Prices, and Prospects for Iran-GCC Relations', 6 May 2020.

64   Author interview with Iranian officials, Berlin, Oslo, New York, London (2016–19).

65   'Iran Sends Five Planes of Vegetables to Help Qatar after Five Arab Nations Cut Ties over "Extremism" Links'.

66   Tweet by Iranian Foreign Minister Zarif, 5 June 2017.

67   Author interview with the director of an Emirati think tank, Dubai, 1 March 2017.

68   Author interview with senior Iranian official, Berlin, 26 June 2017.

69   Ben Hubbard, Palko Karasz and Stanley Reed, 'Two Major Saudi Oil Installations Hit by Drone Strike, and U.S. Blames Iran', *New York Times*, 14 September 2019, https://www.nytimes.com/2019/09/14/world/middleeast/saudi-arabia-refineries-drone-attack.html.

70   Humeyra Pamuk, 'Exclusive: U.S. Probe of Saudi Oil Attack Shows It Came from North – Report', *Reuters*, 19 December 2019, https://www.reuters.com/article/us-saudi-aramco-attacks-iran-exclusive-idUSKBN1YN299.

71   Author interview with military official, Abu Dhabi, 24 November 2021.

72   Ibid.

73   'Qatar Sends More Medical Aid to Iran', *Gulf Times*, 24 April 2020, https://www.gulf-times.com/story/661562/Qatar-sends-more-medical-aid-to-Iran.

74   'Kuwait Sends Aid to Iran to Fight Coronavirus', *Islamic Republic News Agency*, 17 March 2020, https://en.irna.ir/news/83718426/Kuwait-sends-aid-to-Iran-to-fight-coronavirus.

75   'UAE Sends Supplied to Aid Iran in Coronavirus Fight', *Arab News*, 17 March 2020, https://www.arabnews.com/node/1642546/middle-east.

76   Artemis Moshtaghian, 'Iran Threatens to Attach Dubai and Haifa If Country Is Bombed', *CNN News Updates*, 7 January 2020, https://edition.cnn.com/middleeast/live-news/us-iran-soleimani-tensions-intl-01-07-20/h_ec2a577fe833946485ca681a584d980a.

77   Rory Jones and Benoit Faucon, 'Iran, UAE Discuss Maritime Security Amid Heightened Tensions in the Gulf', *Wall Street Journal*, 30 July 2019.

78 'In rare talks, Iran and UAE Foreign Ministers Discuss COVID-19', *Al Jazeera*, 2 August 2020, https://www.aljazeera.com/news/2020/8/2/in-rare-talks-iran-and-uae-foreign-ministers-discuss-covid-19.

79 See Chapter 5.

80 Author interview with Emirati official, Abu Dhabi, 9 March 2022.

81 Author interview with Emirati official, Abu Dhabi, 24 November 2021.

82 Author interview with Emirati official, Abu Dhabi, 9 March 2022.

83 Ibid.

84 Author interview with experts, academics, officials and the military, Abu Dhabi, Dubai, Doha, Kuwait City and Muscat (2014–22).

Conclusion

1 See, for example, Vali Nasr, *The Shia Revival: How Conflicts within Islam Will Shape the Future* (New York: W. W. Norton, 2006); Simon Mabon, *Saudi Arabia and Iran: Power and Rivalry in the Middle East* (London: I.B. Tauris, 2013); Toby Matthiesen, *Sectarian Gulf: Bahrain, Saudi Arabia and the Arab Spring That Wasn't* (Stanford, CA: Stanford University Press, 2013); Frederic M. Wehrey, *Sectarian Politics in the Gulf: From the Iraq War to the Arab Uprisings* (New York: Columbia University Press, 2014); Markus Kaim, *Great Powers and Regional Orders* (Aldershot: Taylor & Francis, 2008); Steven W. Hook and Tim Niblock (eds), *The United States and the Gulf: Shifting Pressures, Strategies and Alignments* (Berlin: Gerlach Press, 2015); Steve A. Yetiv, *America and the Persian Gulf: The Third Party Dimension in World Politics* (Westport, CT: Praeger, 1995).

2 Eleonora Ardemadni, 'UAE's Military Priorities in Yemen: Counterterrorism and the South', ISPI Commentary, 28 July 2016, https://www.ispionline.it/sites/default/files/pubblicazioni/commentary_ardemagni_28_07.2016.pdf.

3 Author interviews with GCC lawmakers, officials, experts and academics, Dubai, Abu Dhabi, Muscat, Doha and Kuwait City (2014–22).

4 Ibid.

5 Ibid.

6 Ibid.

7 Toby Matthiesen, 'Renting the Casbah', in Kristian Coates Ulrichsen (ed.), *The Changing Security Dynamics of the Persian Gulf* (London: Hurst, 2017), 46.

8 David D. Kirkpatrick, 'Who Is Behind Trump's Links to Arab Princes? A Billionaire Friend', *New York Times*, 13 June 2018, https://www.nytimes.com/2018/06/13/world/middleeast/trump-tom-barrack-saudi.html; Kenneth P. Vogel, 'How a Trump Ally Tested the Boundaries of

Washington's Influence Game', *New York Times*, 13 August 2019, https://www.nytimes.com/2019/08/13/us/politics/elliott-broidy-trump.html.

9 See, for example, Alex Emmons, Mathew Cole, 'UAE Enlisted Business to Spy on Trump White House', *The Intercept*, 10 June 2019, https://theinterc ept.com/2019/06/10/trump-uae-businessman-spy/; Sharon LaFraniere, Maggie Haberman, Adam Goldman, 'Trump Inaugural Fund and Super PAC Said to Be Scrutinized for Illegal Foreign Donations', *New York Times*, 13 December 2018, https://www.nytimes.com/2018/12/13/polit ics/trump-inauguration-investigation.html; Sharon LaFraniere, Maggie Habberman, William K. Rashburn, Ben Protess and David K. Kirkpatrick, 'Trump Friend's Ties to Mideast at Heart of Lobbying Enquiry', *New York Times*, 28 July 2019, https://www.nytimes.com/2019/07/28/us/politics/ thomas-barrack-foreign-lobbying.html; 'Trump & the UAE: Connecting the Dots', *Al Jazeera*, 6 April 2018, https://www.aljazeera.com/ news/2018/04/mueller-web-trump-uae-connection-180405113651605. html; Mark Mazzetti, David K. Kirkpatrick and Maggie Haberman, 'Mueller's Focus on Advisor to Emirates Suggest Broader Investigation', *New York Times*, 3 March 2018, https://www.nytimes.com/2018/03/03/ us/politics/george-nader-mueller-investigation-united-arab-emirates. html?smid=tw-bna; Terry Gross, 'UAE's Prince Mohammed Bin Zayed's Growing Influence on the U.S.', *NPR's Fresh Air*, 6 June 2019, https://www. npr.org/2019/06/06/730339596/uaes-prince-mohammed-bin-zayed-s-grow ing-influence-on-the-u-s?t=1565775891581.

10 Jonathan Fenton-Harvey, 'Saudi Arabia and the UAE Fund Academia with Strings Attached', *LobeLog*, 28 August 2019, https://lobelog.com/saudi-ara bia-and-the-uae-fund-academia-with-strings-attached/.

11 Matthew Hedges, 'An Ally Held Me as a Spy – And the West Is Complicit', *The Atlantic*, 25 January 2019, https://www.theatlantic.com/internatio nal/archive/2019/01/matthew-hedges-uae-held-me-spy-west-compli cit/581200/.

12 'NYU Journalism Department Cuts Ties to NYU Abu Dhabi', *Associated Press*, 5 November 2017, https://www.apnews.com/03d65fe3ab40437da da3dd5e7acfd406.

13 David Kenner, 'The Selective Westernization of NYU's Abu Dhabi Campus', *The Atlantic*, 10 May 2018, https://www.theatlantic.com/education/ archive/2018/05/the-selective-westernization-of-nyus-abu-dhabi-cam pus/560096/.

14 See, for example, Ryan Grim, 'Gulf Government Gave Secret $20 Million Gift to D.C. Think Tank', *The Intercept*, 10 August 2017, https:// theintercept.com/2017/08/09/gulf-government-gave-secret-20-mill ion-gift-to-d-c-think-tank/; Eric Lipton, Brooke Williams and Nicholas Confessor, 'Foreign Power Buy Influence at Think Tanks', *New York Times*, 6 September 2014, https://www.nytimes.com/2014/09/07/us/politics/ foreign-powers-buy-influence-at-think-tanks.html; Andrew England and Simeon Kerr, 'Universities Challenged: Scrutiny over Gulf Money',

Financial Times, 13 December 2018, https://www.ft.com/content/fa6d1
5a4-f6ed-11e8-af46-2022a0b02a6c.

15 Sabrina Siddiqui, 'Leading Liberal Thinktank Will No Longer Accept
Funds from UAE', *The Guardian*, 25 January 2019, https://www.theguard
ian.com/us-news/2019/jan/25/united-arab-emirates-funding-center-for-
american-progress.

16 Robbie Gramer and Amy Mackinnon, 'Congress Is Finally Done with
the War in Yemen', *Foreign Policy*, 4 April 2019, https://foreignpolicy.
com/2019/04/04/congress-makes-history-war-yemen-powers-bill/.

17 Joe Gould, 'Key US Democrat Holds Back Support for Gulf Munitions
Sales over Yemen', *DefenseNews*, 3 July 2018, https://www.defensenews.
com/congress/2018/07/03/key-us-democrat-holds-back-support-for-gulf-
munitions-sales-over-yemen/.

18 Patricia Zengerle, 'Defying Congress, Trump Sets $8 Billion-Plus in
Weapons Sales to Saudi Arabia, UAE', *Reuters*, 24 May 2019, https://uk.reut
ers.com/article/uk-usa-saudi-arms/defying-congress-trump-sets-8-bill
ion-plus-in-weapons-sales-to-saudi-arabia-uae-idUKKCN1SU25P.

19 Joe Gould, 'US House Votes to Block Saudi, UAE Arms Sales, Bucking
Trump Veto Threat', *DefenseNews*, 17 July 2019, https://www.defensenews.
com/congress/2019/07/17/us-house-votes-to-block-saudi-uae-arms-sales-
bucking-trump-veto-threat/.

20 Robbie Gramer and Jack Detsche, 'Senate Effort to Stop Trump Arms
Sales to UAE Fails', *Foreign Policy*, 9 December 2020, https://foreignpol
icy.com/2020/12/09/senate-vote-uae-trump-arms-sales-gulf-secur
ity-iran-f-35-drones-middle-east-democrats-biden/.

21 'Dozens of Rights Groups Denounce US Arms Sales to UAE', *Al Jazeera*,
1 December 2020, https://www.aljazeera.com/news/2020/12/1/fuel
ing-harm-us-arms-sales-to-uae-decried-by-29-rights-groups.

22 Matthew Lee, 'US Puts Hold on Foreign Arms Sales, including F-35s
to UAE', AP News, 27 January 2021, https://apnews.com/article/don
ald-trump-politics-united-arab-emirates-b35347c143dcd5a5980b4b886
363c293.

23 Patricia Zengerle, 'Biden Administration Proceeding with $23 Billion
Weapons Sales to UAE', *Reuters*, 14 April 2021, https://www.reuters.com/
business/aerospace-defense/exclusive-biden-administration-proceed
ing-with-23-billion-weapon-sales-uae-2021-04-13/; 'American Official: US
"Fully Committed" to F-35 Sale to UAE', *AP News*, 16 November 2021,
https://www.independent.co.uk/news/joe-biden-american-united-arab-
emirates-saudi-arabia-russia-b1958576.html.

24 Andrew England and Simeon Kerr, 'UAE Suspends Talks with US over
Purchase of F-35 Fighter Jets', *Financial Times*, 14 December 2021, https://
www.ft.com/content/7ab35684-d536-4908-89d6-a730d844c8d6.

25 Statements by Anthony Zinni, former commander of all US forces in the
Middle East, and General James Mattis, quoted in Rajiv Chandrasekaran,
'In the UAE, the United States Has a Quiet, Potent Ally Nicknamed "Little

Sparta"', *Washington Post*, 9 November 2014, https://www.washingtonpost. com/world/national-security/in-the-uae-the-united-states-has-a-quiet-pot ent-ally-nicknamed-little-sparta/2014/11/08/3fc6a50c-643a-11e4-836c-83b c4f26eb67_story.html.

26 Chris Mulls Rodrigo, 'Graham: "I've Got a Real Problem" with Arms Sales to Saudi Arabia', *The Hill*, 26 May 2019, https://thehill.com/ homenews/sunday-talk-shows/445584-graham-i-got-a-real-prob lem-with-arms-sales-to-saudi-arabia.

27 See, for example, Helen Davidson and Christopher Knaus, 'Australian Weapons Shipped to Saudi and UAE as War Rages in Yemen', *The Guardian*, 25 July 2019, https://www.theguardian.com/austra lia-news/2019/jul/25/australian-weapons-shipped-to-saudi-and-uae-as-wa r-rages-in-yemen; Anna Stavrianakis, 'UK Arms Exports Are Still Playing a Central Role in Yemen's Humanitarian Crisis', *The Guardian*, 21 May 2019, https://www.theguardian.com/global-development/2019/may/21/mps-thanking-jeremy-hunt-efforts-peace-in-yemen.

28 See Chapter 5.

29 Round table with senior Qatari Ministry of Foreign Affairs official, London, 20 February 2020.

30 Author interview with Abdullah Baabood, former professor, Qatar University, Doha, London, 28 February 2020.

31 Author interview with a former GCC official, Muscat, 5 March 2017.

32 Ibid.

33 Ibid.

34 Author interview with Omani official, Muscat, 5 March 2017.

35 Author interview with Omani Royal Court official, Muscat, 30 November 2021.

36 Author interview with advisor, Al Jazeera, 24 March 2022.

37 Ibid.

38 Author interview with Abdullah Baabood, former professor, Qatar University, Doha London, 28 February 2020.

39 Author interview with former Emirati national security advisor, New York, 31 October 2019.

40 Statement by Samir Madani in 'UAE Foreign Policy: Beyond the Gulf', Gulf 2000 Webinar, 2 July 2020.

41 Steering Libya Past Another Perilous Crossroad, International Crisis Group Briefing, Number 85, 18 March 2022, https://www.crisisgroup.org/mid dle-east-north-africa/north-africa/libya/b85-steering-libya-past-another-perilous-crossroads.

42 Author interview with Emirati official, Abu Dhabi, 24 November 2021.

43 Statement by Kristian Coates Ulrichsen in 'UAE Foreign Policy: Beyond the Gulf', Gulf 2000 Webinar, 2 July 2020.

44 Kristian Coates Ulrichsen, 'Punching above Its Weight', interview by Michael Young, *Diwan*, Carnegie Middle East Center, 29 June 2020, https:// carnegie-mec.org/diwan/82200, 229.

45   Clark Mindock, 'US Deploys Thousands More Troops to the Middle East after Trump-Ordered Airstrike Kills Iran General', *The Independent*, 3 January 2020, https://www.independent.co.uk/news/world/americas/us-politics/us-iran-war-trump-soleimani-troops-middle-east-pentagon-embassy-airstrike-a9269791.html.

46   'Qasem Soleimani: Iran Vows "Severe Revenge" for Top General's Death', *BBC News*, 3 January 2020, https://www.bbc.co.uk/news/world-middle-east-50986185.

47   Author interview with former Emirati national security advisor, New York, 31 October 2019.

48   Author interview with high-level military official, Abu Dhabi, 24 November 2021.

49   Author interview with Emirati officials and experts, Dubai and Abu Dhabi (2021–2); Kirsten Fontenrose, 'What the Arab Gulf Is Thinking after the Afghanistan Withdrawal', *The Atlantic Council – The New Atlanticist*, 23 September 2021, https://www.atlanticcouncil.org/blogs/new-atlanticist/what-the-arab-gulf-is-thinking-after-the-afghanistan-withdrawal/.

50   Andrew England and Simeon Kerr, ' "More of China, Less of America": How Superpower Fight Is Squeezing the Gulf', *Financial Times*, 20 September 2021, https://www.ft.com/content/4f82b560-4744-4c53-bf4b-7a37d3afeb13.

51   Author interview with Emirati officials and experts, Dubai and Abu Dhabi, March 2022.

52   Author interview with Emirati official, Abu Dhabi, 9 March 2022.

53   Author interview with Emirati officials and experts, Dubai and Abu Dhabi, November 2021 and March 2022.

54   Author interview with Emirati official, Abu Dhabi, 24 November 2021.

55   Ibid.

56   Author interview with Abdulkhaleq Abdulla, Emirati academic, Dubai, 23 November 2021.

57   Author interview with Emirati foreign ministry official, Abu Dhabi, 24 November 2021.

58   Author interview with Emirati official, Abu Dhabi, 24 November 2021.

59   Author interview with Emirati foreign policy analyst, Dubai, 23 November 2021.

60   Author interview with Emirati official, Abu Dhabi, 24 November 2021.

61   Round table with senior Qatari Ministry of Foreign Affairs official, London, 20 February 2020; author interview with Qatari official, London, 3 March 2020.

SELECT BIBLIOGRAPHY

Books

Aarts, Paul, and Carolien Roelants. *Saudi Arabia – A Kingdom in Peril.*
London: Hurst, 2015.

Abdullah, Adel Ali. *The Drivers of Iranian Policy in the Arabian Gulf* (in Arabic).
Al Tanweer Centre for the Studies of Humanities, 2008.

Abrahamian, Ervand. *Khomeinism: Essays on the Islamic Republic.*
Berkeley: University of California Press, 1993.

Allen, Calvin H., and W. Lynn Rigsbee II. *Oman under Qaboos: From Coup to
Constitution, 1970–1996.* London: Routledge, 2013.

Allison, Graham. *Essence of Decision: Explaining the Cuban Missile Crisis.*
Boston, MA: Little, Brown, 1971.

Almezaini, Khalid S., and Jean-Marc Rickli (eds). *The Small Gulf
States: Foreign and Security Policies Before and After the Arab Spring.*
London: Routledge, 2017.

Alsultan, Fahad M., and Pedram Saeid. *The Development of Saudi-Iranian
Relations since the 1990s: Between Conflict and Accommodation.*
London: Routledge, 2017.

Askari, Hossein. *Collaborative Colonialism: The Political Economy of Oil in the
Persian Gulf.* New York: Palgrave Macmillan, 2013.

Bradley, John R. *Saudi Arabia Exposed – Inside a Kingdom in Crisis.*
Basingstoke: Palgrave Macmillan, 2005.

Chubin, Shahram, and Charles Tripp. 'Iran-Saudi Arabia Relations and Regional
Order', *IISS Adelphi Paper* 304 (1996).

Commins, David. *The Gulf States: A Modern History.* London: I.B. Tauris, 2012.

Cooper, Andrew Scott. *The Oil Kings: How the U.S., Iran and Saudi Arabia
Changed the Balance of Power in the Middle East.* New York: Simon &
Schuster, 2011.

Davidson, Christopher M. (ed.), *Power and Politics in the Persian Gulf
Monarchies.* London: Hurst, 2011.

Davidson, Christopher M. *After the Sheikhs: The Coming Collapse of the Gulf
Monarchies.* London: Hurst, 2012.

Dockrill, Michael. *British Defence since 1945.* London: John Wiley, 1989.

Gause III, F. Gregory. *The International Relations of the Persian Gulf*. Cambridge: Cambridge University Press, 2010.

George, Alexander L., and Juliette L. George. *Presidential Personality and Performance*. London: Routledge, 1998.

Glaser, Charles L., and Rosemary A. Kelanic (eds). *Crude Strategy: Rethinking the US Military Commitment to Defend Persian Gulf Oil*. Washington, DC: Georgetown University Press, 2016.

Halperin, Morton H., Priscilla Clapp and Arnold Kanter. *Bureaucratic Politics and Foreign Policy*. Washington, DC: Brookings Institution Press, 2006.

Hanna, Michael Wahid, and Thanassis Cambinis (eds). *Order from Ashes: New Foundations for Security in the Middle East*. New York: Century Foundation, 2018.

Hashemi, Nader, and Danny Poste led. *Sectarianization: Mapping the New Politics of the Middle East*. Oxford: Oxford University Press, 2017.

Hertog, Steffan. *Princes, Brokers, and Bureaucrats: Oil and the State in Saudi Arabia*. Ithaca, NY: Cornell University Press, 2010.

Hook, Steven W., and Tim Niblock (eds). *The United States and the Gulf: Shifting Pressures, Strategies and Alignments*. Berlin: Gerlach Press, 2015.

Jervis, Robert. *Perception and Misperception in International Politics*. Princeton, NJ: Princeton University Press, 1976.

Jones, Toby Craig. *Desert Kingdom: How Oil and Water Forged Modern Saudi Arabia*. Cambridge, MA: Harvard University Press, 2010.

Lacey, Robert. *Inside the Kingdom: Kings, Clerics, Modernists, Terrorists and the Struggle for Saudi Arabia*. London: Penguin, 2009.

Kadhim, Abbas. *Governance in the Middle East: A Handbook*. London: Routledge, 2013.

Kaim, Markus. *Great Powers and Regional Orders*. Aldershot: Taylor & Francis, 2008.

Kamrava, Mehran. *Qatar – Small State, Big Politics*. Ithaca, NY: Cornell University Press, 2013.

Kamrava, Mehran (ed.). *Beyond the Arab Spring: The Evolving Ruling Bargain in the Middle East*. Oxford: Oxford University Press, 2014.

Kaynoush, Banafsheh. *Saudi Arabia and Iran: Friends or Foes?* London: Palgrave Macmillan, 2016.

Krane, Jim. *Energy Kingdoms: Oil and Political Survival in the Persian Gulf*. New York: Columbia University Press, 2019.

Legrenzi, Matteo. *The GCC and the International Relations of the Gulf – Diplomacy, Security, and Economic Coordination in a Changing Middle East*. London: I.B. Tauris, 2015.

Lynch, Marc. *The Arab Uprising – The Unfinished Revolutions of the New Middle East*. New York: Public Affairs, 2012.

Lynch, March. *The New Arab Wars – Uprisings and Anarchy in the Middle East*. New York: Public Affairs, 2016.

Mabon, Simon. *Saudi Arabia and Iran: Power and Rivalry in the Middle East*. London: I.B. Tauris, 2013.

Matthiesen, Toby. *Sectarian Gulf: Bahrain, Saudi Arabia and the Arab Spring That Wasn't*. Stanford, CA: Stanford University Press, 2013.

Matthiesen, Toby. *The Other Saudis: Shiism, Dissent and Sectarianism*. Cambridge: Cambridge University Press, 2015.

McNaugher, Thomas L. *Arms and Oil: US Military Strategy and the Persian Gulf*. Washington, DC: Brookings Institution, 1985.

Milani, Abbas. *The Shah*. New York: St Martin's Press, 2012.

Narizny, Kevin. *The Political Economy of Grand Strategy*. Ithaca, NY: Cornell University Press, 2007.

Nasr, Vali. *The Shia Revival: How Conflicts within Islam Will Shape the Future*. New York: W.W. Norton, 2006.

Nonneman, Gerd(ed.). *Analyzing Middle East Foreign Policies and the Relationship with Europe*. London: Routledge, 2005.

Odysseous, Louiza. *The Subject of Coexistence: Otherness in International Relations*. Minnesota: University of Minnesota Press, 2007.

Pahlavi, Mohammed Reza. *Answer to History*. New York: Stein & Day, 1980.

Peden, G. C. *Arms, Economics and British Strategy: From Dreadnoughts to Hydrogen Bombs*. Cambridge: Cambridge University Press, 2007.

Post, Jerrold M. *The Psychological Assessment of Political Leaders: With Profiles of Saddam Hussein and Bill Clinton*. Ann Arbor: University of Michigan Press, 2005.

Rogan, Eugene. *The Arabs – A History*. New York: Basic Books, 2009.

al Suwaidi, Jamal S. *Iran and the Gulf: A Search for Stability*. Abu Dhabi: Emirates Center for Strategic Studies and Research, 1996.

Ulrichsen, Kristian Coates (ed.). *The Changing Security Dynamics of the Persian Gulf*. London: Hurst, 2017.

Ulrichsen, Kristian Coates. *The United Arab Emirates – Power, Politics, and Policymaking*. Abingdon: Routledge, 2017.

Wehrey, Frederic M. *Sectarian Politics in the Gulf: From the Iraq War to the Arab Uprisings*. New York: Columbia University Press, 2014.

Winfield, Richard Dien. *Freedom and Modernity*. New York: State University of New York Press, 1991.

Yergin, Daniel. *The Prize: The Epic Quest for Oil, Money and Power*. New York: Free Press, 1991.

Yetiv, Steve A. *America and the Persian Gulf: The Third Party Dimension in World Politics*. Westport, CT: Praeger, 1995.

Zahlan, Rosemarie Said. *The Making of the Modern Gulf States: Kuwait, Bahrain, Qatar, the United Arab Emirates and Oman*. London: Routledge, 2016.

Journal articles

Chen, Dinding, and Xiaoyu Pu, 'Correspondence: Debating China's Assertiveness', *International Security*, vol. 38, no. 3 (Winter 2013/14): 176–83.

Darvishi, Farhad, and Ameneh Jalilvand, 'Impacts of US Military Presence in the Arabic Countries in the Persian Gulf', *Geopolitics Quarterly*, vol. 6, no. 4 (Winter 2010): 168–80.

Friedberg, Aaron L. 'The Sources of Chinese Conduct: Explaining Beijing's Assertiveness', *Washington Quarterly*, vol. 37, no. 4 (2014): 133–50.

Greenwood, David. 'Constraints and Choices in the Transformation of Britain's Defence Effort since 1945', *Review of International Studies*, vol. 2, no. 1 (April 1976): 5–26.

Johnston, Alastair Iain. 'How New and Assertive is China's New Assertiveness?' *International Security*, vol. 37, no. 4 (Spring 2013): 7–48.

Li, Mingjiang. 'Reconciling Assertiveness and Cooperation? China's Changing Approach to the South China Sea Dispute', *Security Challenges*, vol. 6, no. 2 (Winter 2010): 49–68.

Longinotti, Edward. 'Britain's Withdrawal from East of Suez: From Economic Determinism to Political Choice', *Contemporary British History*, vol. 29, no. 3 (2015): 318–40.

Mearsheimer, John J. 'The Gathering Storm: China's Challenge to US Power in Asia', *Chinese Journal of International Politics*, vol. 3, no. 4 (Winter 2010): 381–96.

Raine, Sarah. 'Beijing's South China Sea Debate', *Survival*, vol. 53, no. 5 (2011): 69–88.

Sato, Shohei. 'Britain's Decision to Withdraw from the Persian Gulf 1964–68: A Pattern and a Puzzle', *Journal of Imperial and Commonwealth History*, vol. 37, no. 1 (2009): 99–117.

Smith, Simon C. 'Britain's Decision to Withdraw from the Persian Gulf: A Pattern Not a Puzzle', *Journal of Imperial and Commonwealth History*, vol. 2, no. 44 (2016): 328–51.

Thayer, Carlyle A. 'The United States and Chinese Assertiveness in the South China Sea', *Security Challenges*, vol. 6, no. 2 (Winter 2010): 69–84.

Yahuda, Michael. 'China's New Assertiveness in the South China Sea', *Journal of Contemporary China*, vol. 22, no. 81 (2013): 446–59.

Papers/reports

Ardemadni, Eleonora. 'UAE's Military Priorities in Yemen: Counterterrorism and the South', *ISPI Commentary*, 28 July 2016, https://www.ispionline.it/sites/default/files/pubblicazioni/commentary_ardemagni_28_07.2016.pdf.

Barzegar, Kayhan. 'Balance of Power in the Persian Gulf: An Iranian View', *Middle East Policy*, vol. 17, no. 3 (Fall 2010): 74–87.

Guzansky, Yoel, and Nizan Feldman, 'Plunging Oil Prices: The Challenge for the Gulf Oil Economies', INSS Insight, no. 675, 22 March 2015.

Al-Khatteeb, Luay. 'Gulf Oil Economies Must Wake Up or Face Decades of Decline', Middle East Economic Survey, 14 August 2015.

Lbish, Hussein. 'The UAE's Evolving National Security Strategy', The Arab
    Gulf States Institute in Washington Report, 6 April 2017, https://agsiw.org/
    wp-content/uploads/2017/04/UAE-Security_ONLINE.pdf.
Roberts, David B. 'Qatar's Domestic Stability and the Gulf Crisis', The
    Washington Institute Policy Watch 2847, 18 August 2017.
Sadjadpour, Karim. 'The Battle of Dubai: The United Arab Emirates and the
    U.S.-Iran Cold War', The Carnegie Papers (2011).
Wehrey, Frederic, Theodore W. Karasik, Alireza Nader, Jeremy Ghez, Lydia
    Hansell and Robert A. Guffey, Saudi-Iranian Relations since the Fall of
    Saddam (RAND, 2009).
Wehrey, Frederic, David E. Thaler, Nora Bensahel, Kim Cragin, Jerrold D.
    Green, Dalia Dassa Kaye, Nadia Oweidat and Jennifer Li, Dangerous but
    Not Omnipotent: Exploring the Reach and Limitations of Iranian Power in the
    Middle East. Santa Monica, CA: RAND, 2009.
Westphal, Kirsten, Marco Oberhaus and Guido Steinberg, 'The US Shale
    Revolution and the Arab Gulf States: The Economic and Political Impact of
    Changing Energy Markets', SWP Research Paper, November 2014.
'Neo-Piracy in Oman and the Gulf: The Origins of British Imperialism in the
    Gulf', MERIP Reports, no. 36 (1975).

Speeches

Supreme Leader Ayatollah Ruhollah Khomeini. 'We Shall Confront the World
    with Our Ideology', speech on Radio Tehran, 21 March 1980.

Official documents

(Supreme Leader Ayatollah Ruhollah) Imam Khomeini. Governance of
    the Jurist: Islamic Government. Tehran: The Institute for Compilation
    and Publication of Imam Khomeini's Works – International Affairs
    Department, 1970.
The Question of Bahrain, UN Security Council Resolution 278, 11 May 1970,
    http://unscr.com/en/resolutions/doc/278 (accessed 6 July 2022).
UAE Cable. 'Abu Dhabi Crown Prince Warns DOE DepSec Poneman about
    Iran', 17 December 2009.
US Department of State. 'Strong Words in Private from MBZ at IDEX – Bashes
    Iran, Qatar, Russia', 25 February 2009.
US Department of State. 'US-UAE Cooperation against Taliban Finance
    Continues', 24 January 2010.

INDEX

2008 Financial crisis 15, 32
2017 GCC split 8, 99, 101, 102–3, 105, 110–11, 113, 124

9/11 30, 33, 59, 80, 142, 209

Abdulla, Abdulkhaleq 16, 19, 81, 90
al Nahyan, Abdullah bin Zayed 85, 96, 112
al Nahyan, Khalifa bin Zayed 52
al Nahyan, Mohammed bin Zayed (MBZ) 5–6, 82, 86, 88, 92, 111, 119, 121
al Nahyan, Tahnoon bin Zayed 86, 104
al Nahyan, Zayed bin Sultan 6
Abraham Accords 84
Abu Dhabi 1, 3, 4, 6, 9, 12, 15, 16, 22, 36, 39, 40, 41, 43, 47, 48, 49, 50, 51, 52, 53, 57, 58, 59, 60, 61, 62, 63, 64, 65, 66, 68, 69, 70, 71, 72, 73, 74, 75, 76, 77, 78, 79, 80, 81, 82, 83, 85, 86, 88, 89, 90, 91, 92, 93, 94, 95, 96, 97, 99, 100, 104, 106, 118, 124
Aden 75
Afghanistan 27, 30, 31, 33, 34, 35, 41, 107, 108, 121, 122
Ahmadinejad, Mahmoud 20, 48
Al Islah 16, 73–4
Al Jazeera 14, 104, 108
Al Otaiba, Youssef 50, 67, 68, 87
Al Qaeda 30, 74, 104
Al Saud family 1, 44
al Thani, Khalifa bin Hamad 2, 104
al Thani, Sheikh Mohammed bin Abdulrahman 103, 107

Al Ula agreement 8, 103, 104, 107, 109, 119
Arak heavy water reactor 45, 46
al Assad, Bashar 20, 23, 83, 84, 85, 86, 144, 204

Bab al Mandab 74, 89
Bahrain 2, 3, 14, 15, 21, 24, 30, 40, 75, 94, 100, 101, 102, 104
Belt and Road initiative 82
Ben Ali, Zine el Abidine 17
Biden, Joe 39, 108, 118, 121
bin Said, Qaboos 2, 119
bin Salman, Mohammed (MBS) 56–8, 104, 119
bin Tariq, Haitham 100
Blinken, Anthony 108
Bosnia 60
Bouazizi, Mohammed 11, 12
breakout time 43
Bush, George 27, 29, 30
Bushehr nuclear power plant 48

Carter, Jimmy 29, 35
China 27, 31, 32, 33, 34, 35, 43, 45, 64, 71, 72, 82, 83, 118
Clinton, Hillary 27, 29, 32, 34, 39
Cold War 23, 28, 84, 122
Communism 5, 28
counterterrorism 74, 77, 89
Crimea 35

Dabaiba, Abdul Hamid 96, 120
Dempsey, Martin 62
Dhofar 2, 125
Donilon, Tom 31, 34

DP World 66, 67, 69, 80
dual containment 29
Dubai 4, 5, 15, 29, 31, 49, 58, 66, 71, 87, 109, 112

Eastern province (Saudi Arabia) 14
Egypt 11, 12, 13, 17, 22, 23, 25, 27, 30, 41, 63, 67, 68, 70, 71, 72, 76, 77, 82, 88, 95, 102
El Sisi, Abdel Fattah 67
enrichment (uranium) 45, 47, 49
Erdogan, Recep Tayyip 84, 86
Eritrea 8, 64, 78

Fadlallah, Mohammad Hussein 20
France 43, 45, 63, 66, 69, 96, 118

Gargash, Anwar 73, 95, 103, 104
Gulf Cooperation Council (GCC) 3, 4, 15, 17, 18, 19, 24, 25, 29, 38, 47, 48, 49, 51, 57, 60, 75, 76, 82, 88, 99, 100, 101, 105, 109, 110, 111, 113, 119, 123, 124
Germany 43, 45, 53, 66
Ghaddafi, Muammar 17, 75
Giants Brigades 89, 92
Goldberg, Jeffrey 32, 37, 55

Hadi, Abdrabbuh Mansur 74, 75, 93
Haftar, Khalifa 75, 77, 78, 83, 94, 95, 96
Hamas 85
Hedges, Matthew 118
Herzog, Isaac 92
Hezbollah 48, 50, 53, 57, 102
Hodeida 73, 90, 91, 121
Houthis 13, 50, 53, 54, 62, 72, 73, 74, 75, 84, 89, 90, 91, 92, 93, 103, 111, 112, 115
Hu Jintao 32
Hussein, Saddam 30, 33, 48

Iran 1–6, 8, 12, 17–21, 23–6, 28, 29, 35, 38–9, 41, 43–61, 64–7, 71–3, 85, 89, 91, 93, 99, 100–2, 105–6, 109–16, 124

Iraq 1, 27–30, 33–5, 41, 48, 50, 52–5, 102
Iran nuclear deal (JCPOA) 1, 6, 8, 41, 43, 44, 46–7, 50, 51, 52, 53–9, 66, 68, 105, 111, 115, 116
Iranian Revolutionary Guards (IRGC) 54
Islamic State (ISIS) 53, 54, 63, 78, 141, 174
Islamic Revolution of Iran 1, 2, 28, 44
Islamism 6, 16, 18, 25, 35, 71, 76–7, 94, 102
Israel 3, 20, 28, 48, 84, 85

Japan 27, 32, 33, 72
Joint Plan of Action (JPOA) 46

Kamrava, Mehran 18
Kerry, John 51
Khamenei, Ayatollah Ali 49
Khashoggi, Jamal 57, 119
Khatami, Mohammad 45, 54
Khomeini, Ayatollah Ruhollah 1, 44
Kosovo 3
Kuwait 2, 6, 15, 28, 29, 40, 44, 45, 57, 111, 112

Lebanon 20, 52
Libya 9, 12, 13, 17, 18, 23, 63, 64, 72, 75, 76, 77, 78, 80, 83, 86, 89, 94, 95, 96, 99, 105, 109, 117, 120, 121
Lynch, Marc 16

maximum pressure 38, 111, 112
Morsi, Mohamed 70, 88
Mubarak, Hosni 12, 17, 22, 23, 27, 41, 54, 67, 68, 88
Muslim Brotherhood 16, 22, 23, 25, 57, 70, 71, 74, 76, 86, 88, 101, 102, 104

Natanz power plant 45, 167
North Atlantic Treaty Organization (NATO) 40, 75, 76, 81, 94, 107

al Nimr, Sheikh Nimr 106
Nixon, Richard 28
North Korea 32, 152

Obama, Barack 1, 6, 21, 22–3, 27,
    30–41, 46, 49, 51, 54–6, 68, 77,
    115, 121
Oman 2, 15, 24, 38, 44, 45, 49, 93, 100,
    101, 110, 112, 119
Operation Desert Storm 81

Palestinian Islamic Jihad 85
Pan-Arabism 14
Peninsula Shield Force 21, 24, 57
Presidential Council (Yemen) 93

Qatar 2–4, 8, 11, 14, 18, 24–5, 38,
    44–5, 49, 68, 76–7, 86, 99, 100,
    101–13, 117, 119, 120, 123–4

Rafsanjani, Akbar Hashemi 45
Red Sea 73, 74, 90, 91, 104
Rhodes, Ben 30
Rice, Susan 35, 38
Rouhani, Hassan 45, 46, 52
Russia 35, 43, 45, 64, 65, 66, 72, 82, 83,
    84, 85, 96, 119

Saleh, Ali Abdullah 74, 93
Saudi Arabia 1–6, 8, 14–15, 18, 24–5,
    28–30, 38, 40, 44, 49, 55–8, 72–5,
    81, 88, 90, 93–4, 99–103, 105–11,
    113, 115, 118–19, 124
Second World War 28
self-sufficiency 3–4, 6–7, 9, 17, 18, 22,
    36, 41, 47, 52, 56, 58, 63, 65, 78,
    86, 106, 113, 116, 122
Shah of Iran 4, 44
Shia 14, 20, 21, 25, 38, 48, 102
small power 4, 6
social media 12, 14, 15, 37
Somalia 60, 195
South China Sea 32
Soviet Union 28
Southern Transitional Council (STC)
    75, 83, 89

Stockholm Agreement 91
Syria 11, 17, 18, 20, 23, 52, 53, 54, 55,
    56, 68, 72, 83, 84, 85, 86, 102,
    105, 122

Tahrir 22, 102
Taliban 33, 107, 108
Tillerson, Rex 68
Tripoli 77, 78, 94, 95, 96
Trump, Donald 38, 39, 68, 78, 102,
    103, 107, 111, 112, 117, 118, 121
Tunbs 2, 4
Tunisia 11, 12, 13, 14, 22
Turkey 31, 84, 86, 95, 102, 104,
    106, 122
Twin Pillar policy 28
twin towers 29

Ukraine 21, 80, 83, 84, 119, 120, 122
UN General Assembly 84
UN Human Rights Council 84
UN Security Council 43, 45, 53, 76,
    84, 199, 241
United Kingdom 2, 4, 28, 43, 45, 63,
    66, 118
United States 2, 3, 6, 8, 11, 12, 22, 23,
    26, 27, 28, 29, 31, 32, 33, 34, 36,
    37, 38, 39, 40, 41, 43, 45, 46, 47,
    48, 49, 50, 51, 52, 53, 54, 55, 56,
    58, 59, 60, 61, 62, 63, 64, 67, 68,
    69, 71, 72, 75, 76, 77, 81, 82, 83,
    84, 86, 87, 88, 91, 92, 94, 95, 102,
    107, 108, 111, 112, 116, 117, 118,
    119, 121, 122, 123, 124
US invasion of Iraq 1, 30, 33

Wagner Group 95

Xi, Jinping 71, 82

Yemen 8, 9, 13, 18, 25, 52, 54, 55, 57,
    58, 64, 72, 73, 74, 75, 80, 83, 89,
    90, 91, 92, 93, 102, 109, 111, 113,
    115, 117, 118, 119, 121
Yemeni National Resistance
    Coalition 89